BLACK AMERICAN WRITERS
Bibliographical Essays

*Volume 2   RICHARD WRIGHT, RALPH ELLISON,
JAMES BALDWIN, AND AMIRI BARAKA*

Black American Writers
Bibliographical Essays

Volume 2   *RICHARD WRIGHT,*
   RALPH ELLISON, JAMES
   BALDWIN, AND AMIRI BARAKA

Edited by
M. THOMAS INGE
MAURICE DUKE
JACKSON R. BRYER

New York   *St. Martin's Press*

Library of Congress Calalog Card Number: 77–85987
Copyright © 1978 by St. Martin's Press, Inc.
All Rights Reserved.
Manufactured in the United States of America.
2109
fedcb
For information, write St. Martin's Press, Inc.,
175 Fifth Avenue, New York, N. Y. 10010

cover design: Mies Hora

ISBN: 0–312–08295–9

PREFACE

The last two decades have witnessed a great proliferation of scholarship devoted to the history and culture of Afro-Americans. And out of this increasing recognition of the contribution of blacks to the development of this nation has come a significant reassessment of the aesthetic and humanistic achievements of black writers.

Black American Writers: Bibliographical Essays is intended as an appraisal of the best biographical and critical writings about America's seminal black writers, as well as an identification of manuscript and special resources for continued study. It is also intended to give an overview of the current state of scholarly recognition of the lives and careers of these authors and an appreciation of their works.

The coverage is intentionally selective, both in the figures involved and the material examined in each chapter. Yet we feel that, within our self-imposed chronological limit, no major Afro-American literary figure has been overlooked. Volume 1 covers the early black writers of the eighteenth century, the slave narratives, the early modern writers, the Harlem Renaissance, and Langston Hughes. Volume 2 focuses on four major twentieth-century black writers: Richard Wright, Ralph Ellison, James Baldwin, and Amiri Baraka (LeRoi Jones). A bibliographical survey of the great number of black American writers who have come to prominence since Wright, Ellison, Baldwin, and Baraka would require another volume or volumes and, given the rich and vigorous production of black writers today and the continual emergence of new figures, would perhaps be premature.

Our hope is that the bibliographical essays in these volumes, all by specialists on their topics, will aid and encourage further study of black American writers and literature.

M. Thomas Inge
Maurice Duke
Jackson R. Bryer

KEY TO JOURNAL ABBREVIATIONS

ABC	American Book Collector
AH	American Heritage
AHR	American Historical Review
AI	American Imago
AJS	American Journal of Sociology
AL	American Literature
ALR	American Literary Realism, 1870–1910
AmerS	American Studies
AQ	American Quarterly
AR	Antioch Review
ArQ	Arkansas Quarterly
ASch	American Scholar
ASoc	Arts in Society
AtM	Atlantic Monthly
BALF	Black American Literature Forum
BARev	Black Academy Review
BB	Bulletin of Bibliography
BlackBB	Black Books Bulletin
BlackD	Black Dialogue
BlackR	Black Review
BlackSch	Black Scholar
BlackW	Black World
CathW	Catholic World
CE	College English
ChiR	Chicago Review
CLAJ	College Language Association Journal
ColQ	Colorado Quarterly
ConL	Contemporary Literature
CP	Concerning Poetry
Crit	Critique
DAI	Dissertation Abstracts International
DB	Down Beat
EA	Etudes Anglaises
EAL	Early American Literature

EH	Eastern Horizon (Hong Kong)
EJ	English Journal
EngR	English Record
ETJ	Educational Theatre Journal
EvR	Evergreen Review
Expl	Explicator
FourQ	Four Quarters
GaR	Georgia Review
GC	Graduate Comment
HC	Hollins Critic
IJAS	Indian Journal of American Studies
JAF	Journal of American Folklore
JAH	Journal of American History
JAmS	Journal of American Studies
JBlS	Journal of Black Studies
JBP	Journal of Black Poetry
JEGP	Journal of English and Germanic Philology
JHR	Journal of Human Relations
JML	Journal of Modern Literature
JNE	Journal of Negro Education
JNH	Journal of Negro History
JNT	Journal of Narrative Technique
JPC	Journal of Popular Culture
JSH	Journal of Southern History
KanQ	Kansas Quarterly
KR	Kenyon Review
L&I	Literature and Ideology
LanM	Langues Modernes
LJ	Library Journal

MarkhamR	Markham Review	*S&S*	Science and Society
MASJ	Midcontinent American Studies Journal	*SAQ*	South Atlantic Quarterly
		SatR	Saturday Review
MD	Modern Drama	*SBL*	Studies in Black Literature
MFS	Modern Fiction Studies		
MidwestJ	Midwest Journal	*SCR*	South Carolina Review
MinnR	Minnesota Review	*SEP*	Saturday Evening Post
MissQ	Mississippi Quarterly	*SF*	Social Forces
ModQ	Modern Quarterly	*SFQ*	Southern Folklore Quarterly
MQ	Midwest Quarterly		
MQR	Michigan Quarterly Review	*SHR*	Southern Humanities Review
MR	Massachusetts Review	*SLJ*	Southern Literary Journal
N&Q	Notes and Queries		
NALF	Negro American Literature Forum	*SNL*	Satire Newsletter
		SNNTS	Studies in the Novel (North Texas State University)
NAR	North American Review		
NConL	Notes on Contemporary Literature		
		SR	Sewanee Review
ND	Negro Digest	*SSF*	Studies in Short Fiction
NEQ	New England Quarterly	*SWR*	Southwest Review
NewL	New Letters	*TAY*	Twice-A-Year
NHB	Negro History Bulletin	*TDR*	The Drama Review (Formerly Tulane Drama Review)
NL	New Leader		
NR	New Republic		
NY	New Yorker	*TQ*	Texas Quarterly
NYHTBW	New York Herald Tribune Book Week	*TSLL*	Texas Studies in Language and Literature
NYRB	New York Review of Books		
		UKCR	University of Kansas City Review
NYTBR	New York Times Book Review	*UR*	University Review
PBSA	Papers of the Bibliographical Society of America	*VQR*	Virginia Quarterly Review
		WHR	Western Humanities Review
PMLA	Publications of the Modern Language Association of America	*WLB*	Wilson Library Bulletin
		WSCL	Wisconsin Studies in Contemporary Literature
PoeS	Poe Studies		
PR	Partisan Review	*WWR*	Walt Whitman Review
PubW	Publishers Weekly	*XUS*	Xavier University Studies
QJS	Quarterly Journal of Speech		
QQ	Queen's Quarterly	*YR*	Yale Review
QRL	Quarterly Review of Literature	*YULG*	Yale University Library Gazette
RAL	Research in African Literature	*ZAA*	Zeitschrift für Anglistik und Amerikanistik (East Berlin)
RALS	Resources for American Literary Study		

CONTENTS

BLACK AMERICAN WRITERS
Bibliographical Essays

Volume 2   *RICHARD WRIGHT, RALPH ELLISON,*
JAMES BALDWIN, AND AMIRI BARAKA

RICHARD WRIGHT

JOHN M. REILLY

Early in his career Richard Wright was asked to prepare a brief autobiographical note for *The New Caravan* (edited by Alfred Kreymborg et al. [New York: Norton, 1936]), which included his short story "Big Boy Leaves Home." He devoted most of the sketch to external detail: his race; his birth in 1908 in Mississippi; his moves with his family to various southern towns; the end of his schooling at the age of fifteen; and the series of menial jobs he had held. It was characteristic of Wright to stress such objective facts, for his early encounter with Jim Crow society, his poverty and limited opportunity for education or employment, and his migration in 1927 to the South Side of Chicago made him a representative participant in black social history and gave him his inevitable literary topic. It was just as appropriate, however, that Wright concluded his early autobiographical note with the statement, "At present I'm busy with a novel," because the assertion of the presence of an artistic sensibility despite unprepossessing circumstances announced his consistent literary theme—the struggle for self-determination. Works such as *Native Son* and *Black Boy* greatly changed American literature, because the power of Wright's craft secured such a large audience and affected it so deeply that it became impossible for readers or critics to continue to ignore black American writing.

Richard Wright died in 1960, after thirteen years of self-chosen exile in Paris. For a while, before and after his death, his reputation was in decline. Other writers appeared to speak for blacks. Today, though, because of the artistic power of his characteristic theme of the struggle for self-determination, Wright seems securely established as a major author. We are coming to understand what he meant by saying, in his essay "The Literature of the Negro in the United States" (in *White Man, Listen!* [Garden City, N.Y.: Doubleday, 1957]) that the experiences of most people during the twentieth century are comparable to those undergone by blacks in America for three centuries. The author who describes that experience may be "the most representative voice of America and of oppressed people anywhere in the world today."

1

Bibliography

Michel Fabre and Edward Margolies have provided the fullest listings of works by Richard Wright. Their compilation first appeared in *Bulletin of Bibliography* (January–April 1965). It was reprinted in Constance Webb's biography *Richard Wright* (New York: Putnam, 1968), and was included in *Negro Digest* (January 1969), where its authorship was not acknowledged. A revised version, enlarged by the addition of twenty items, appeared in *New Letters* (Winter 1971). In its most recent form, once again revised and enlarged by Fabre, this basic bibliography serves as a valuable appendix to Fabre's biographical study *The Unfinished Quest of Richard Wright* (New York: Morrow, 1973). In addition to providing a comprehensive listing, the bibliography indicates the extent of Wright's output through division into sections for poetry, fiction, and nonfiction, the latter including books, articles and essays, reviews and comments on books, prefaces and introductions, journalism, and published correspondence. Arrangement within sections is chronological, giving the year of composition when it differs from the date of publication. Reprints are included when they differ from original versions. This bibliography, then, provides a basic outline of Wright's public career as artist and committed intellectual.

Translations and foreign editions of Wright's major publications can be identified through *A Bibliography of Neo-African Literature* by Jahnheinz Jahn (New York: Praeger, 1965), which chronologically lists ninety-five items in the entry on Richard Wright. Indication of the availability of those works for research in the United States must be sought in *A Dictionary Catalogue of the Schomburg Collection of Negro Literature and History,* 9 vols.; first supplement, 2 vols.; second supplement, 4 vols. (Boston: G. K. Hall, 1962, 1967, 1972).

Bibliographic aids to locating research and criticism on Wright began with Jackson R. Bryer's selected checklist of criticism (*WSCL,* Fall 1960). His compilation includes annotations on American and foreign books containing references to Wright, newspaper and magazine articles, and an extensive listing of American reviews of Wright's books with the exceptions of *Savage Holiday,* which did not receive reviews in the United States because of its original publication in paperback, and *Lawd Today,* unpublished until 1963. For more recent criticism, students may turn to the directory provided by Russell C. Brignano in "Richard Wright: A Bibliography of Secondary Sources" (*SBL,* Summer 1971). Brignano includes no reviews, but his bibliography is otherwise complete as of 1971, providing information about the reprints of essays and dividing the bibliography into seven sections: "Books About Wright"; "Pamphlets About Wright"; "Books Containing Individual Chapters or Major Sections on Wright"; "Other Books Offering

Significant Discussions of Wright"; "Journal Special Numbers Devoted to Wright"; "Essays About Wright"; and "Other Essays Containing Discussions of Wright." Brignano does not annotate but, like Bryer in his pioneering checklist, includes foreign essays and books.

As studies of Wright and of black literature proliferate, selective listings and evaluative guides become helpful. In the first category, Richard Abcarian's *Richard Wright's "Native Son": A Critical Handbook* (Belmont, Calif.: Wadsworth, 1970) offers both an amplification of the list of reviews of *Native Son* and a listing of some American discussions of Wright that have appeared since Bryer's checklist. Also significant is Darwin T. Turner's entry on Wright in his *Afro-American Writers* (New York: Appleton, 1970). The value of Turner's listing is enhanced by its inclusion in a volume providing references to research aids, background material, general black literary history and criticism, and works of 134 Afro-American authors in addition to Wright. And in *Five Black Writers* (New York: New York University Press, 1970), Donald B. Gibson includes among works he judges useful references to some of the doctoral dissertations on Wright that appeared in the 1960s.

Gibson is also the author of the first bibliographical essay on Wright (*CLAJ*, June 1969). Although he is highly selective among references, by dividing the "criticism" section into aesthetic criticism, sociological criticism, and philosophical criticism, he guides the reader into the growing specialization of Wright studies. The most complete work of this sort, however, is John M. Reilly's "Richard Wright: An Essay in Bibliography" (*RALS*, Autumn 1971). Reilly's essay, patterned on the format of *Sixteen Modern American Authors,* edited by Jackson R. Bryer (New York: Norton, 1973), provides, in the section devoted to criticism, a discussion of the first responses to Wright's publications in the United States, with an attempt to identify reviewers' political and aesthetic perspectives; an evaluation of the critical treatment Wright received during his career in exile and because of the special circumstances of the postwar mood; and an identification of the issues that have demanded critical attention since Wright's death and his recognition as a major American writer.

Editions

Four of Richard Wright's seven published volumes of fiction are currently available in paperback editions. *Uncle Tom's Children: Four Novellas* (1938), published with additions as *Uncle Tom's Children: Five Long Stories* (1940), appears in Harper & Row's Perennial Library, along with *Native Son* (1940) and *The Outsider* (1953). *Eight Men* (1961) is published by Pyramid. Hardcover reprints of *Savage Holiday* (1954) and *The Long Dream* (1958) have been issued, in 1975 and 1969, respectively, by

Chatham Booksellers (Chatham, N.J.); and "Five Episodes," from the unpublished "Island of Hallucinations," is accessible in the hardcover collection of Afro-American writing *Soon, One Morning* (New York: Knopf, 1963), edited by Herbert Hill. The novel *Lawd Today* (1963), which was published posthumously and used to be available in paperback from Avon, is no longer in print.

Wright's autobiography, *Black Boy: A Record of Childhood and Youth* (1945), is also published in the Perennial Library by Harper & Row. Originally the manuscript of *Black Boy* continued his story through his experiences in Chicago and with the Communist party, but before publication Wright agreed to the publisher's suggestion that he conclude with his departure from the South. Fragments of much of the final portion of the manuscript were published in such short pieces as "What You Don't Know Won't Hurt You" (*Harper's Magazine,* December 1942), "American Hunger" (*Mademoiselle,* September 1945), "Early Days in Chicago" (in *Cross Section,* edited by Edwin Seaver [New York: McClelland, 1945]; also with the title "The Man Who Went to Chicago" in *Eight Men),* and "I Tried to Be a Communist" (*AtM,* August 1944 and September 1944). In 1977 Harper & Row issued the entire second portion of the autobiography under the title *American Hunger.*

Arno Press (New York, 1969) has reprinted *12 Million Black Voices: A Folk History of the Negro in the United States* (1941), with photographs selected by Edwin Rosskam; and Wright's study of the Gold Coast before it emerged as the nation of Ghana, *Black Power: A Record of Reactions in a Land of Pathos* (1954), is now available from Greenwood Press (Westport, Connecticut, 1974). Lamentably, the essays collected as *White Man, Listen!* (1957), once available in a Doubleday Anchor paperback, have gone out of print, while Wright's report on the Afro-Asian Conference at Bandung, *The Color Curtain* (1956), and the record of his study of European underdevelopment, *Pagan Spain* (1956), were never reissued when the first editions were exhausted.

The situation is the same for the dramatic version of the story of Bigger Thomas, *Native Son: The Biography of a Young American, A Play in Ten Scenes* (1941), of which Wright was coauthor with Paul Green; and Wright's adaptation of Louis Sapin's play *Papa Bon Dieu,* produced in New York on June 4, 1968, by the Negro Ensemble Company under the title *Daddy Goodness,* has never been published.

Recently, some of Wright's notable short pieces have been reprinted. The lecture "How Bigger Was Born," published as an essay in *Saturday Review* (June 1, 1940) and later as an enlarged pamphlet by Harper & Row, has been included in new printings of the Perennial Library edition of *Native Son.* Wright's fullest statement of literary theory, "Blueprint for Negro Literature" (*New Challenge,* Fall 1937), appears in its earlier and longer version in *Amistad 2,* edited by John A. Williams and

Charles F. Harris (New York: Vintage, 1971). The journal *New Letters* (in a special issue devoted to Wright [Winter 1971], reprinted as *Richard Wright: Impressions and Perspectives,* edited by David Ray and Robert Farnsworth [Ann Arbor: University of Michigan Press, 1973]) has published "The American Problem—Its Negro Phase," an unfinished first draft of a lecture Wright prepared for a French audience in the 1950s. In addition, there is a sample of ten haiku taken from the 3,000 Wright composed in the last year of his life. A subsequent issue of *New Letters* (Fall 1972) provides an example of an early essay in "Ethnological Aspects of Chicago's Black Belt," together with a "Bibliography on the Negro in Chicago," both of which Wright prepared for the Federal Writers' Project in 1936.

Gratifying as it is that much of Wright's fiction is in print and that the steady sales of *Native Son* and *Black Boy* confirm them as two of the most important books of the century, it must be noted that Wright was more than the author of two powerful books. As Wright scholars seek the early verse, shorter works, and out-of-print social essays, they discover that he wrote consistently and variously of the fundamental historical experiences of the twentieth century. Thus, we need a convenient collection of such works. Michel Fabre has made an important contribution to our need for scholarly editions of Wright's work with a bilingual edition of *The Man Who Lived Underground,* translated by Claude Edmonde Magny (Paris: Aubier, 1971), which includes a lengthy critical introduction. Let us hope that this will be matched by other projects, for nothing less than complete, reliably edited publication of all Wright's works will do.

Manuscripts and Letters

Most of Wright's papers have been acquired recently by the Beinecke Rare Book and Manuscript Library at Yale University. This archive is comprised of more than one thousand items, including: successive versions of *American Hunger* and typescripts of other published and unpublished autobiographical writings; travel diaries for *Black Power* and *The Color Curtain;* daily journals from 1945 and from Wright's early days in Paris; typescripts of book reviews and other critical writing; six short dramatic pieces and a typescript of *Daddy Goodness;* typescripts for writings on social and political topics (many unpublished); twenty-four unpublished poems, versions of some published ones, as well as more than three thousand haiku Wright was preparing for publication at the time of his death. Materials related to his fiction include typescripts of the novel "Black Hope" (unfinished), the stories collected in *Eight Men,* "A Father's Law" (unfinished novel), early versions of *Lawd Today,* "Freedom's Lonely Son" (unfinished novel), a number of unpublished short stories, and film scenarios. Episodes from "Island of Hallucination," as published in *Soon, One Morning,* are in the archive, but the final complete version (unpublished) is restricted. Additional items providing insight into Wright's work are typescripts of interviews he gave in Paris, notes and outlines for uncompleted projects, notes on his reading, and a proposal for a magazine. The archive also contains many pieces of Wright's correspondence, among them letters discussing his plans for novels, individual letters from Wright to Langston Hughes and Dorothy Peterson, five letters and cards to Carl Van Vechten, seven letters and a cable to Gertrude Stein, and eighty pieces of correspondence with Dorothy Norman. It is also likely that the papers in the Langston Hughes Estate at Yale contain additional correspondence.

A number of research libraries in the United States have interesting materials. The New York Public Library has a typescript of *Native Son,* the manuscript of the unpublished novel "Monument to Memory," the second draft of *The Long Dream,* a mimeographed copy of the screenplay for *Native Son* produced by Wright and Pierre Chenal in 1951, as well as some photographs and photocopies of personal papers. The New York Public Library also lists among its holdings a typescript of *Daddy Goodness.*

The Princeton University Library has Wright materials in three of its special collections. The Sylvia Beach Papers includes a typescript with the author's corrections of the earliest version of "The Man Who Lived Underground," signed December 9, 1946. The files of *Story* magazine contain another, shorter typescript of the same story together with a typescript of the first rough draft of Wright's unproduced film script about the Jubilee Singers entitled "Melody Limited" (1944). The *Story* files also contain a typescript of his foreword to *The Violent Conflict,* carbon copies of letters from Whit Burnett to Richard Wright and to Ellen Wright, miscellaneous biographical and publicity materials relating to Wright's winning the *Story* prize for *Uncle Tom's Children* in 1938, and a letter from Sinclair Lewis regarding the prize. In addition, Princeton holds selected papers of Harper and Brothers, which include copies or originals of approximately five hundred letters exchanged among Wright; his agent, Paul R. Reynolds, Jr.; his editor at Harper's, Edward Aswell; and Aswell's successor, John Fischer, between 1938–1957.

Other scattered Wright materials include: typescripts of "Blueprint for Negro Writing" and "Black Boy" in the Chicago Public Library; the manuscript of *Black Power* at Northwestern Univerity; page proofs of *Native Son,* indicating revisions, in the Fales Library at New York University; and carbon copies of several typescripts held by Walter Goldwater of the University Place Bookshop in New York. (It should be noted that the entry in *American Literary Manuscripts* [Austin: University of Texas Press, 1960] indicating the Hartford Seminary Foundation holding of eight letters of Richard Wright does not refer to the novelist.)

Ten letters held by Kent State University Libraries from Wright to a boyhood friend have been edited by Thomas Knipp as *Richard Wright: Letters to Joe C. Brown* (Kent, Ohio: Kent State University Press, 1968). Knipp provides extensive annotation of personal references. The Kent State manuscript collection also includes a typescript of the unpublished essay "I Choose Exile" (c. 1956).

A clutch of correspondence has been published in *New Letters* (Winter 1971), including letters from Wright to Owen Dodson and letters to Wright from Henry Miller, Albert Camus, André Gide, Claude Lévi-Strauss, Cesare Pavese, and Jean-Paul Sartre. Translations and notes are provided by Michel Fabre and constitute a preview of the edition of selected correspondence to be included in the forthcoming *Letters of Richard Wright,* edited by Fabre, Ellen Wright, and Edward Margolies. Harper & Row will publish the items selected from over eight hundred letters in two volumes, the first covering the years 1935 to 1946 and the second from 1946 to Wright's death in 1960.

Until the Harper's edition appears, Edward Margolies's "The Letters of Richard Wright" (in *The Black Writer in Africa and America,* edited by Lloyd W. Brown [Los Angeles: Hennessey & Ingalls, 1973]) must serve as a description of the correspondence. Although Wright did not regard the letter as a literary genre, he was prolific in its production, carefully attending to style and argument if he thought the writing publishable. More than half the letters were written to Paul Reynolds, another batch to Edward Aswell, and a large group to Margrit de Sablonière, a translator and agent for Wright in Europe. The letters are, of course, biographically valuable, especially in detailing problems Wright encountered politically, but their greatest help to critics and scholars lies in their revelations of his literary processes. Apparently the drafts of his manuscripts were always twice as long as the published volumes, and for cuts and revisions he nearly always accepted editorial advice. The letters also indicate that a major source for *The Long Dream* was autobiographical material excluded from *Black Boy,* while *Savage Holiday,* like "The Man Who Lived Underground," was stimulated by Wright's reading of the popular press. As for a portrayal of the artist's mind, the exclusively professional correspondence in the forthcoming volumes shows that Wright was considerably less sanguine in letters than in books about the future of Africa and Asia and that he was even uncertain about his desire to continue as a writer of fiction, especially during his last year, when he lived alone in Paris, reduced to writing texts for recording companies.

Biography

Biographical study of Richard Wright must be concerned with two equally important levels of truth. The first is Wright's own vision of his life, which he presents in *Black Boy* and a number of shorter published autobiographical pieces such as "The Ethics of Living Jim Crow," "How Bigger Was Born," "American Hunger," "I Tried to Be a Communist," "What You Don't Know Won't Hurt You," and "Early Days in Chicago." Reading these, one comes to realize that nearly all Wright's fiction has been informed by his own felt experience, that his non-fiction writing extended such experience to cognition, and that interpretation of his work and career is well advised to attend closely to the subjective accounts. On the other hand, critics have been too quick to assume that Wright's subjective accounts of his experience are sufficient, when in fact a complementary level of truth—objective biographical fact—is needed if we are fully to understand the writer who sought to engage and never to evade reality.

The early biographical account of Wright by Edwin R. Embree in *13 Against the Odds* (New York: Viking, 1944) makes a start toward combining the levels of biographical truth. Embree relies heavily on published autobiographical materials, but supplements them with interviews that enable him to provide a valuable discussion of Wright's program of self-education in psychology and sociology.

The first published full-length biographical appraisal of Wright is Constance Webb's *Richard Wright: A Biography* (New York: Putnam, 1968). Webb had a long friendship with Wright and nourished the idea of writing an interpretation for more than twenty years. When a publisher's decision forced Wright to cut the final third of *Black Boy* before publication, he gave her the galley sheets of the unpublished portion, which she then had printed privately. A copy of the privately circulated work exists in the Sylvia Beach Papers at Princeton as published with the twenty-four pages of Webb's commentary described as "Notes Preliminary to a Full Study of the Work of Richard Wright." The burden of the notes, actually a discourse, appears in Webb's critical article "What Next for Richard Wright?" (*Phylon,* Spring 1949), but the biographical interest evidenced in the fact of the privately circulated publication waited until Wright's death for fulfillment. At that time Webb began to expand her collection of data for a full-length biography. Through Fabre and Margolies she gained access to collected correspondence and from Ellen Wright the opportunity to go over manuscript materials; in addition, Webb interviewed a number of Wright's contemporaries. But despite these enviable working conditions, the completed biography is a disappointment. Among its strengths is a detailed accounting of Wright's various literary plans. Its great weakness, however, lies in the attempt to avoid a dry rendition of details by the use of a novelist's style. Not only does this lead Webb to describe immediate feelings and impressions of which she could have no knowledge, it also makes her inclined to fill the narrative with portentous episodes of conflict between Wright and the Communist party, sometimes anticipatory, at other times vaguely speculative, but never with an effort at substantiation.

W. Edward Farrison, in reviewing Webb's work (*CLAJ,* June 1969), makes the pertinent observation that relying so heavily on *Black Boy* obscures the distinction between anecdote and fact, to which might be added that the basis for many of the anecdotes from Wright's life is so slight as to be documented only by references to "conversations with Richard Wright."

Ten years of solid research in all Wright's papers, extensive interviews with principal and secondary figures in Wright's life, and a long-term commitment to the critical study and teaching of Afro-American literature have resulted in the biography that scholars will trust and depend on for many years. In *The Unfinished Quest of Richard Wright* (New York: Morrow, 1973), translated from the French by Isabel Barzun, Michel Fabre uses both autobiography and objective detail to demonstrate conclusively the thesis that Wright must be accepted as an author continuously proceeding through cycles of development interrupted only by death—not by exile, abandonment of his true subject, loss of touch with American reality, or whatever had been advanced previously as an attractive explanation of a presumed decline in Wright's power between the early and late periods of his life. Fabre intends that his book give a detailed chronology in which the works, published and unpublished, can be situated; and while *The Unfinished Quest* is not intended to be a critical work, it offers an assessment of Wright that is salutary for criticism.

Fabre says that neither technical innovation nor originality of political and social thought accounts for Wright's importance. That is to be found—and it is the mark of Wright's originality—in his understanding of the exceptional significance of blacks in twentieth-century history. Afro-Americans, and later Wright would say all colonized people, represent mankind arriving in the industrial world. A quest for liberation from racial caste in Mississippi broadened for Wright into a quest for liberation of the Third World and then into struggle against all oppression. As writer and intellectual militant in the cause of what he saw as the representative experience of our time, says Fabre citing Ralph Waldo Emerson, Wright became himself a representative man.

Fabre correctly takes it for granted that a literary biography need not be limited to evidence of published works, and this assumption gives us for the first time a clear picture of Wright's life in exile, incidentally demonstrating that his output did not diminish after 1945. A good deal of that period for Wright was occupied with concern about American government activities that affected him personally, and in a concluding section Fabre judiciously examines the evidence for and against the presence of a plot to ruin Wright, even to kill him. In addition to the bibliography of Wright's works, the volume contains listings of important books dealing with his life, interviews with Wright that appeared in publications in Europe and the United States, foreign and American articles on events in his career, and some obituary notices.

Reviews of Fabre's volume give it high approval. In his review-essay, Melvin Dixon (*BlackW,* March 1974) remarks especially on the structure of the study, which counterpoints the rhythm of Wright's life against the rhythm in the works the life produced. The cogency of the structure lies in its representation of Wright's career as a reflection of the development of twentieth-century Afro-American thought. Blyden Jackson (*AL,* November 1974) finds the value of Fabre's work in its great expansion of verified biographical knowledge and its suggestive remarks about Wright's exile years. However, Jackson departs from total approval, saying that Fabre never penetrates the private black world that had so much to do with shaping Wright's consciousness.

Jackson insists, contrary to what he finds in Fabre, that Richard Wright's creative home was the Delta South. This belief sustains Jackson's own biographical essay "Richard Wright: Black Boy from America's Black Belt and Urban Ghettos" (*CLAJ,* June 1969). Using the scenes from *Black Boy* in which Wright confronts his peasant father as the presiding metaphor in his essay, Jackson recounts Wright's growing up in distinctively black worlds from which he carried the folk knowledge and emotional set of black America into the milieu of artists and intellectuals.

The significance of Richard Wright's career to later black writers is notable, of course, and is properly considered an aspect of his biography. A negative view of that significance appears in various essays by James Baldwin. Most of these document Baldwin's dispute with what he understands to be the assumptions and practice of Wright's protest fiction; but in "The Exile" (*Encounter,* April 1961; reprinted in Baldwin's *Nobody Knows My Name* [New York: Dial, 1961]), he offers his point of view on Wright's life in Europe, finding him to be politically isolated, even foolish, and describing Wright's attitude toward individual American blacks as contemptuous. An analysis of the particular relationship that generated this opinion appears in Maurice Charney's "James Baldwin's Quarrel with Richard Wright" (*AQ,* Spring 1963), and the Fabre biography adds a further dimension. However, John A. Williams testifies most positively about the significance of Wright to other black authors. His novel *The Man Who Cried I Am* (Boston: Little, Brown, 1967) is a *roman à clef* featuring Wright in the character Harry

Ames as the father of all black American writers. The fundamental racism of Western societies and the black writer's perception of it are central themes in the novel; so, too, do they provide the dynamics of a short biography that Williams has written for younger readers entitled *A Biography of Richard Wright: The Most Native of Sons* (Garden City, N.Y.: Doubleday, 1970).

Numerous others of Wright's contemporaries have published recollections and evaluations. *Anger and Beyond,* edited by Herbert Hill (New York: Harper & Row, 1966), contains a symposium, "Reflections on Richard Wright," in which Arna Bontemps, Horace Cayton, and Saunders Redding participated. Cayton speaks of knowing Wright in Chicago when Wright was gathering material for *12 Million Black Voices,* and observes the influence of the Chicago School of sociology on Wright's work. Bontemps, too, speaks of Wright's confirmation of his insights with the data of social science, while Redding characterizes Wright as an extraordinarily zealous intellectual. Horace Cayton adds to the description of his early relationship with Wright in his own autobiography *Long Old Road* (New York: Trident, 1965); and in an account of a train ride with Wright in 1943, "The Curtain" (*ND,* December 1968), he provides an anecdote illustrating Wright's sensitivity to racial mores. Ralph Ellison casts light on Wright's interest in literary craft and familiarity with master writers in a brief section of "A Very Stern Discipline— An Interview with Ralph Ellison" (*Harper's Magazine,* March 1967); and in *Goodbye, Union Square* (Chicago: Quadrangle, 1970), Albert Halper reminisces about meeting Wright during the period when Wright was identified with the proletarian literary movement.

New Letters (Winter 1971) includes personal impressions of others who knew Wright during this period, including Benjamin Appel, Harry Birdoff, Henrietta Weigel, Winburn T. Thomas, Owen Dodson, Frank K. Safford, Jack Conroy, Horace Cayton, and Sidney Williams. Grace McSpadden White contributes an article to the same volume on Wright in Memphis. Another outstanding contribution to the issue is Margaret Walker Alexander's memoir of the years 1936 to 1939 during which she and Wright exchanged views of writers and philosophy and Wright corresponded with her to secure clippings on the notorious Nixon murder trial in Chicago, which later formed part of the background for *Native Son.* Mrs. Alexander has decided opinions about Wright and *Native Son,* and her personal relationship with him makes them important to know. Also important are articles by John Houseman, producer of the stage version of *Native Son,* who describes the difficult arrangements for production and points out for those who know the play only in its printed version how it differs from that viewed on Broadway; and by Thomas Cripps, who recounts the background and production of the film version of Bigger's story.

Jerre Mangione's *The Dream and the Deal: The Federal Writers' Project 1935–1943* (Boston: Little, Brown, 1972) contains scattered comments on the relationship between Wright and many contemporaries. Commentary by a fellow author who knew Wright in both New York and Paris appears in Chester Himes's autobiography, *The Quality of Hurt* (Garden City, N. Y.: Doubleday, 1972), and in an interview conducted by John A. Williams with Himes for *Amistad 1*, edited by Williams and Charles F. Harris (New York: Vintage 1970).

Another perspective on Wright is provided by two people who knew him through his interest in psychiatry. In "An Unconscious Determinant in *Native Son*" (*Journal of Criminal Psychopathology*, July 1944) Fredric Wertham, who worked closely with Wright on a project for a Harlem psychiatric clinic, describes Wright's evident personal interest in psychopathological problems in forming his fiction. Related is an article by Helen V. McLean on "Racial Prejudice" (*American Journal of Orthopsychiatry*, October 1944). Mentioning that in 1943 Wright spoke to the Chicage Institute for Psychoanalysis about the effects of racial fear, she relates racial fear and its effects to the concept of "overdetermination."

Simone de Beauvoir describes a period with the Wrights in New York in *America Day by Day*, translated by Patrick Dudley (New York: Grove, 1953); and in an interview conducted by Fabre (*SBL*, Fall 1970), she gives a firsthand account of Wright's contributions to *Les Temps Modernes* and refers briefly to his political association with Sartre in the 1950s. Dorothy Padmore (the widow of the Pan-Africanist George Padmore who, like Wright, was once a Communist), in a letter to Fabre (*SBL*, Fall 1970), stresses Wright's involvement in anticolonialist work, making clear that he was widely regarded as having transformed his struggle against racism into an international position when he moved to Europe.

Criticism

The accessibility of Reilly's bibliographical essay (*RALS*, Autumn 1971, discussed previously) and the incorporation of many reviews into Fabre's biography and a book by Keneth Kinnamon, to be discussed shortly, preclude repetition of a specialized treatment of the development of Wright's reputation. It should be enough to observe here that Wright received his most informed estimates in the early years of his career from critics who shared his involvement in the literary culture of the left or who felt sympathy with his social protest. Even the considerable praise his work earned for its frankness and its projective power was often qualified by suggestions that his inevitable topic might have only temporary appeal or was exaggerated in a way that made its appearance in his writing unrealistic. After *Native Son* and *Black Boy* had fully established Wright as a major talent, there was a tendency to measure all his subsequent work by their standard, a procedure that could not help overlooking his development and casting him in the role of the author losing touch with his inspiration and surviving long past his peak.

Nearly all serious criticism of Wright today takes it for granted that he is a major author whose assertion that "the Negro is America's metaphor" provides a fundamental description of modern life, abroad as well as in the United States. Consequently, discussion of Wright's politics is moving away from partisanship; analysis of racial references in his work increasingly focuses on questions of nationalism, culture, and class; and Wright's craft can be studied as a resolution of technical problems or an expression of his world view rather than as a formal envelope.

BOOKS

Edward Margolies centers his study, *The Art of Richard Wright* (Carbondale: Southern Illinois University Press, 1969), on themes of social psychology. His thesis is that Wright's fiction and nonfiction are complementary in describing a pattern, which Wright's life also demonstrated, of progression among oppressed peoples from emotional and political bondage, through acts of self-liberation, to the position of "free outsiders." In the first part of his book, Margolies supports his thesis with a careful analysis of the seldom-discussed works of nonfiction as illustrations of Wright's conceptions of "the fractured personality" of oppressed individuals and "the shattered civilization" of their cultures. Having rooted the study conceptually, Margolies is prepared to study design and style as Wright's vehicle. He is highly appreciative of *Lawd Today,* observing in it the stylistic influences of James T. Farrell, John Dos Passos, and Gertrude Stein on Wright's documentation of the erosion of black folk culture. *Native Son* he describes as Wright's attempt to fuse political ideology with his understanding of black experience. From this point of view, Margolies finds the famous novel only a partial success that made it necessary for Wright to examine his material again in *The Outsider* and *Savage Holiday.* At the nadir of pessimism, neither existentialism nor Freudianism afforded the means to reconcile beliefs and feelings in a convincing narrative of freedom, and Wright returned, in *The Long Dream,* to quasi-autobiographical fiction.

The author of the first full-length study of a literary figure opens himself to considerable criticism and, of course, Margolies is no exception. Interestingly, though, the shortcomings observed seem the result of a scholarly method sound in itself but too narrow in scope. Thus, Harry L. Jones (*CLAJ,* June 1969) wishes for more attention to the influences of existentialism and folklore, and raises as his only serious objection Margolies's attempt to deduce biography from Wright's works—a comment, by the way, applicable to much criticism of any writer and a weakness only in excess. Louise Blackwell (*JML*, Summer 1970) wonders if Margolies's study does not demonstrate that the "disinterested intellectual criteria" of a scholar are insufficient to judge works devoted to self-definition. More than anything else this is a remark aimed at a white critic's attempting unapologetic evaluation of a black author; but Blackwell finds the work a valuable introduction to Wright and thereby agrees with the estimate of Blyden Jackson (*AL*, January 1970), who says the work is a long overdue appreciation of Wright's remarkable *art*.

Margolies also discusses Wright in *Native Sons: A Critical Study of Twentieth-Century Negro American Authors* (Philadelphia: Lippincott, 1968), where he argues that *Native Son* contains three types of revolutionism: nationalist, embodied in Bigger's hate; metaphysical, in his challenge of the conditions of being; and communist, as introduced by the characters of Max and Jan. As in the full-length study, Margolies here finds Wright unable to fuse the themes successfully.

The latent thesis of Dan McCall in *The Example of Richard Wright* (New York: Harcourt Brace Jovanovich, 1969) is a justification of Wright's mode of protest writing. In the process he also attempts to illuminate the intimate relationship between Wright's personal psychology and his works. No writer, he aptly says, "happens" to be black. Race is the determining factor of an Afro-American author's identity, and no valid criticism can be made of his dealing with reality as he lives it. One finds, then, that Wright's self-exploration carried him to the depths of social experience and provided him the vision of sexually inspired interracial confrontation, so prominent in his plots, as well as dreams of camaraderie and mobility that provide a positive myth to his works. Some excellent readings of Wright's fiction substantiate the representation of his archetypal myth, but the book, almost devoid of documentation and exploration of historical particulars, hardly advances our understanding of Wright. On the contrary, McCall's "new criticism," imaginatively applied as it is, limits the significance of Wright's career to the works of the 1940s, and so underplays the importance of ideas, particularly Marxism, in his life, that Wright appears largely an intuitive author. A detailed analysis of the study's amateurism and the more serious charge of misuse of scholarly sources can be found in Keneth Kinnamon's review (*JEGP*, January 1971).

Another unsatisfactory book-length study is Russell C. Brignano's *Richard Wright: An Introduction to the Man and His Works* (Pittsburgh: University of Pittsburgh Press, 1970). Race relations in the United States, Marxism, international affairs, and Wright's changing philosophy are Brignano's categorical topics, each of which is assigned a major chapter, while a final chapter considers fragmentary pieces written in Wright's last years and offers a summary of the importance of his career. The approach, as Jackson R. Bryer observes (*AL,* January 1972), prevents aesthetic judgments. An even more serious weakness is in the substance of the discussion the categorical arrangement supports. Brignano wishes to demonstrate that Wright was essentially a Western humanist, rational and full of "faith in man's unfettered will to accomplish good and justice." This, he believes, appears in Wright's conflict with the Communist party, underlies the rhetorical purpose of much of his writing, and explains his philosophical concerns. To make his point, Brignano must represent Marxism as a system of "rigid" and "strict" laws of historical development that forces its adherents to adopt ingenious devices to account for exceptions such as those to be found in Afro-American history, and to play down cultural attitudes such as racism. Thus, Brignano's conception of Marxism appears as simplistic as his idea of humanism. Similar charges of reductionism may be found in the review by Richard Abcarian (*JML,* Summer 1971), who points out that Brignano is not only blinded to Wright's art by his own anticommunist sentiments but also seems unaware of the work of black critics as well as of central documents in contemporary Afro-American literature that could modify his own rigid scheme. In fairness, it must be mentioned that Nancy Tischler's tandem review of the books by Margolies and Brignano (*SNNTS,* Fall 1970) prefers the critical vitality she observes in the latter's concentration on Wright's strongest works and his attempt to generalize the problems Wright faced.

Keneth Kinnamon, who has been contributing articles to Wright studies for several years, is the author of the fourth full-length study: *The Emergence of Richard Wright: A Study in Literature and Society* (Urbana: University of Illinois Press, 1972). The importance of this work is two-fold. First, it marks a new degree of specialization in Wright studies, for it concentrates on Wright's career through publication of *Native Son* without in any way suggesting it is the whole of the story. Rather, it is Kinnamon's view that 1940 was a first climax for Wright and a point of achievement in Afro-American letters. The second value of the study lies in Kinnamon's methodological sophistication, which leads him to seek the dialectical relationships among Wright's consciousness, his works of aesthetic and moral imagination, and the conditions of American racism that demand protest. Daniel Aaron, commenting on the first point (*AL,* November 1973), finds the book to be a first-rate introduction to Wright, and W. Edward Farrison (*CLAJ,* September 1973) approves highly of the careful research Kinnamon accomplishes within the precise limits he sets for himself. A review by John M. Reilly (*JEGP,* October 1973) qualified the success in application of intended method, but otherwise observes that no one has done a better job than Kinnamon of situating literary works in the objective world Wright knew, and no full-length work is as illuminating about the evolution of Wright's art, because it carefully studies the experience with communism as well as Wright's refinement of his view of personality.

Katherine Fishburn brings another sort of specialization to the list of books on Wright with a study of thematic unity. *Richard Wright's Hero: The Faces of a Rebel-Victim* (Metuchen, N.J.: Scarecrow Press, 1977) alters the chronological order of Wright's composition to show a progression from representation of the initiation of blacks into American society (*Black Boy* and *The Long Dream*) through the divergent rebellions of Jake Jackson (*Lawd Today*) and Bigger Thomas (*Native Son*) and culminating in the existential careers of the arrogantly "free" Cross Damon (*The Outsider*) and prophetic everyman Fred Daniels ("The Man Who Lived Underground"). Fishburn illuminates relationships among these selected works of Wright's; and her applications of Karen Horney's concept of neurosis, significant interpretations of existentialist philosophy, and critical approaches derived from Northrop Frye's *Anatomy of Criticism* (Princeton, N.J.: Princeton University Press, 1957) and Wayne Booth's *The Rhetoric of Fiction* (Chicago: University of Chicago Press, 1961) produce interpretations that integrate theme and text. Still, one must recognize here, as in other criticism described in this survey, the limitation of a method that supplants the complex relationships of an author and the world of historical experience, as he encountered it in the chronology of composition, with a critical abstraction.

Richard Wright, a short monograph by David Bakish (New York: Ungar, 1973), cannot be considered a critical study, but it is not without merit as an introductory volume for new students of Richard Wright. Bakish organizes his presentation chronologically, using Webb as his authority for biography, discussing each significant text in an effort to point up its continued relevance. Sometimes he indulges in plot summary, but more often than not his presentation incorporates useful critical points; thus, the work contains an able elucidation of the structure of *Lawd Today* and of a rhythmic pattern in "Long Black Song." Treating Wright's ideas, Bakish indicates ways in which *12 Million Black Voices* and later nonfiction mix black nationalism and Marxism, a theme of considerable interest to critics today; and his attention to the craft and themes of *Pagan Spain* takes that work with a seriousness that is long overdue.

As an indication of critical views of Richard Wright in Japan, where he has been the most popular Afro-American author since publication of a translation of *Native Son* in 1940, a book by Masao Takahashi is of interest. *Higeki no Henrekisha: Richard Wright no Shōgai* [The Tragic Wanderer: the Life of Richard Wright] (Tokyo: Chūō Daigaku Shuppanbu, 1968) concentrates on Wright after what Japanese critics call his extrication from America. Takahashi stresses Wright's struggle to overcome the destiny his race forced upon him, concluding that after choosing exile he still could not find satisfactory literary expression.

PAMPHLETS

Two pamphlets have appeared on Wright, presumably directed toward readers seeking a brief introduction. The first, *Richard Wright* by Robert Bone (Minneapolis: University of Minnesota Press, 1969), divides Wright's works into American and French periods, with a secondary emphasis on his relationship to communism during each. Bone finds Wright's best work in the American period: *Black Boy,* the story of his attempt to liberate himself from systematic oppression; *Native Son,* an internalized picaresque occurring in a setting of urban nihilism; and "The Man Who Lived Underground," his most flawless work, treating the fear of nothingness that was at the root of the author's personality. The spiritual crisis he suffered as an ex-Communist Wright tried to surmount in a combination of existentialism, Third World politics, and images of the outsider. In the process he devised a theory of modern history as a transition from rural traditional culture that is, in Bone's view, the principal challenge to T. S. Eliot's view of tradition. By stressing the congruity of Wright's biography and art, Bone gives strength to his explanation that Wright's apparent aesthetic failure in his later work was the result of a conflict between rebelliousness, through which Wright established identity, and the desire for community, which could not contain his rootlessness.

The second pamphlet, Milton and Patricia Rickels's *Richard Wright* (Austin, Texas: Steck-Vaughn, 1970), stresses the themes of Wright's art that "grow from Southern soil." The approach is unique in Wright criticism. By careful analysis of imagery the authors show, particularly in those works dealing directly with the South, the presence of characters, language, and legend of black folk culture. While the presentation follows the chronological outline of biography, attention is paid throughout to style, authorial point of view, and dominant patterns of imagery in the literary texts.

A booklet by Karl-Heinz Wirzberger, *Probleme der Bürgerrechtsbewegung in der Amerikanischen Prosaliteratur* [The Problem of the Civil Rights Movement in American Prose Literature] (Berlin: Akademie-Verlag, 1967), provides a valuable discussion of Wright from a Marxist viewpoint representative of opinion in the German Democratic Republic. The booklet generally places Wright in the context of black influence on American culture. It also views him in relationship to the forms the struggle for liberation has taken from the time of the Harlem Renaissance of the 1920s through the recent civil rights movement. After *Black Boy* Wright seems to have been unable to find a formula for continuing the fight, and consequently he adopted a general concept of humanism to replace his previous political conviction. Wirzberger relates this development in Wright's career to the differences that have emerged since the 1940s between progressive black intellectuals and the political left, differences he sees as conflicts about strategies appropriate to the needs of a simultaneous fight against fascism and for civil rights.

PARTS OF BOOKS

The earliest study of Afro-American literature to devote space to Wright is Hugh M. Gloster's *Negro Voices in American Fiction* (Chapel Hill: University of North Carolina Press, 1948), which considers Wright the chief proletarian spokesman of his race, a judgment substantiated by elementary reference to the sociological content of the fiction. In an entirely different class is Carl Milton Hughes's study *The Negro Novelist: A Discussion of the Writings of American Negro Novelists, 1940–1950* (New York: Citadel, 1953), which places *Native Son* among psychological novels, asserting that Wright drove home his environmental thesis by dramatizing Bigger's incurably neurotic personality. For Hughes, the novel is a modern tragedy when understood through analysis of leading symbols within the narrative. Limited as it is in coverage, Hughes's book remains a highly suggestive discussion, supplemented by a valuable survey of reviewers' opinions and indications of Wright's influence on a school of protest authors that includes Chester Himes, Curtis Lucas, and Ann Petry.

Robert Bone, in *The Negro Novel in America* (New Haven, Conn.: Yale University Press, 1958; rev. ed., 1965), considers Wright against an even broader canvas. Arguing that Wright's significance in the history of Afro-American literature lies in his fusion of "pronounced racialism with a broader tradition of social protest," Bone describes Wright as being responsible for stimulating imitation of his protest fiction and reaction against it, a cycle that for Bone provides the pattern for more than two decades of twentieth-century black writing. His analysis of *Native Son* within the historical scheme is sensitive to the metaphor and psychological dynamics of the narrative, but neither Bone's historical pattern nor his aesthetic judgment permits him to give serious attention to Wright's work after *Native Son*.

A number of other books devoted to fiction include extensive discussions of Wright as a spokesman for Afro-American culture. David Littlejohn's *Black on White: A Critical Survey of Writing by American Negroes* (New York: Grossman, 1966) gives Wright a central place in his interpretation of black writing as the literature of racial strife. To Littlejohn, Wright is a "figure of almost primeval simplicity" whose conviction of righteousness made him unable to see people in other than morally simple terms. There is never any question for Littlejohn about Wright's art—he has none. Perhaps it is Littlejohn's expressed purpose of helping white readers deal with the rhetoric of black writing that accounts for the continuance of his book in print, but it is to be hoped that no one takes his view of Wright seriously, for his presumption passes belief. He is so persuaded of the inferiority of black literature that it is impossible to conceive of his having an equitable opinion of the people whose cultural expression lies in that literature.

Nelson M. Blake's *Novelists' America: Fiction as History 1910–1940* (Syracuse, N.Y.: Syracuse University Press, 1969) devotes a chapter to Wright that offers no new interpretation. In view of the persistence of such attitudes as Littlejohn's, however, it deserves attention because it presents a point of view one might have hoped would be commonplace in general treatments of Wright. Blake is well aware of the difficulties in using fiction as social documentary; yet, combining literary texts with pictorial illustrations of the black ghetto, he asserts the historical validity of the contention that Wright and Bigger manifest the rebelliousness and anger induced by oppression and prophesy the inevitability of violent attempts to break out of confinement.

Arthur P. Davis's *From the Dark Tower: Afro-American Writers 1900 to 1960* (Washington, D. C.: Howard University Press, 1974) is conceived as a survey on the model of Vernon Loggins's earlier book on black writers before the twentieth century, *The Negro Author: His Development in America to 1900* (New York: Columbia University Press, 1931). Davis includes Wright in the second section of his book, "Toward the Mainstream," where he characterizes Wright's fiction as a portrayal of the bleakness of life, decidedly at variance with the current slogan that "Black is Beautiful." For Davis *Native Son* is a culmination of Wright's powers, blending his naturalism, Marxism, sense of loss of religious faith, and his themes of flight and death as affirmation. Much of the essay is assertion rather than demonstration and therefore leaves much to debate: Is *The Long Dream* anachronistic? Was Wright's commitment to communism never more than halfhearted? At least one assertion, though, is a fruitful suggestion for a conception of Afro-American literary tradition: *Black Boy* continues the pattern of slave narratives.

Even more provocative in its suggestion of Wright's place in Afro-American tradition is Bernard W. Bell's *The Folk Roots of Contemporary Afro-American Poetry* (Detroit: Broadside, 1974), which describes Richard Wright, Ralph Ellison, and Amiri Baraka (LeRoi Jones) as the spiritual fathers of the contemporary black arts movement. By examination of theory and practice from the Harlem Renaissance to the present day, Bell attempts to demonstrate a persistent theory of folk art related to Johann Gottfried von Herder's. Although he uncovers no direct reference or borrowings from Herder among his subjects, Bell nevertheless argues a congruence between Herder's ideas of the historical continuity of a people transmitting a heritage through language, the effect of *Zeitgeist* (the spirit of the times) as a transforming power, and the ideas debated by black aestheticians. Wright's place in the continuity of black aesthetic concerns derives from his essay "Blueprint for Negro Literature," which urges writers to deepen their involvement with the oral and musical culture of the black masses while at the same time consciously expressing the forces that historically lead to liberation. Thus, Wright theoretically calls for a reconciliation of high art and folk art in lieu of writing that is only derivative from Anglo-American tradition and therefore sterile. Situating Wright as he does in the theoretical matrix of Afro-American literature, Bell does a great deal to enhance our ideas of Wright's influence (he says, for example, that Baraka's "Myth of a Negro Literature" constitutes an updating of Wright's "Blueprint") and to suggest a dimension to his aesthetic greater than any we are led to by concentration solely on Wright's "protest."

In *The Way of the New World: The Black Novel in America* (Garden City, N.Y.: Doubleday, 1975), Addison Gayle, Jr., also ascribes paternity of the contemporary literary movement to Wright. For Gayle, however, it is the truth of Wright's demonstration of the precarious peace between African-Americans and the eternal assassin at the door that made possible a viable literary tradition. *Native Son* is weakened by the incident of Bessie Mears's murder and by Wright's tendency to put faith in moral rules, since both reduce the racial content of Bigger's actions; but if Bigger's life is understood intuitively as occurring in an upside-down world, it teaches the power of the forces arrayed against blacks. The complementary work is *The Long Dream,* whose protagonist, Tyree Tucker, provides similar lessons about life in the South. Gayle's study of Afro-American fiction is devoted to the process of development in which other authors have gone beyond Wright in creating more complex characters and producing new, positive images and myths.

In contrast, Roger Rosenblatt's *Black Fiction* (Cambridge, Mass.: Harvard University Press, 1974) conceives of Afro-American writing as locked in cyclic patterns in which protagonists cannot reciprocate the world's impact upon them and must realize their wish to be free in self-disintegration. Thus, for Rosenblatt, although the reversal of reason in stories of blacks fighting each other and the images of fire and furnace in *Native Son* may give lessons, above all else they are images of captivity. An extensive critique of Rosenblatt's distinction between literature and history in his approach to black literature, as well as of the general weakness of his book's plan, can be found in W. Edward Farrison's "Much Ado About Negro Fiction: A Review Essay" (*CLAJ*, September 1975).

Stephen Butterfield's *Black Autobiography in America* (Amherst: University of Massachusetts Press, 1974) studies Wright's place in literary tradition through examination of *Black Boy,* the greatness of which, Butterfield claims, is matched in American autobiography only by Henry David Thoreau's *Walden*. The patterns of *Black Boy* are common in black literature: a developing theme of resistance as in the slave narratives, exhibition of the ironies inherent in racism, and experiences of alienation and the crisis of identity. Wright renders the materials into great literature, however, by the achievement of a totally functional style that avoids any self-consciousness and by relating the history and politics essential to an understanding of black life "*through* the individual experience of the boy Richard, without ever leaving his personal story."

Because he is himself a very promising writer, Clarence Major's comments on Wright are attractive. He is disappointing, though, in the chapter he devotes to Wright in *The Dark and Feeling: Black American Writers and Their Work* (New York: Third Press–Joseph Okpaku, 1974), for his presentation is limited to well-known biographical data and information on the content of works. Major's view of Wright is capsulized by his chapter title, "Richard Wright: The Long Hallucination," refering to the ideologies Major believes corrupted Wright's original innocence.

Catherine Juanita Starke's *Black Portraiture in American Fiction: Stock Characters, Archetypes, and Individuals* (New York: Basic Books, 1971) refers briefly to the environmental and internalized construction of Bigger Thomas and classifies Cross Damon among characters moving, like Ellison's narrator in *Invisible Man,* from subservience to self-assertion. Sam Bluefarb, in *The Escape Motif in the American Novel: Mark Twain to Richard Wright* (Columbus: Ohio State University Press, 1972), sees the story of Bigger Thomas completing a pattern in American literature that began with escape to the West. Bigger's escape, internalized as it is, and placed in an unusual manner within the urban setting of the naturalistic novel, carries the strategy of escape to a dead end.

Shorter estimates of Wright in book-length studies of literature vary according to the specificity of the context in whch he is viewed. Chester E. Eisinger, whose major black entry in his study of *Fiction of the Forties* (Chicago: University of Chicago Press, 1963) is Wright, emphasizes the naturalism of *Native Son,* marking it as a survival from the 1930s, and finds that because of deeply felt indignation Wright had difficulty assimilating his feelings into effective narrative even with the aid of the sociological concepts of the Chicago School. Seymour L. Gross, in his introduction to *Images of the Negro in American Literature,* edited by Gross and John Edward Hardy (Chicago: University of Chicago Press, 1966), is also concerned with Wright in the context of ideas of the 1930s, although he stresses the class concept that helped revive dreams of equality by providing black authors with both a way of identifying with all oppressed peoples and an audience receptive to their narratives of exploitation. For Harold Cruse in his examination of the experience of blacks in the white-dominated left, *The Crisis of the Negro Intellectual* (New York: Morrow, 1967), Richard Wright provides the example of a black intellectual sincerely trying to cope with black nationalism but failing to go beyond his Marxist starting point to observe that in the special American circumstance the path to ethnic liberation is through culture. S. P. Fullinwider contradicts Cruse in *The Mind and Mood of Black America* (Homewood, Ill.: Dorsey, 1969), which describes Wright as a participant in the general dialectic of myth and sociological imagination at the heart of modern Afro-American culture. As a representative of the sociological imagination, Wright exceeded earlier social thinkers in rejecting American society totally, and thus established a thesis of a counter-community that would embody the values absent from white-dominated American society.

ARTICLES ON WRIGHT'S CAREER AND LITERARY INFLUENCE

The severest criticism of Wright's social protest appears in two essays by James Baldwin. The first, "Everybody's Protest Novel" (*Zero,* April 1944; *PR,* June 1949; reprinted in *Notes of a Native Son* [Boston: Beacon, 1955]), is a critique of *Uncle Tom's Cabin;* it concludes by remarking that Bigger Thomas is a descendant of Uncle Tom, and that in creating Bigger Wright conceded the validity of Harriet Beecher Stowe's stereotype. Baldwin elaborated this criticism in "Many Thousands Gone" (*PR,* November–December 1955; reprinted in Baldwin's *Notes of a Native Son*), an essay concentrating on *Native Son.* By his account in that essay, the novel fails even in its social premise, for it provides no real knowledge of Bigger. What is more, even in putting Bigger forth as a warning to white society of black rage, Wright did not tell the whole story: whites know they created Bigger but still they want to destroy him. Failing to recognize such wickedness, the novel suggests a resolution of racial conflict that is merely a liberal dream of good will in which blacks obliterate their personalities and become as whites.

Baldwin's dispute with Wright is fully discussed in the article by Maurice Charney mentioned previously ("James Baldwin's Quarrel with Richard Wright" [*AQ*, Spring 1963]). Heinz Wüstenhagen (*ZAA*, 1965) interprets the relationship of the two authors for a German audience in "James Baldwins Essays und Romane: Versuch einer ersten Einschäteung" [James Baldwin's Essays and Novels: a Preliminary Estimate]. An article by B. K. Mitra, "The Wright–Baldwin Controversy" (*IJAS*, July 1969), takes the view that the younger Baldwin's criticism of Wright's work shows primarily the differences between generations. For Albert Murray, in "Something Different, Something More" (in *Anger and Beyond*, edited by Herbert Hill [New York: Harper & Row, 1966]), the controversy becomes a stimulus for evaluation of the achievements of Baldwin and Wright. Taking a balanced view, Murray rejects Baldwin's disdain for protest by indicating how extensive it is in all of black culture, especially music; but he also finds Baldwin's criticism of *Native Son* essentially valid, for Wright, unfortunately in Murray's opinion, always chose to work within the framework of his political ideology. A contrasting view is presented by Kichung Kim, in "Wright, the Protest Novel, and Baldwin's Faith" (*CLAJ*, March 1974), who explains that although Baldwin certainly knows of the existence of Bigger Thomas types, he denies their literary validity because they fail to meet Baldwin's ideal of what man might be.

More to the point than general description of the dispute is Irving Howe's extensive essay "Black Boys and Native Sons" (*Dissent*, Fall 1963). Howe develops a strong argument against the position of Baldwin and others by focusing upon the honesty of Bigger's portrayal and the projective power of the narrative, in which Wright departed from conventional naturalism, yielding himself to a nightmare vision that made *Native Son* a book that changed American culture forever. According to Howe, criticism of the novel's lack of poise by Alfred Kazin in *On Native Grounds* (New York: Harcourt Brace Jovanovich, 1972) denies the impact of its social authenticity; and criticism like Baldwin's of the sociological conception of black life ignores the likelihood of imbalance in a novel depending on expressionistic effect.

For a sense of the various disputes that Wright's protest still generates, one should read Howe in light of Cecil M. Brown's "Richard Wright: Complexes and Black Writing Today" (*ND*, December 1968). Brown argues that there is a difference between social actuality and Wright's view of it, saying that to reject Wright's mode of protest is only to reject the negative form that was accepted among whites. Brown's model is the "creative protest" of Amiri Baraka, who never accedes to white views of appropriate themes.

Recognizing the importance of a revival of interest in Wright, Stanley Edgar Hyman undertakes a survey of his works in today's intellectual climate in "Richard Wright Reappraised" (*AtM*, March 1970). In so doing he finds Wright remarkably prescient. There is, he says, in contrast to Baldwin and Brown, a fundamental radicalism in the challenge to white liberalism in *Native Son*. But Hyman's essential interest is in Wright's craft. He believes it is now possible to see that the period of Wright's most important writing was marked by his break with conventional realism, the outstanding example being "The Man Who Lived Underground." The early poetry and short stories he sees as being tractarian; while the last phase of Wright's career, dating from the publication of *Black Boy*, is typified by mechanical parallels to Feodor Dostoevsky and spurious existentialism.

A contrary view is found in Martha Stephens's "Richard Wright's Fiction: A Reassessment" (*GaR*, Winter 1971). Taking issue with exclusive concentration on *Native Son* and later work, Stephens stresses the realism of Wright's rendering of emotional states and the dramatic quality of his earlier fiction. Characters such as Mann in "Down by the Riverside," she says, are positive and heroic; and *Lawd Today*, with its poignant and comic character of Jake, is, of all Wright's fiction, the "most readable, technically the most interesting, and the most honest and convincing in its depiction of Negro life."

A number of articles seeking basic themes in all Wright's works have appeared recently. An invaluable example is George E. Kent's "Richard Wright: Blackness and the Adventure of Western Culture" (*BlackR*, No. 1, 1971), describing the ambivalent themes of consciousness and the author's relationship to black and white culture. *Black Boy*, for example, is seen as representing the growth of an alienated consciousness, but at the same time the author reveals himself as an exaggerated Westerner in his expression of the individual's life motivated by revolutionary will. Richard Kostelanetz's narrower focus in "The Politics of Unresolved Quests in the Novels of Richard Wright" (*XUS*, Spring 1969) uncovers a tortuous development for Wright as "themes for collective action suggested in his earlier writing are modified or even repudiated in later fiction, and character-types portrayed as saviors in youthful works become false messiahs in mature ones."

Two articles by Raman K. Singh seek a pattern through observation of Wright's treatment of Marxism, communism, and Christianity. In the first, "Some Basic Ideas and Ideals in Richard Wright's Fiction" (*CLAJ*, September 1969), Singh traces a progression from Wright's acceptance of Marxist and Communist party ideology coupled with rejection of Christian passivity, through a period of rejection of the party but retention of the Marxist fundamentals in combination with existentialism and Freudianism, finally to a period of suspicion of all systems but dependence on broad Marxist ideals. The second article, "Christian Heroes and Anti-Heroes in Richard Wright's Fiction" (*NALF*, Winter 1972), schematizes the progression more fully.

The existentialist parallel to Singh's readings is contained in Donald

B. Gibson's "Richard Wright and the Tyranny of Convention" (*CLAJ*, June 1969). Gibson asserts Wright's leading theme to be the individual in conflict with social convention. Violations of social control rather than morality is the issue, and Gibson distinguishes Wright's narrower view in the early works and *The Long Dream*, where the response to tyrannical convention is flight, from deliberate assaults on convention such as those in *Native Son* and *The Outsider*.

Attempts since his death to estimate Wright's achievement by referring him to the tradition of black literature may properly be said to have begun with Blyden Jackson's "The Negro's Image of the Universe as Reflected in His Fiction" (*CLAJ*, September 1960). Using *Native Son* as a chief illustration, and thereby implying its high validity and effective influence, Jackson's brilliant essay describes the shape, feel, and peculiar eschatology of the black fictional universe. As *Native Son* makes most clear, the universe consists of two parts: the ghetto (including the rural South in this category) and the nonghetto. The feel of the universe is manifest in Wright's title *Native Son*—it is pervasively ironic. Finally, the world of black fiction is static in Jackson's view, for characters like Bigger are engaged in the elemental process of a holding action which, regardless of outcome, does not alter the objective world. In a later article, "The Negro's Negro in Negro Literature" (*MQR*, Fall 1965), Jackson offers another angle of interpretation that reinforces his description of Wright's importance: there was a time when black literature was designed to show whites how much blacks were like them, but Wright exemplifies the drastic change to portrayal of black character as a challenge and a menace to whites.

Innovation in black literature is also the subject of two essays on Wright by Saunders Redding. "The Problems of the Negro Artist" (*MR*, Autumn–Winter 1964–1965) speaks of the salutary effect Wright's manner of negating stereotypes has on writers hoping to break through the walls of a literary ghetto. The point is amplified in Redding's essay "The Negro Writer and American Literature" in *Anger and Beyond*, where, by an analysis of Wright's departure from stereotype in the portrayal of the effects of repression on personality, Redding asserts that Wright defied the expectations of both the white audience and the black audience, which had been used to a "monotypical glorified picture."

Frank D. McConnell, in "Black Words and Black Becoming" (*YR*, Winter 1974), describes Wright's achievement as making us aware of an older tradition of storytelling, one which is not premised on the ideas of psychological realism, where changing one's perceptions amounts to changing the world. Rather, Wright and black authors before him such as Frederick Douglass and Jean Toomer provide narratives in which individual consciousness exists to illuminate the existing dimensions of an inhuman universe. The landscape for Bigger Thomas is maddeningly unalterable by individual effort; but through acquisition of the power to name his deeds and himself as the haunting figure in the fears of whites, Bigger achieves ponderousness. McConnell's essay excites us with its proposal that we consider Wright a phenomenological fictionalist.

Anne O. Cauley's intention in her consideration of Wright's achievement is to inspire. "A Definition of Freedom in the Fiction of Richard Wright" (*CLAJ*, March 1976) describes major characters from Jake in *Lawd Today* to Cross Damon of *The Outsider* in terms of their search for self-mastery in an irrational world. This is certainly not an incorrect way to view Wright's characters, but the essay tends, as do many purely thematic studies, to leave the dynamics of literature behind.

A more successful thematic study than Cauley's can be found in "Violence in Afro-American Fiction: An Hypothesis" (*MFS*, Summer 1971), by Stephen B. Bennett and William W. Nichols. Since violence is not only an inevitable topic in criticism of Wright, but also one that exposes the animating core of his narratives, the authors' hypothesis is that Wright is an outstanding illustration of the disposition of black writers to use violence as the route to discovery of meaning. In works of Baldwin or Toomer it may lead to self-destruction that salvages individual dignity; in "Bright and Morning Star," *Native Son,* and *The Outsider,* violence is a creative means to self-discovery. The best-known white American authors usually emphasize the horror of violence and the popular culture romanticizes it, but Afro-American literature has long employed violence to create a "culture of revolution," as has become widely evident in the apocalyptic writings of the 1960s. The Bennett and Nichols article should be read together with "Richard Wright: The Meaning of Violence," by David P. Demarest, Jr., (*NALF,* Fall 1974), which explicates "Between the World and Me" and short passages from *Black Boy* to show the care Wright gave to details of violence, insistently establishing group identity in the individual consciousness of his characters.

Consideration of Wright in the context of "Cultural Nationalism in Afro-American Literature" is undertaken by O. B. Emerson (in *The Cry of Home: Cultural Nationalism and the Modern Writer,* edited by Ernest Lewald [Knoxville: University of Tennessee Press, 1972]), who concurs in the general opinion that *Native Son* constitutes a high point in the achievement of black writing because of the power of its ethical and sociological implications. Related to the work of Ellison, Baldwin, John A. Williams, and Ishmael Reed, as well as to that of earlier authors such as Toomer, Wright's fiction appears as one of the most eloquent examples of protest writing and an essential dimension of the black cultural heritage. In smaller scope, June Jordan's essay "Richard Wright and Zora Neale Hurston: Notes Toward a Balancing of Love and Hatred" (*BlackW,* August 1974) also insists on a continuum of black literature by rejecting the necessity for choosing either the affirmative work of Hurston or the protest of Wright as exemplary. Despite the differences Wright and Hurston display and the criticisms each made of the other, they are, according to Jordan, part of the whole, not antipathetic.

Two critics who disagree with the general attribution of success to Wright's attempts to change the nature of black literature are Karl Shapiro and Theodore Gross. Shapiro argues, in "Decolonization of American Literature" (*WLB,* June 1965), that although *Native Son* embodies the recognition of decolonization as the central thrust of American experience, the novel is itself fashioned in the pattern of the colonializing white forms. Gross's purpose in "Our Mutual Estate: The Literature of the American Negro" (*AR,* Fall 1968) is to call for *professional* studies on black literature rather than the enthusiasm that overlooks, for example, that "Wright is a mediocre novelist, and mediocre in a fundamental sense: he does not inform his experiences with a meaning deeper than their representational value." Despite his expressed concern with respectability for black literary studies, Gross's call for judgment by standards similar to those applied to other, nonblack, writers appears to be an effort to reassert the priority of a "mainstream" dominated by values derived from white literature and culture.

The value of an insistently black orientation in assessing Wright can be seen in Lance Jeffers's "Afro-American Literature: The Conscience of Man" (*BlackSch,* January 1971). Afro-American literature deserves consideration as a profoundly moral creation, according to Jeffers, because it protests against wickedness, affirms man's infinite potential for good, and admonishes man to be true to his deepest positive identity. Jeffers makes the important point that despite the violence and hatred that make up narratives such as Wright's, the purpose in protesting by such means is to insist upon the innate possibilities of the characters to flourish as human beings if their shackles can be broken. A reinforcement of Jeffers's argument can be found in the previously cited "Violence in Afro-American Fiction: An Hypothesis" by Bennett and Nichols. Quoting Frantz Fanon on the "zone of non-being" where authentic upheaval can begin, and ranging widely over modern black writing with many examples from Wright, the authors propose that black fiction does not associate violence with chaos but rather uses it to demonstrate the value of a culture of revolution.

In an article on "The Future Study of Richard Wright" in the special Wright number of the *College Language Association Journal* (June 1969), George E. Kent notes a need, among others, for studies of Wright's literary apprenticeship, his relationship with the Communist party, and his early reading. Several such articles have recently appeared, at least initiating such a study. Daniel Aaron, in "Richard Wright and the Communist Party" (*NewL,* Winter 1971), describes the attraction Wright had for the party as the type of revolutionary proletarian artist the Communist literary program needed. Wright responded favorably because the party, alone at the time, had a program that appealed to him; but although he served faithfully in politics, he regularly challenged the literary practices of functionaries. Monika Plessner's "Richard Wright—Vorkämpfer der II 'Amerikanscher Revolution' " [Richard Wright—Advocate of a Second American Revolution] (*Frankfurter Hefte,* 1965) argues that after *Uncle Tom's Children* Wright began to doubt the possibility of a political solution to the racial problem, for hatred seemed to him to make class solidarity impossible. Marxism remained his tool of analysis throughout his career, but his fear and anger led him to existentialism.

Another view of Wright's relation to communism, and an indication that feelings about him still run high, can be found in Mary Ellen Brooks's "Richard Wright's Artistic Conscience" (*L&I,* No. 13, 1972), which describes Wright as an opportunist linking himself to the Communist party for self-advancement and unable to liberate himself from the bourgeois idea of an artistic conscience above class. The literary result may be seen, according to Brooks, in the anti-working-class portrayal of Bigger. A positive analysis of the literary fruits of Wright's association with the Communist party and Marxism provides the content of John M. Reilly's "Richard Wright's Apprenticeship" (*JBlS,* June 1972), which argues that membership in the party offered the intellectual support of a comprehensive theory of social relations to the intuitively radical Wright, thus providing him with a direction and purpose for his early writing as well as means and opportunity to work out an aesthetic that had continued effect throughout his career.

Although the effect of H. L. Mencken and the great realists and naturalists on Wright is well known from his autobiography, there has been very little research on peculiarly literary aspects of his apprenticeship. Michel Fabre has begun to correct that oversight with his essay on "Richard Wright's First Hundred Books" (*CLAJ,* June 1973). Based upon examination of surviving books from Wright's personal library collected before 1940 and other indications of his reading, this study suggests the importance to the aspiring writer of the fiction of Henry James, James Joyce, D. H. Lawrence, Gertrude Stein, and Ernest Hemingway, in addition to the works of Frank Norris, Stephen Crane, Sherwood Anderson, and Wright's contemporary proletarian authors. Fabre also reports Wright's lack of reading at that time in literary theory, specifies the influential works of Marxism—books by Lenin and Stalin—and indicates that Wright's extensive reading in psychology, social science, and philosophy occurred at a later date.

ARTICLES ON WRIGHT'S EXILE

Until the recent studies of the early years, the most persistently discussed extra-literary event in Wright's life has been his self-imposed exile. Although no one suggests that emigration was not a suitable move for Wright to make in 1947, a number of critics have been making plain, since his first writing from Europe began to appear, their conviction that Wright's art suffered from exile. A leading exponent of that view in contemporary reviews and later essays is Saunders Redding. His essay "The Alien Land of Richard Wright" (in *Soon, One Morning,* edited by Herbert Hill [New York: Knopf, 1963]), contains the most thoughtful expression of the viewpoint. Wright, he says, was never at home in France and was never able to write about it successfully in fiction, because his home was the ghetto of the soul, "an America that Negroes only know." Taking his black identity to Europe, Wright could not take the America that fed his consciousness.

A more general interpretation is developed in the essay "Richard Wright no Dasshutsu" [The Extrication of Richard Wright] by Fukuo Hashimoto, a pioneer Japanese translator and scholar of Afro-American literature, in his book *Kokujin Bungaku no Sekai* [The World of Negro Literature] (Tokyo: Miraisha, 1967). Hashimoto finds in Wright a repeated pattern of extrication, from one community after another, and emphasizes that such extrication was the result of his peculiar situation as an Afro-American author. Elsewhere, an exposition of Wright's career in France that suggests an increased maturity in the work he did while exiled appears in Jean-François Gournard's "Richard Wright as a Black American Writer in Exile" (*CLAJ,* March 1974).

Specific and well-documented responses to the negative view of Wright's exile can be found in Michel Fabre's essay "Wright's Exile" (*NewL,* Winter 1971) and in Harold T. McCarthy's study of Wright's exile publications, "Richard Wright: The Expatriate as Native Son" (*AL,* March 1972). Fabre attempts to describe the exile from Wright's own point of view, similar to the work he does in his biography, and represents Wright as stating "I am an American, but . . . ." While Fabre thus describes Wright's consciousness of his position, McCarthy analyzes its results. Essentially, he argues that Wright was always an alien, a position easily documented in the fiction, and only after leaving the United States was he able to relax his intensely rationalistic approach to American black life. This process of relaxation occurs in the nonfictional studies of preindustrial societies where Wright senses the power of race and spirit in cultural life. In effect, then, exile permitted him to acknowledge the ways in which his people have kept their folk identity and to feel a sense of identity that on an emotional level amounted to coming home to Afro-America.

STUDIES OF THE WORKS

Early Verse Wright's first published works—the 1924 story "The Voodoo of Hell's Half Acre," of which he speaks in *Black Boy,* and the piece titled "Superstition," which appeared in *Abbott's Monthly Magazine* in April 1931—were in the mode of Gothic fiction; but his career as an author got underway only when he began to publish the verse stimulated by his participation in the literary culture of the left wing. Although the earliest published critical notice Wright received was the essay by Edward Clay, "The Negro and American Literature" (*International Literature,* No. 6, 1935), linking the young John Reed Club poet to Langston Hughes and Sterling Brown, Wright's verse has been virtually ignored until recently.

Russell C. Brignano's book *Richard Wright: An Introduction to the Man and His Works* (Pittsburgh: University of Pittsburgh Press, 1970), for example, considers the verse as evidence of the process by which Wright gained experience in literary possibilities of language; and Keneth Kinnamon's *The Emergence of Richard Wright: A Study in Literature and Society* (Urbana: University of Illinois Press, 1972) incorporates the discussion of his article "Richard Wright: Proletarian Poet" (*CP,* June 1969), which appraises Wright's attempt to synthesize revolutionary feeling and black experience in his poetry as generally a failure, with the exception of the deeply felt "Between the World and Me." John M. Reilly's essay on Wright's apprenticeship also treats the verse, much as Kinnamon does, as representative of experiments in technique. Going beyond verse itself to a consideration of Wright's "lyric vein," Michel Fabre, in "The Poetry of Richard Wright" (*SBL,* Fall 1970), follows an analysis of the early proletarian verse with observations on the poetic techniques used in *12 Million Black Voices* to translate sociological concepts into metaphor and epiphanies in *Black Boy.*

Lawd Today Repeated rejections from publishers prevented the appearance of Wright's apprentice novel, *Lawd Today* (*c.*1936), until 1963, when it provided readers a backward look at the recently deceased author. Its reception from reviewers varied from the acclaim by which Granville Hicks (*SatR,* March 30, 1963) compared its naturalistic power with work by Theodore Dreiser and James T. Farrell to the disdain of Nick Aaron Ford (*CLAJ,* March 1964), who found it difficult to believe Wright had written the book. Similar to a reviewer's acclaim is Lewis Leary's declaration in *"Lawd Today:* Notes on Richard Wright's First/ Last Novel" (*CLAJ,* June 1972) that the book stands high as one in which the figure of Jake reveals through mind and action the culture that condemns him.

More extensive studies include Edward Margolies's examination of the antihero Jake in *The Art of Richard Wright* (Carbondale: Southern Illinois University Press, 1969); Kinnamon's *"Lawd Today:* Richard

Wright's Apprentice Novel" (*SBL,* Summer 1971)—an article also incorporated into his book—which studies the novel as a relative failure in execution but significant in staking out concerns Wright would develop later; and Reilly's argument in "Richard Wright's Experiment in Naturalism" (*SBL,* Autumn 1971) that the premises of *Lawd Today* so contradict the world view Wright was developing that he effectively abandoned naturalism after the novel was finished.

A departure from other criticism, resulting in an assertion that sociopolitical interpretations of Wright's apprentice novel cannot work at all, is found in Don B. Graham's *"Lawd Today* and the Example of *The Waste Land"* (*CLAJ,* March 1974), which studies the work as a novel of spiritual desiccation explicitly derived from T. S. Eliot.

Uncle Tom's Children Most sophisticated among studies of *Uncle Tom's Children,* and also the first extended critical treatment the volume received, is Edwin Berry Burgum's "The Art of Richard Wright's Short Stories" (*QRL,* Spring 1944; reprinted in Burgum's *The Novel and the World's Dilemma* [Oxford: Oxford University Press, 1947]). In an effort to show the workings of Marxism in craft and authorial outlook, Burgum compares Wright's stories of the southern American black peasantry with John Millington Synge's treatment of Irish peasants. Wright evidently aims to clarify, to raise the people's consciousness of the forces that affect their lives, rather than to add to their feelings of impotence before mystifying circumstances. "Long Black Song," for example, through description of the reciprocity between developing events and changing personality, shows Silas, the leading male character, developing a limited power to control his fate. In fact, Burgum argues, this dialectical narrative structure constitutes the form of modern tragedy, showing "sin" operating through men who rule, and tragic action through the contradictions between the external state of life and a character's strong internal feelings of rebellion.

After a thirty-year hiatus, Burgum's suggestion of tragic form has been taken up by P. Jay Delmar, whose "Tragic Patterns in Richard Wright's *Uncle Tom's Children"* (*NALF,* Spring 1976) greatly enriches our understanding of characterization in the early short stories. Delmar defines the tragic pattern as one in which the protagonist, because of weaknesses in himself, fails to resolve successfully a dilemma brought on by hostile forces surrounding him. Accordingly, Big Boy is a victim of his own pride and impulsiveness as well as of the socially determined fear of interracial sexuality; Mann is helped to death by his indecisiveness; and the twin protagonists of "Long Black Song" are undone by sensuality and again pride. Such analysis also leaves one sensitive to the possibility that "Fire and Cloud" contains a resolution imposed by its author contrary to the implications of the first part of the story and at odds with endings of patterns in other stories in the volume. "Bright and Morning Star," then, appears to be a reorganization of elements mishandled in the previous story to achieve an ending in keeping with the tragic form of the book.

Another reappraisal of Wright's first volume appears in James R. Giles's "Richard Wright's Successful Failure: A New Look at *Uncle Tom's Children*" (*Phylon*, Fall 1973). As do most critics, Giles concentrates on thematic elements, but he does so to demonstrate that in the short stories Wright used with more sophistication images and themes he would repeat in *Native Son*. There is, by Giles's reading, the same progression in militancy and understanding but without Wright's later editorializing.

Campbell Tatham, in "Vision and Value in *Uncle Tom's Children*" (*SBL,* Spring 1972), unconvincingly dismisses any radical political content in the stories. Nevertheless, he writes a cogent description of the themes of the volume: the discovery of internal sources of strength, the overcoming of impediments to freedom inherent in traditional culture and white-fostered stereotypes, and the necessity for joining in collective struggle. Among the strengths of Tatham's discussion of the book, which he considers possibly Wright's one real masterpiece, is his willingness to name and take issue with other critics.

Several essays focus on the individual stories in *Uncle Tom's Children,* but the only unqualified success is Blyden Jackson's "Richard Wright in a Moment of Truth" (*SLJ,* Spring 1971). Jackson fully explores possible biographical sources, but the main burden of the article consists of a reading of the story that demonstrates in detail how the psychology and anthropology of American racism find form in "Big Boy Leaves Home." Of the remaining two essays on particular stories, John Timmerman's "Symbolism as Syndetic Device in Richard Wright's 'Long Black Song' " (*CLAJ,* March 1971) has interest for the character contrasts it describes, but is far from conclusive in its argument for the existence of a nationalist hero in the story; and Carole W. Oleson's "The Symbolic Richness of Richard Wright's 'Bright and Morning Star' " (*NALF,* Winter 1972) does no more than note the presence of symbols in the story and say how they might affect a reader.

Native Son As would be expected, *Native Son* stimulates an abundance of critical discussion. The reader seeking an overview of the issues raised by Wright's most famous book will find Richard Abcarian's *Richard Wright's "Native Son": A Critical Handbook* (Belmont, Calif.: Wadsworth, 1970) a convenient source of pertinent essays by Wright (including responses he made to two particularly outrageous attacks), twenty contemporary reviews, a section of Abcarian's choices of the "best and most representative critical essays," and a selection of excerpts from other, more recent, important black social writers.

Three extended essays from the decade in which the novel appeared retain critical interest for us today. Melvin B. Tolson, in "Richard Wright: Native Son" (*ModQ,* Winter 1939), attributes Wright's success in the novel to his independence from the bourgeois experience and aspiration that infused earlier black fiction. It was an independence that allowed him to synthesize personal knowledge of frustration and social barriers with his expression to construct episodes that move breathlessly through "economically and socially predestined cycles" with the inevitability of Greek tragedy. "The Promise of Democracy in Richard Wright's *Native Son*" by Edwin Berry Burgum (*S&S,* 1943; reprinted in Burgum's *The Novel and the World's Dilemma*) goes to the heart of Bigger's motivation in a discussion of the social limits on perception, and establishes the parameters of psychological realism in the novel. In this way Burgum anticipates the subject of the best criticism on *Native Son,* and in a concluding treatment of the contradiction between Bigger's anarchistic individualism and Max's contention that collective organization is necessary, Burgum also introduces a discussion of the book's ending, destined to be interpreted over and over again.

The third early essay is not intended as a critical piece but as a full analysis of the psychology in the novel. C. V. Charles's "Optimism and Frustration in the American Negro" (*Psychoanalytic Review,* July 1942), an article recommended to Wright by his editor, Edward Aswell, studies the ideational life of all Bigger Thomases through an examination of Wright's fictional character as a neurotic individual who chooses crime to relieve the unbearable tension caused by his own conflicting emotions. As Charles's title suggests, there is an optimistic significance to the interpretation because Bigger's drive is, of course, for self-expression and fulfillment. Although it is unlikely that this article has been widely read by literary critics, it should be, because it puts in detailed psychological perspective a dynamic conception of character only gradually emerging in the criticism.

Native Son, however, strikes readers as social and racial comment before anything else. Indeed, there can be no doubt that Wright intended it that way, so it is to be expected that much of the criticism deals with those themes. For example, David Britt, in "*Native Son:* Watershed of Negro Protest Literature" (*NALF,* Fall 1967), states that Bigger must be considered in social terms because the controlling metaphor of nightmare and the racial dimension of each incident demonstrate that white society governs the Negro's self-image. This is a familiar point, and we shall see that it leads to possibilities for the study of epistemology and imagery within the novel.

Concentration on the social perspective has been fruitful also for stimulating attention to the racial viewpoint, as in two essays by Addison Gayle, Jr. The first, "A Defense of James Baldwin" (*CLAJ,* March 1967), disputes (as does Baldwin) the social resolution Wright implies in *Native Son*. All society has to do is live up to the American creed and Bigger's rage will be stifled; but at the time he wrote the novel, Wright could not allow for the possibility that American white people have no intention of living up to the mythic creed and are unfrightened by the consequences if they do not. The second essay seems to be a reconsideration on Gayle's part, anticipating his viewpoint in *The Way of the New World: The Black Novel in America* (Garden City, N. Y.: Doubleday, 1975). "Cultural Nationalism—The Black Novelist in America," in Gayle's *The Black Situation* (New York: Horizon, 1970), links Wright to the nationalist Martin Robison Delany, whose emphasis on black uniqueness Gayle sees revived in urban novels, beginning during the Harlem Renaissance. In this connection *Native Son* appears as an unsurpassed rendition of the reality of black separateness, and therefore a departure from the romantic views of racial assimilationists.

An analysis, as distinct from an assertion, of the specific blackness of *Native Son* appears in the chapter by Houston A. Baker, Jr., on "Racial Wisdom and Richard Wright's *Native Son*" in Baker's *Long Black Song: Essays in Black American Literature and Culture* (Charlottesville: University Press of Virginia, 1972), which Baker uses as an introduction to the volume *Twentieth Century Interpretations of "Native Son"* (Englewood Cliffs, N.J.: Prentice-Hall, 1972). In this essay Baker accounts for Wright's commitment to communism, at the time of writing the novel, in terms of fundamental cultural assumptions about a united black community. He also describes Bigger first in relation to the existential characters of fugitive slave narratives and then as a conscious literary projection of the folk hero of the "bad nigger" embodied in Shine and Stackolee. According to Baker, Wright thus completes the work begun by Paul Laurence Dunbar and James Weldon Johnson of translating values from oral black literature into written form.

An attempt to pursue the social meaning of the novel in terms of the proletarian implications within it appears in James G. Kennedy's "The Content and Form of *Native Son*" (*CE,* November 1972). For Kennedy, the work grows out of the world view of a colonial subject in the period of imperialism. Wright's controlled point of view provides Bigger with a high degree of working-class consciousness, apparent in his perception of bourgeois characters as antagonists and developed through a plot showing the impossibility of relating across class lines. Although Max fails to encourage his antagonism, Bigger nevertheless moves to purposefulness in the ending of the novel and becomes a Communist. Annette Cohn, in a commentary published with the article, makes sufficient criticism of Kennedy's scheme when she says that Bigger is both more complicated than Kennedy assumes him to be and more limited in his possibilities because of racism, and consequently possesses only a rudimentary class consciousness.

As a critique of American society, *Native Son* has often been paired with *An American Tragedy,* Theodore Dreiser's novel of an American youth destroyed. A recent example can be found in the East German critic Friederike Hajek's "*American Tragedy—Zwei Aspekte . . . [American Tragedy*—Two Aspects]" (*ZAA*, 1972), which focuses on the differences in the two authors' responses to youth destroyed by a capitalist society: Wright presents rebellion; Dreiser documents resignation.

Critics observing the frequency of insistence upon social content in *Native Son* have sometimes argued explicitly for what might be termed a desocializing interpretation. A highly effective example of such an argument is Donald B. Gibson's "Wright's Invisible Native Son" (*AQ*, Winter 1969). Gibson cites passages from the concluding section of the novel to demonstrate that it is about Bigger's coming to terms with himself, not about his trial and not about Max. Feeling wonder and separateness, Bigger becomes every man whose death is imminent.

Also concentrating on the final appearances of Bigger, Edward Kearns argues in "The 'Fate' Section of *Native Son*" (*ConL*, Spring 1971) that the ironies and paradoxes of the novel's third book, when formally analyzed, show a conflict between abstract definitions of existence (such as those imposed by Max) and the concrete realities that provide Bigger with means for escaping from stereotypes. Kearns builds his essay as an explicit answer to what he terms the conventional view of the "Fate" section expressed by John M. Reilly in the afterword to the Harper Perennial Library edition of *Native Son*. Another essay intending to correct the same view is Charles L. James's "Bigger Thomas in the Seventies: A Twentieth Century Search for Relevance" (*EngR*, Fall 1971). James rejects interpretations of Bigger as being dehumanized by stressing his understandable human needs, in particular the need to revolt against the violence done to his sensibilities by white oppression and the need to reject a passive submission common among the oppressed.

Richard E. Baldwin joins the discussion in "The Creative Vision of *Native Son*" (*MR*, Spring 1973) for the purpose of arguing that the last book of the novel brings the character of Bigger to completion as a critic of American culture and an affirmative representative of the creative power of human personality. The ironic image of Bigger, solitary in a cell, realizing a vision of a social world without walls, fulfills the "significant action" of a murder done to reorder social relations and to give Bigger the feeling of participation in life necessary to his growth. Baldwin traces a by now familiar theme, of course, but he adduces additional imagery to assure consideration of the theme as part of the aesthetic form of *Native Son*.

Jeffrey A. Sadler's "Split Consciousness in Richard Wright's *Native Son*" (*SCR*, April 1976) rehearses once again the argument that Bigger's struggle for self-knowledge is consistently central to the novel, including its last book. Sadler provocatively employs R. D. Laing's conception of the "divided self" in explaining Bigger's behavior, but otherwise he is intent on reiterating Max's blindness and the idea that Wright was subtly undercutting Communist party positions in the novel's conclusion. The latter is a very debatable proposition, depending in large measure for its proof on uncritical acceptance of Wright's description in "I Tried to Be a Communist" (*AtM,* August 1944 and September 1944) of his breaking with the party as early as 1936.

Probably the most useful discussion of the meaning of the novel's final section is provided by Paul N. Siegel in "The Conclusion of Richard Wright's *Native Son*" (*PMLA,* May 1974). To begin with, Siegel corrects the prevalent interpretations of Boris Max's political affiliations. He is, according to Siegel, neither a Stalinist nor a revolutionary but rather a man seeking redress of wrongs to avert the cataclysm he foresees. Analyzing Max's courtroom speeches, Siegel shows that the images and themes they embody are so recurrent in the narrative that it is a grave mistake to continue, as critics have done, to view Max's exposition as less than integral to the novel. Finally, he argues that Max's shock at the remarks Bigger makes in his cell about killing does not represent failure to comprehend. Instead, it is recognition of the inescapable catastrophe the society will not permit to be averted. For his part, Bigger has reached a level of hatred of oppression and an intimation of comradeship in his acceptance of Jan. Attached to a motor idea (Marxism) in Wright's work, these attainments of Bigger's presage a struggle for another American Revolution.

Still another attempt to remedy presumed citical errors is Amritjit Singh's "Misdirected Responses to Bigger Thomas" (*SBL,* Summer 1974). Singh's concern is that critics have been so overwhelmed by Bigger's presence that they have ignored the early pages of establishing detail presented in the authorial voice as social and environmental description. If readers attend properly to this detail, according to Singh, there can be no criticism of the novel as being merely negative protest or as being overwhelmed by violence. Nor would Bigger's thoughts be read as inconsistent. Singh sees some weakness in the novel, particularly in Bigger's exceptionally rapid realization of possibilities in his life after the murders, but he strongly denies the descriptions of inadequacy made by James Baldwin (in "Many Thousands Gone" and "Everybody's Protest Novel," both mentioned earlier) and Cecil Brown (in "Richard Wright: Complexes and Black Writing Today," mentioned earlier). Baldwin merely tells us his preferences for his own writing and is not talking about *Native Son* at all; and Brown is reactionary and irresponsible in saying that Wright's powerful protest was an attempt to curry favor with whites.

Sheldon Brivic's "Conflict of Values: Richard Wright's *Native Son*"

(*Novel,* Spring 1974) also contributes a reassessment, this one concentrating on Bigger's character. Rather than viewing Bigger as an ambivalent character, Brivic contends that we must see in him a personality split that adds political and social value to the novel. Bigger's irrational aspect, for example, relates to an intuitive nationalism in his character and is the level on which he takes responsibility for murder. The rational aspect, in contrast, provides Bigger with politically progressive significance. Providing diagrams of all the values embodied in Bigger's personality conflict, Brivic's essay becomes a very suggestive analysis of the ways in which Wright portrayed socially observable contradictions through the medium of human personality.

As debate about the thematic burdens of *Native Son* proceeds, it becomes necessary for any argument to ground itself in an understanding of the subtleties of the art that goes beyond naturalistic premises. James A. Emanuel, in "Fever and Feeling: Notes on the Imagery in *Native Son*" (*ND,* December 1968), provides a start in one direction. Bigger, he observes, knows life most surely in images, and his desire for wholeness can be fulfilled "only when his feelings merge with some equivalent object around him." Because of the frustration of this desire to merge with the world, the psychological substance of the novel is conveyed in images of light and dark, isolation, blotting out, white blurs, walls, and curtains. Emanuel, providing a count of the occurrences of each such image and an idea of the functions served by many, intends his essay to be suggestive, but he has done enough to support well the contention that it is through imagery as dramatized subjective experience that Wright achieves the remarkable effect of making Bigger a sympathetic character.

There have been five other studies of imagery in the novel. James Nagel, in "Images of 'Vision' in *Native Son*" (*UR,* December 1969), takes blindness as a metaphor for lack of understanding and shows it functioning, similarly to W. E. B. Du Bois's veil in *The Souls of Black Folk,* as a curtain or wall separating people. Going over much the same ground is Thomas LeClair's "The Blind Leading the Blind: Wright's *Native Son*" (*CLAJ,* March 1970). According to LeClair, Bigger moves from one kind of blindness to another after killing Mary and can only begin to see clearly at the end of the novel. Max, who must grope his way out of the cell after learning what Bigger has come to see as the meaning of the crimes, is a further extension of the metaphor, as are numerous references to concealment and inadequate understanding. These are ingenious essays that would profit from application of a controlling concept such as that Burgum used as early as 1943 in "The Promise of Democracy in Richard Wright's *Native Son*."

An example of an idea insufficiently rather than ingeniously developed appears in the third essay on imagery in *Native Son,* "The White

Self-Image Conflict in *Native Son*," by Louis Graham (*SBL*, Summer 1972), which simply observes the ironic descriptions of white characters such as the Daltons, who speak liberalism while engaging in exploitation. A pole away is Lloyd W. Brown's "Stereotypes in Black and White: The Nature of Perception in Wright's *Native Son*" (*BARev*, Fall 1970). Brown shows that initially Bigger's "perceptual values are merely passive reflections of white categorizations." After the murder of Mary, however, Bigger is forced by the treatment he receives to analyze his actions through introspective awareness, and he achieves definition in his own terms. Brown's essay is successful criticism not because it is the most comprehensive treatment of vision in the novel, although it is that, but because it goes well beyond the limits of a formal analysis into socially informed discussion.

Finally, a more limited but still useful examination of imagery is found in Robert Felgar's " 'The Kingdom of the Beast': The Landscape of *Native Son*" (*CLAJ*, March 1974), which takes off from Max's statement that Bigger comes from "the land of the beast" to tally occurrences of animal images that enforce tone.

Studies that will perhaps contribute to fuller understanding of *Native Son* by focusing on specific aspects of technique include Michel Fabre's "Black Cat and White Cat: Richard Wright's Debt to Edgar Allan Poe" (*PoeS*, June 1971), which brings to bear upon the links between the white cat, fire, and guilt in the furnace-room scene a solid description of Wright's great interest in Gothic and mystery literature; R. B. V. Larsen's study of "The Four Voices of Richard Wright's *Native Son*" (*NALF*, Winter 1972), which distinguishes among the speeches of Max, the voice of the "establishment," Bigger's speech, and the third-person narration in rhetorical terms; and Phyllis R. Klotman's "Moral Distancing as a Rhetorical Technique in *Native Son*: A Note on 'Fate' " (*CLAJ*, December 1974), which attempts an explanation of the way guilt is shifted from the protagonist, with whom we identify, to society.

Interesting notes on detail in the novel, also perhaps useful in small ways, are Jerold J. Savory's "Bigger Thomas and the Book of Job: The Epigraph to *Native Son*" (*NALF*, Summer 1975), which explains the aptness of a quotation from the impatient, rebellious Job, who is to be distinguished from the patient and pious figure of the folktale; Linda Prior's "A Further Word on Richard Wright's Use of Poe in *Native Son*" (*PoeS*, December 1972) and Seymour L. Gross's "*Native Son* and 'The Murders in the Rue Morgue': An Addendum" (*PoeS*, June 1975), both of which present internal and external evidence, respectively, for intentional allusions to Poe's "Murders in the Rue Morgue"; and a discussion by Gross of Wright's possibly deliberate use of the name "Dalton" (" 'Dalton' and Color Blindness in *Native Son*" [*MissQ*, Winter 1973]).

There are also a few notes that are unlikely to be very helpful.

Eugene E. Miller's "Voodoo Parallels in *Native Son*" (*CLAJ*, September 1972) may remind us of Wright's interest in folk culture, but implicitly it rewrites the novel in searching out parallels between Haitian rites for deliberate entry into cosmic unity and the spontaneous murder of Mary Dalton. Similarly, Edward A. Watson's rewriting of Bessie's speeches in the tradition of Ma Rainey and Bessie Smith in "Bessie's Blues" (*NewL*, Winter 1971) presents a representation of Bessie's character that is isolated from the dynamics of the novel.

The remaining subject of major critical interest regarding *Native Son* is its existentialist quality. This is discussed in several of the general articles, such as those by Raman K. Singh ("Some Basic Ideas and Ideals in Richard Wright's Fiction" [*CLAJ*, September 1969]; and "Christian Heroes and Anti-Heroes in Richard Wright's Fiction" [*NALF*, Winter 1972]), and is a theme of Gibson's essay on the "invisible native son." Hiromi Furukawa's essay on *Native Son* in *Kokujin Bungaku Nyūmon* [*Introduction to Negro Literature*] (Osaka: Sōgensha, 1973) represents a reevaluation of Wright that stresses his existentialism; and Esther Merle Jackson's earlier work "The American Negro and the Image of the Absurd" (*Phylon*, Winter 1962) includes Wright's novel as a second stage of a progression—starting with William Faulkner's *Light in August* and ending with Ralph Ellison's *Invisible Man*—that represents a modern sense of alienation derived from awareness of the condition of Afro-Americans.

Black Boy   Interest in *Black Boy*, Wright's second great popular success, has been high since its publication. W. E. B. Du Bois (*NYHTBW*, March 4, 1945) departs from the favorable reviewer response with the comment that the self-centered hero of what appears to him a fictionalized biography misjudges black people and unconvincingly exaggerates Wright's picture of experience; but most commentators accept the work as a valuable representation of personal and general black life. Horace Cayton, for example, in "Frightened Children of Frightened Parents" (*TAY*, Spring–Summer/Fall–Winter 1945), finds *Black Boy* an adaptation of the European tradition of autobiography to the special purpose of describing the fear-hate-fear complex wherein a black person's insecurities are reinforced by the environment; efforts to rebel, brought on by hatred of a humiliating position, result in fear of punishment, leading to a deep-seated feeling of guilt.

Ralph Ellison's "Richard Wright's Blues" (*AR*, June 1945; reprinted in Ellison's *Shadow and Act* [New York: Random House, 1964]) also discusses Wright's efforts to reveal problems of a psychological nature. Ellison's model for explanation is the blues, which he explains as a chronicle of personal catastrophe expressed lyrically and functioning, through emotional probing, to keep the painful details alive. With a blues attitude, Wright describes the historical process of black life in terms of one childhood, thereby dramatizing what happens when a black person's sensibility attempts to fulfill itself. Whites repress individuality in blacks in order to maintain supreme power; blacks repress each other as a means of self-defense against the reprisals an independent black can bring down on the whole community.

Another indication of the social and psychological validity of Wright's personally derived view of minority life is found in David Riesman's "Marginality, Conformity, and Insight" (*Phylon*, Fall 1953). In Riesman's opinion, Wright demonstrates a significant technique of social survival through his powers of imagination and a conceptual reeducation. The later process has particular applicability to the continuation of Wright's autobiography in "I Tried to Be a Communist," for Riesman says that adoption of a map of reality such as Wright found in Marxism, which says that one's suffering can be explained by a theory of generalized class and ethnic oppression, may serve, as it did Wright, to transform marginal status into a design for affirmative living.

These insightful readings of social content find an interesting parallel in the report of a statistical analysis contained in Ralph K. White's *"Black Boy*: A Value Analysis" (*Journal of Abnormal and Social Psychology*, October 1947). Codifying values stated in the narrative and tabulating the frequency of their appearance and application to individuals, White discovers, for example, 1,205 references to frustration and 349 references to positive satisfaction. White in no way contradicts an impressionistic reading of the autobiography, but the statistical evidence of Wright's lack of expressed interest in sex and love, the high percentage of people toward whom he showed 100 percent disapproval, and the absence of expressions of concern for other blacks is, to say the least, startling.

John M. Reilly's "Self-Portraits by Richard Wright" (*ColQ*, Summer 1971) extends the findings of the social analyses of *Black Boy* to an account of the development of Wright's artistic expression. The congruity between Wright's sense of the structure of his own personality in the autobiography and in his fictional narratives is illustrated by a study of "The Man Who Lived Underground," which leads to the conclusion that as Wright is continually concerned with representing the defensive outsider seeking self-definition through acts of rebellion, "it is only a slight exaggeration to argue that . . . all of his works are self-portraits."

There have also been three significant efforts in articles to go beyond the apparent isolation of the narrator in *Black Boy* and determine relationships between the book and black culture. Joseph Bruchac's study of "Black Autobiography in Africa and America" (*BaRev*, Spring–Summer 1971) attempts to explicate the African quality of Wright's inner strength by noting the similarity of historical context for *Black Boy* and Camara Laye's recounting of his youth in Guinea in *The Dark Child*.

Although Bruchac observes the many differences in the authors' views of family, education, and childhood, he makes a case for their identity in their mutual necessity to assert personal integrity against the dehumanizing Western assumptions about black colonials. Sidonie Ann Smith, in "Richard Wright's *Black Boy:* The Creative Impulse as Rebellion" (*SLJ,* Fall 1972), follows Ellison's lead in reading the autobiography as the story of an education, describes the essential metaphor within the story as warfare between self and environment, and makes a valuable connection to Afro-American tradition by describing the similarities found in fugitive slave narratives to Wright's theme of "freeing" an authentic identity. Then Ronald Primeau, in "Imagination as Moral Bulwark and Creative Energy in Richard Wright's *Black Boy* and LeRoi Jones' *Home*" (*SBL,* Summer 1972), completes the circle by delineating a common pattern of intensified perception creating the world anew in Wright's autobiography and in the essays of a contemporary cultural nationalist.

An example of close reading technique applied to Wright's autobiography can be found in Gayle Gaskill's "The Effect of Black/White Imagery in Richard Wright's *Black Boy*" (*NALF,* Summer 1973). Observing positive images of blackness and the fear of engulfing whiteness that Wright reports from a dream, Gaskill suggests that Wright purposely attempts to reverse the conventional Western values assigned to light and dark.

The Outsider   With the passing of the cold-war mentality that cast Wright as an exponent of an outmoded style of fiction, and the encouraging recent developments in biographical research, Wright's work in his exile years may soon gain the critical attention it deserves. Meanwhile, however, it is only *The Outsider* for which a genuine critical discussion can be reported.

The first feature of the novel to which critics must attend is the deemphasis of race. Arthur P. Davis, in *"The Outsider* as a Novel of Race" (*MidwestJ,* Winter 1955–1956), describes the technical means by which Wright allows readers to take Cross Damon's race as a given; and George Knox, in "The Negro Novelist's Sensibility and the Outsider Theme" (*WHR,* Spring 1957), indicates how the creation of an ambiguous Christ figure converts the black protagonist into a general representative of modern man.

Concerned with a tendency to see *The Outsider* as a departure from Wright's earlier work, Nathan A. Scott writes in "Search for Beliefs: Fiction of Richard Wright" (*UKCR,* Autumn 1956 and Winter 1956) of a predilection for existentialism always present in Wright's work as a result of his life experiences. Returning again to the subject in "The Dark and Haunted Tower of Richard Wright" (*GC,* July 1964), Scott discusses the novel as the one "emphatically existentialist novel in contemporary American literature," but finds it disappointing, nevertheless, because Cross Damon achieves no more than destructive revenge. Scott explains his judgment in terms of Wright's ignorance of the universal nature of evil and his lack of defense against his own radicalism. The point, however, seems to be that Wright lacked a Christian understanding.

Interesting but different rebuttals of Scott are offered by Raman K. Singh and Lewis A. Lawson. Singh, in "Wright's Tragic Vision in *The Outsider*" (*SBL*, Fall 1970) argues that the concept of original sin has been secularized in the narrative of Cross Damon, for whom the cause of doom is being born, and that Wright intentionally led him along the pathway to his fate by providing him with an exaggerated belief in his own intellect. On the other hand, Lawson's article "Cross Damon: Kierkegaardian Man of Dread" (*CLAJ*, March 1971) identifies the novel as quite Christian by reading Cross's behavior in the light of the existential conception of guilt expounded in Søren Kierkegaard's *The Concept of Dread*.

Two serious essays by Charles I. Glicksberg examine Wright's novel against the background of European existentialism. One, titled "Existentialism in *The Outsider*" (*FourQ*, January 1958), finds the novel inspired by the works of Sartre and Camus and gives a section-by-section analysis showing Cross evading the ideological traps set for him while acknowledging no power superior to his own. In "The God of Fiction" (*ColQ*, Autumn 1958), Glicksberg again relates the novel to Camus's description of the metaphysical rebel as one whose rebellion in behalf of a dream of order and a reign of justice must lead him to inhumanity unless he accepts the limits of his own responsibility. According to Glicksberg, Wright's novel—enforcing the point by its nightmare of inhumanity as Cross invalidates all sanctions including his personal ones—is the most consistent example of nihilistic philosophy in fiction.

Richard Lehan's "Existentialism in Recent American Fiction: The Demonic Quest" (*TSLL*, Summer 1959) is also concerned with relationships between European existentialists and American writers, and a specific discussion of Wright adds a treatment of literary structure that does much to explain readers' dissatisfaction with *The Outsider*. The problem, Lehan explains, is that despite his philosophical theme with its insistence on subjective limits, Wright continues to use an omniscient point of view and a naturalistic narrative structure. The result is a contradiction between theme and form.

Probably the fullest discussion of the workings of explicit philosophy within Wright's novel is found in Kingsley Widmer's "The Existential Darkness: Richard Wright's *The Outsider*" (*WSCL*, Fall 1960). Treating the book as an American fable of guilt and anguish, Widmer describes the choices available to Cross as assertions of nonexistence, since they have to be made in a world of dehumanizing conflicts. Cross's premises demand that he descend into the darkness of defiant nihilism for enlightenment, but in his American situation, where outsider status is actual as well as metaphysical alienation, there are not even negative limits to prevent Cross from hovering in ambiguity. In a recent revision of the essay, appearing under the title "Black Existentialism: Richard Wright" in *Modern Black Novelists: A Collection of Critical Essays,* edited by M. G. Cooke (Englewood Cliffs, N.J.: Prentice-Hall, 1971), Widmer places *The Outsider* in a line of development from existential paradigms in "The Man Who Lived Underground" and *Black Boy.*

Another link between *The Outsider* and Wright's earlier fiction is provided by Darwin T. Turner's *"The Outsider:* Revision of an Idea" *(CLAJ,* June 1969), which describes the novel as another effort to deal with the idea at the core of *Native Son* and in the process create a protagonist whose powers of conceptualization are more adequate to philosophical exploration than Bigger's. The essence of similarity between the novels is that both Bigger and Cross are metaphysical rebels who become free to choose through a death, and who carry their freedom to the extent of symbolically divesting themselves of the socially conditioned black personality.

A complete departure from the previous lines of critical interest in *The Outsider* appears in the attempt of Phyllis R. Klotman and Melville Yancey (in "The Gift of Double-Vision: Possible Political Implications of Richard Wright's 'Self-Consciousness' Theme" [*CLAJ,* September 1972]) to relate the novel's "dreadful objectivity" positively to the consciousness of roles and rules developed in the study of learning theory, sociolinguistics, and the sociology of knowledge. If such a consciousness were widespread among whites and blacks, it might lead to the understanding necessary for political coalition. One cannot doubt that Wright would have been interested.

Works from the Exile Period Other works Wright published during his exile period necessarily receive critical treatment in the book-length studies and biographies and in the best of the essays on the general question of the meaning of his exile. But considering that the thirteen years he spent in Europe represent two-thirds of his career as a known author, it is an instruction in the limits of American literary criticism to observe what slight attention the products of those years receive in journals. Katherine Sprandel (Fishburn) has incorporated her reading of the initiation theme in *The Long Dream (NewL,* Winter 1971) into her book on Wright's hero (cited earlier). The only other essay on that novel is Linda Bearman Hamalian's "Richard Wright's Use of Epigraphs in *The Long Dream" (BALF,* Winter 1976). James Baldwin makes a notable contribution to the discussion of *Eight Men* in "The Survival of Richard Wright" *(Reporter,* March 16, 1961; reprinted as "Eight Men" in Baldwin's *Nobody Knows My Name* [New York: Dial, 1961]) by modifying his earlier description of Wright's work as a reinforcement of stereotypes. "It now begins to seem," he writes with particular reference to "The Man Who Lived Underground," " . . . that Wright's unrelentingly bleak landscape was not merely that of the Deep South, or of Chicago, but that of the world, of the human heart."

The only discussion of the social essays that equals Edward Margolies's *The Art of Richard Wright* (Carbondale: Southern Illinois University Press, 1969) and Harold T. McCarthy's "Richard Wright: The Expatriate as Native Son" (*AL*, March 1972) in comprehensiveness, while offering a different interpretation, is the section devoted to Wright's view of the Third World in Harold R. Isaacs's "Five Writers and Their African Ancestors" (*Phylon*, Fall 1960; reprinted in Isaacs's *The New World of Negro Americans* [New York: John Day, 1963]). The burden of Isaacs's discussion is that Wright disavowed the color mystique of both African nationalists and Afro-American authors. In combination with a strong feeling against religion and tradition, this disavowal made Wright respond to Africa as a Westerner and, moreover, as one who had converted the condition of outsider forced upon him by racism into a life-style he had come to believe permitted him to observe the world freely. Testimony to the success of Wright's free observation is put forth in John A. Williams's introduction to the Doubleday edition of *White Man, Listen!*, where Williams explains that Wright's importance to other writers is due above all to a "fantastic sense of perception," which in the case of his essays on Africa and Asia enabled him to see by the acts of the past what the future would bring.

THE FUTURE OF WRIGHT CRITICISM

Some indication of the direction for future developments in Wright criticism can be found by taking "The Man Who Lived Underground" as a test case. Of all his short pieces, Wright's story of the underground man has been most interesting to critics. As previous discussion shows, they have seen the story as a break with conventions of realism, as one of the clearest projections of Wright's personality into fiction, and as evidence of an inclination to existentialism predating his European exile. Appropriately, then, several articles have appeared that attempt to assess the story's novelty and significance. The first, by Ronald Ridenour, " 'The Man Who Lived Underground': A Critique" (*Phylon*, Spring 1970), sees the story as a move beyond protest to a consideration of the struggle faced by all men to find meaning in their lives. The argument, though, is derivative and undeveloped, so it does little to indicate how Wright deracializes the protagonist, so obviously black in early versions of the story. Shirley Meyer, in "The Identity of 'The Man

Who Lived Underground' " (*NALF,* July 1970), finds that Fred Daniels achieves authentic identity when he realizes through his underground experiences that all men are inherently evil and goes above ground to accept responsibility by communicating his existential vision. The reading is plausible—as far as it goes. David Bakish, in "Underground in an Ambiguous Dreamworld" (*SBL,* Autumn 1971), intends to fill out a thematic reading with examination of light and dark imagery, the former positive and the latter ambiguous. Again plausible, but essentially a reading confirming an impressionistic feeling that there is ambiguity in the story. In "The Death of Richard Wright's American Dream: 'The Man Who Lived Underground' " (*CLAJ,* March 1974), Mildred W. Everette goes somewhat further in analysis of the story to observe images of deadness throughout it and to link the tone and theme to a disillusionment Wright experienced after he went to Chicago with some hope that life could be lived humanely and found out otherwise.

A contrast to these competent but limited essays is Michel Fabre's "Richard Wright: The Man Who Lived Underground" (*SNNTS,* Summer 1971). Fabre begins by establishing the details of Wright's composition of the story, situating it in relation to other works, published and unpublished, that occupied Wright during the time of its composition. He then makes a multileveled analysis that subsumes imagery and the critical problem of racial identity into exploration of Wright's philosophical concerns in the story. Constantly aware of the dynamics of the story and influences that went into its composition, he builds an analysis that indicates the cyclic alternations among quasi-mythological, fantastic, realistic, and parabolic elements that serve as vehicles for meaning.

The contrast to be stressed among these essays is not one of degrees of sensitivity in reading literature; it is methodological. The practice of American literary studies depends heavily on the assumption that an ideal critic is an ideal reader, who benefits from awareness of other disciplines but basically is engaged in empirical observation of texts. Certainly such practice explains the heavy concentration of interest on a few of Wright's works, both because of a need to deal with (that is, read) books that have become classics and because of the preference in "ideal reading" for internally complex books. The best books and articles in this survey of Wright studies, however, go well beyond such limits in an effort to discover through a study of his biographical, historical, political, and social contexts the sources of his animation, in life and writings.

Much remains to be done. Analysis of Wright's relationships with other authors and his choices of literary influences, along with continued examination of his connection with Afro-American sources, will clarify Wright's place in cultural tradition. Some of the same factors might usefully extend the beginnings that have been made in interpreting his aesthetics. Comprehensive study of later works and the social and political ideas Wright developed in his exile years must be undertaken if we are fully to understand his relevance to our time. For these tasks, and the projects to which others give priority, all factual information and unpublished material as is practicable should be made available. Above all, however, in our critical approach to Wright we must be as sensitive as he is to the interrelationship among personal experience, social history, culture, and the forms of literature. American literary criticism will be the better for it, and Wright will be understood as a major author deserves to be.

I should like to acknowledge the contributions of the following people who have helped me in preparing successive versions of this essay. Michel Fabre, Keneth Kinnamon, Edward Margolies, and Raman K. Singh have freely shared materials and information about their projects. Gerald A. Kirk, managing editor of *Studies in the Novel,* and Joyce E. Smith, reference librarian of the Medical-Dental Library at Howard University, provided photocopies of important essays. Nafi Donat, archivist at the Hartford Seminary Foundation; Donald Gallup, curator of the American Literature Collection at Beinecke Library, Yale University; Walter Goldwater, the University Place Bookshop; Dean H. Keller, curator of Special Collections at Kent State University; and Wanda M. Randall, assistant to the curator of manuscripts at Princeton University, provided detailed information about library holdings. Shunsuke Kamei of the University of Tokyo supplied annotated references to Japanese criticism, as did Manfred Severin of Humboldt University for German criticism.

RALPH ELLISON

JOANNE GIZA

In a recent interview in *Interviews with Black Writers* (New York: Liveright, 1973), John O'Brien mentioned that Ralph Ellison seemed to "have had the misfortune of having written a classic American novel the first time out."

"That's something other people decided, I didn't," Ellison replied. "It was just a book I wrote. I didn't have anything to lose. I didn't think that I was writing a classic. I didn't think the book would sell."

It has been more than twenty-five years since Random House published *Invisible Man,* and in that time the book has never once been out of print. The number of critical articles devoted to Ellison's one novel runs into the hundreds, and whether they are favorable or unfavorable, there is no doubt of the profound impact the novel has had on American literature which followed it, by both black and white authors.

Bibliography

As late as 1968, bibliographical study of Ralph Ellison was still virgin territory. In that year R. S. Lillard published "A Ralph Waldo Ellison Bibliography (1914–1967)" (*ABC,* November 1968), the first bibliography of Ellison's works. Listing them in chronological order from 1937 to 1967, Lillard identified each piece as a vignette, short story, book review, essay, interview, or public address. Because many of the periodicals in which Ellison's early works first appeared are difficult to locate, Lillard provided reprints where possible. He also compiled a brief listing of foreign translations of *Invisible Man.* A year later Carol Polsgrove published "Addenda to a Ralph Waldo Ellison Bibliography (1914–1968)" (*ABC,* November–December 1969) which not only added new articles to Lillard's list, but also noted new editions of *Invisible Man* as well as the most accessible reprints of Ellison's most popular short stories, "Flying Home" and "King of the Bingo Game."

In 1971, Bernard Benoit and Michel Fabre brought out "A Bibliography of Ralph Ellison's Published Writings" (*SBL,* Autumn 1971). They divided their bibliography into four sections: fiction, literary criticism and book reviews, essays–lectures–interviews, and art and music criticism, with the works listed chronologically within each category. The main virtue of this bibliography is that it brings material by Ellison up to date to June 1971; however, it does not add any new material prior to 1967, and in fact misses several items contained in the Lillard and Polsgrove compilations. Two glaring errors become apparent immediately in Benoit and Fabre: "And Hickman Arrives" is listed as appearing in Volume I (1956) of *The Noble Savage*, the first volume of which did not appear until 1960; and Ellison's contribution to Granville Hicks's *The Living Novel* is incorrectly titled "Sociology, Morality and the Novel," instead of the correct "Society, Morality and the Novel." Finally, their bibliography does not list reprints. Another Ellison listing is offered in *Black American Writers Past and Present: A Biographical and Bibliographical Dictionary*, Vol. I, by Theresa Gunnels Rush, Carol Fairbanks Myers, and Esther Spring Arata (Metuchen, N.J.: Scarecrow, 1975).

A source of data on secondary comment about Ellison is Jacqueline Covo's *The Blinking Eye: Ralph Waldo Ellison and His American, French, German and Italian Critics, 1952–1971* (Metuchen, N.J.: Scarecrow, 1974). In addition to updated versions of two earlier bibliographical essays and checklists on American and French criticism (*CLAJ*, December 1971 and June 1973), this book adds information on Ellison's reputation in Germany, Italy, and Britain. The first half of the volume consists of essays about Ellison criticism from 1965 to 1971 in each country except Britain, and the remainder is devoted to checklists for each essay. In addition to a regular index, Covo includes an author-editor index to her checklists, a helpful and noteworthy feature. Covo's work appears dependable and thorough, and despite some strange errors in the text (Addison Gayle, Jr., is once referred to and indexed as Gayle Addison, Jr., for example) and an incomplete list of reviews from the United States, this book is the most valuable source of information on Ellison criticism.

Other useful but brief lists include a short (seven page) but representative annotated bibliography in David E. Pownall's *Articles on Twentieth Century Literature: An Annotated Bibliography 1954 to 1970* (Millwood, N.Y.: Kraus–Thompson, 1973); the list in *A Bibliographic Guide to the Study of Southern Literature*, edited by Louis D. Rubin, Jr., (Baton Rouge: Louisiana State University Press, 1969); Frank E. Moorer and Lugene Baily's listing in *Black World* (December 1970); and the bibliographies in Richard Kostelanetz's *Master Minds* (New York: Macmillan, 1969), *Five Black Writers*, edited by Donald B. Gibson (New York: New York University Press, 1970), Darwin T. Turner's *Afro-American Writers* (New York: Appleton, 1970), and *A Casebook on Ralph Ellison's "Invisible Man"* edited by Joseph Trimmer (New York: T. Y. Crowell, 1972).

Written in a tone highly critical and contemptuous of white reviewers and critics is Ernest Kaiser's "A Critical Look at Ellison's Fiction and at

Social and Literary Criticism By and About the Author" (*BlackW*, December 1970), which must be read as one man's personal opinion of the state of Ellison criticism and not as an attempt at any kind of objective evaluation.

Editions

Both *Invisible Man* and *Shadow and Act* are readily available in paperback editions. *Invisible Man*, first published by Random House in 1952, appeared as a Signet paperback the following year. Random House published a Modern Library edition of the novel in 1963, and the most accessible edition at present is the paperback offered by Vintage Books (New York, 1972). *Invisible Man* was made available in England in hardcover by Victor Gollancz (London, 1953) and in paperback by Penguin (London, 1966).

Shadow and Act, a collection of Ellison's critical articles, interviews, and addresses, was also first published by Random House (1964). Signet Books issued the original paperback edition in 1966, and the collection is now available in a Vintage printing (1972). Secker and Warburg offered the collection to British readers (London, 1967).

Although Ellison has written enough short stories to warrant a collection, none has appeared to date. Aside from the "Battle Royal" excerpt from *Invisible Man*, "Flying Home" and "King of the Bingo Game" seem to be the two short stories most consistently reprinted. Both are available in *Dark Symphony*, edited by James A. Emanuel and Theodore Gross (New York: Free Press, 1968). "Flying Home" also appears in Langston Hughes's very popular anthology, *The Best Short Stories by Negro Writers* (Boston: Little, Brown, 1967). For Ellison's other short writings and for excerpts from his forthcoming novel, the reader must go to the periodicals in which they first appeared. The best sources of information about where this material appeared are the bibliographies by Lillard, Polsgrove, and Benoit and Fabre.

Biography

Although no full-length biography of Ralph Ellison has appeared to date, there is sufficient material, though scattered, to piece together a reasonable outline of the author's life. Two general works, *Contemporary Authors: A Bio-Bibliographical Guide to Current Authors and Their Works,* edited by James M. Ethridge and Barbara Kopala (Detroit: Gale Research, 1965), and *Current Biography Yearbook,* edited by Charles Moritz (Bronx, N.Y.: H. W. Wilson, 1969), have several pages of discussion of the highlights of Ellison's life and career in each, and thus are good starting points.

In the many interviews he has granted over the years, Ellison frequently talks about his boyhood in Oklahoma, his years at Tuskegee Institute, his first visit to New York and his meeting with Richard Wright, all of which were significant to his success as a writer and the ultimate form of his art. "That Same Pain, That Same Pleasure" and "The Art of Fiction," both of which appear in *Shadow and Act* (New York: Random House, 1964), are essential reading not only for Ellison's reminiscences of his youth, but also for his ideas about writing and the influences on his own writing. Important autobiographical as well as "craft" information is supplied in "On Initiation Rites and Power: Ralph Ellison at West Point," edited by Robert H. Moore (*ConL*, Spring 1974), in which Ellison explores the influence of his college reading, specifically T. S. Eliot's *The Waste Land*, along with his life experiences. Probably the most in-depth and revealing interview yet to appear serves as the introduction to the recent *Ralph Ellison: A Collection of Critical Essays*, edited by John Hersey (Englewood Cliffs, N.J.: Prentice-Hall, 1974). In this interview with Hersey, Ellison gives the fullest and most detailed account to date of his father and mother and of their important influence upon him. The discussion of the art of fiction which dominates the interview enriches and probes further into the points made in Ellison's original essay of that title.

Along these same lines, James A. McPherson, a young black writer whose work Ellison admires, has written one of the finest articles on Ellison, "Indivisible Man" (*AtM*, December 1970). Employing an unusual format, McPherson combines interview and correspondence with Ellison, personal impressions of the man and his work, and the reactions of young students who have heard Ellison lecture, to present a composite picture of the novelist. This kaleidoscopic presentation fosters a kind of immediacy which makes readers feel they have themselves spent time in Ellison's company. "Indivisible Man" is unique for the many anecdotes Ellison relates and for several personal details he mentions, such as his first marriage. Ellison also talks frankly about his relationship with other members of the black community, and he is most eloquent in his ideas about black culture and black youth.

Some details of Ellison's Oklahoma background are given in Jim Simpson's folksy, hometown account of Ellison's youth in Oklahoma City (*Daily Oklahoman*, August 23, 1953). And in an interview conducted by Hollie I. West (*Washington Post*, August 21, 1973), Ellison devotes himself to a discussion of the frontier, specifically Oklahoma, as it affected black life, his own included. Jervis Anderson provides the most comprehensive account of Ellison's early life in Oklahoma in a recent *New Yorker* essay (November 22, 1976), "Profiles: Going to the Territory." Anderson accompanied the Ellisons on a trip to Oklahoma for the dedication of the Ralph Waldo Ellison Branch Library. In this fifty-three-page essay

Anderson recounts Ellison's conversations with old acquaintances and their impressions of him, as well as his own impressions of Ellison's style, irony, and sense of self. Anderson briefly relates the history of black settlement in Oklahoma to lead up to a "history" of Ellison's family, and gives one of the only descriptions of Ellison's father, Lewis, and of his "adopted" grandfather, J. D. Randolph (who apparently was a tremendous influence on him). Anderson discusses Ellison's early love of music, both classical and jazz, as well as why Ellison has never forgotten that he is an Oklahoman and indeed considers himself a frontiersman. While this is an informative essay, it is somewhat jumbled, jumping from Ellison's concept of the frontier to his first marriage to a description of his second wife, Fanny, to Ellison's hobbies and daily routine. Richard Kostelanetz's essay on Ellison in his *Master Minds* is one of the most thorough accounts of Ellison's early days from Oklahoma to New York. At the same time, Kostelanetz takes the reader into Ellison's more recent life and into his apartment on Riverside Drive in New York by describing the furnishings of his home, his hobbies, his manner of dress, even the tobacco he uses. Kostelanetz attempts to give a complete picture of the man, both public and private. John Corry's article "An American Novelist Who Sometimes Teaches" (*New York Times Magazine*, November 20, 1966) was written for the same purpose.

The Richard Wright–Ralph Ellison relationship has been and continues to be of great interest to critics. These two giants of black literature met for the first time during Ellison's early days in New York when he was still making the transition from musician to sculptor to writer and Wright had already made a name for himself as an author of some note. Neither the details of the friendship nor Wright's precise influence on Ellison are known. The now-famous Ellison–Howe debate clarified the question somewhat. In "Black Boys and Native Sons" (*Dissent*, Autumn 1963), Irving Howe could not find words eloquent enough to praise Richard Wright for the art of his protest novels in contrast to the novels of James Baldwin. In connection with Baldwin, Howe described Ellison as the "Negro writer who has come closest to satisfying Baldwin's program of rejecting the protest novel." How, he asks, could "a Negro put pen to paper, how could he so much as breathe, without some impulsion to protest, be it harsh or mild, political or private, released or buried?" Ellison did not take what he saw as a prescription for the proper subject matter of black literature lightly, and was most eloquent in his response, "The World and the Jug" (*NL*, December 9, 1963; reprinted in *Shadow and Act*). In the course of his answer he necessarily examines his relationship with Wright and reveals his thoughts about Wright's kind of writing as well as his own. For the first time, Ellison had attempted to clarify the nature of that very important friendship, and for that many, among them Henry F. Winslow, Sr., (in a letter to the editor of *New Leader* printed in the January 6, 1964 issue), are grateful. The only other detailed account of this relationship is in Constance Webb's biography *Richard Wright* (New York: Putnam, 1968). Webb recounts events and conversations between the two men that appear nowhere else and that do much to fill out the few facts Ellison himself has related about that friendship. Michel Fabre's new biography of Richard Wright, *The Unfinished Quest of Richard Wright* (New York: Morrow, 1973), is disappointing in that it does not add to what Webb has already chronicled.

Willie Morris has written one of the few personal accounts of Ellison as a friend and social companion in *North Toward Home* (Boston: Houghton Mifflin, 1967). In *The Dream and the Deal: The Federal Writers' Project 1935–1943* (Boston: Little, Brown, 1972), Jerre Mangione recalls some of Ellison's activities as a writer with the Federal Writers' Project and quotes Ellison about those years and how his association with the project may have influenced his writing. And Albert Murray, in his *South to a Very Old Place* (New York: McGraw-Hill, 1971), recalls early days with Ellison at Tuskegee, and portrays in detail a young English professor, Morteza Drexel Sprague, who had a great influence on Ellison and to whom *Shadow and Act* is dedicated.

Two other pieces by Ellison, "Tell It Like It Is, Baby" in *The Nation* (September 20, 1965) and "February" in *Saturday Review* (January 1, 1965), contain important autobiographical material, the first about his childhood, the second about his mother's death.

Criticism

In 1965, *Book Week* conducted a poll of two hundred prominent authors, critics, and editors to determine "which works of fiction between 1945 and 1965 are the most memorable and likely to endure." *Invisible Man,* winner of the 1952 National Book Award, was voted number one. In that issue of *Book Week* (September 26, 1965), F. W. Dupee suggested that the novel's continuing popularity stemmed from its "astonishing scope and defiant audacity," its "appalling vividness or touching truthfulness," and called it "a veritable *Moby Dick* of the racial crisis." This was high praise indeed for a novel of which Ellison has said, "I failed of eloquence."

Though Ellison may feel that he failed, the critics obviously do not agree. Attention, if not always scholarly, has been steady since the novel's publication in 1952; and since the *Book Week* poll a boom in Ellison criticism has taken place in both periodicals and books. Three collections of criticism dealing with *Invisible Man* have appeared since 1970: John M. Reilly edited *Twentieth Century Interpretations of "Invisible Man"*(Englewood Cliffs, N.J.: Prentice-Hall, 1970), Ronald Gottesman,

The Merrill Studies in "Invisible Man" (Columbus, Ohio: Merrill, 1971), and Joseph Trimmer, *A Casebook on Ralph Ellison's "Invisible Man"* (New York: T.Y. Crowell, 1972). The last is unique in that background essays by such notables as Marcus Garvey, W. E. B. Du Bois, and Richard Wright are included in order to put the novel into historical and social perspective. A more recent compilation is the previously cited *Ralph Ellison: A Collection of Critical Essays,* edited by John Hersey, which reprints essays not only on *Invisible Man* but on Ellison and his ideology. Two journals concerned primarily with black studies, the *College Language Association Journal* (March 1970) and *Black World* (December 1970), have devoted entire issues to appraisals of Ellison and his work.

Despite such attention, Ellison's popularity among the new generation of black authors and critics would seem to be on the decline. In a survey conducted among thirty-eight black writers by *Negro Digest* (January 1968), Ellison was tied with James Baldwin for third place as most important black writer, behind Richard Wright and Langston Hughes. Although individual responses of those surveyed were recorded, Ellison's name was rarely mentioned. Don L. Lee criticized Ellison for losing the "black forces that live within the body" to create black art, and John A. Williams mentioned that Ellison has lost ground as *the* black novelist by "producing so slowly," an opinion expressed more acidly by Nikki Giovanni in *Gemini* (Indianapolis: Bobbs-Merrill, 1971): " . . . as a writer Ellison is so much hot air, because he hasn't had the guts to go on writing." In 1968 Larry Neal noted in the Afterword to Amiri Baraka (LeRoi Jones) and Neal's anthology *Black Fire* (New York: Morrow, 1968) that Ellison was not included because his writings have "little bearing on the world as the 'New Breed' sees it." Neal later regretted this statement in "Politics as Ritual: Ellison's Zoot Suit," a lengthy article defending Ellison and his politics against the attacks of the left (*BlackW,* December 1970).

Addison Gayle, Jr., also criticized Ellison "who, like Brown, Johnson, and Baldwin, remains wedded to the concept of assimilation at a time when such a concept has ceased to be the preoccupation of the black writer" (*The Black Aesthetic* [Garden City, N.Y.: Doubleday, 1971]). In a more recent publication, *The Way of the New World: The Black Novel in America* (Garden City, N.Y.: Doubleday, 1975), Gayle reiterates the same point when he cites Ellison's political beliefs as being responsible for the central flaw in the hero's character. Ellison's protagonist in *Invisible Man* could have emerged as a black man but instead he "chooses death over life, opts for noncreativity instead of creativity, chooses the path of individualism instead of racial unity." Despite this flaw, Gayle praises the novel for its richness of imagery, myth, and legend, and for its "soul."

Ellison has suffered continuous assaults from the black Left since 1952. Harold Cruse, in *The Crisis of the Negro Intellectual* (New York: Morrow, 1967), provides a most comprehensive account of the position held by the Left with regard to Ellison and describes a Negro Writers Conference staged by John O. Killens and the Harlem Literary Guild in 1965 at which Ellison came under heavy attack by Killens, John Henrik Clarke, and Herbert Aptheker. William Walling has coolly and objectively analyzed the basis of this disagreement in " 'Art' and 'Protest': Ralph Ellison's *Invisible Man* Twenty Years After" (*Phylon*, June 1973) in which he examines Ellison's "retreat into pure aesthetics" and his insistence on the freedom of the imagination, which is, "in reality, his criticism of even the best intentioned ideologues."

INVISIBLE MAN

In "The Ambivalence of Ralph Ellison" (*BlackW*, December 1970), Nick Aaron Ford suggested that the ambivalence of many of the scenes in *Invisible Man* encouraged various interpretations of the novel and at the same time provided intellectual stimulation. Certainly the avalanche of articles which continues to appear each year attests to this. Critics have attempted to deal with this highly complex work through a variety of motifs. For convenience, therefore, I have divided the section on criticism of *Invisible Man* into subsections, each dealing with a different motif. Contemporary reviews of the novel preface the more recent criticism.

Contemporary Reviews The publication of *Invisible Man* in April 1952 caused a minor sensation, indicated by the fact that this novice's first attempt was reviewed and recognized almost immediately as a significant publication by major newspapers and journals across the country. One theme which ran through much of the criticism was that Ellison was unique among black authors because he had gone beyond them. Webster Schott (Kansas City *Star*, May 31, 1952) stated the case directly: "It's a paradox, but the quality which classifies Ralph Ellison's *Invisible Man* as one of the best novels yet written by an American Negro is that it's concerned with themes which are . . . universal rather than racial." This note of universality sounded through most of the prominent reviews, including those by Anthony West (*NY*, May 31, 1952), Saul Bellow (*Commentary*, June 1952), Harvey Curtis Webster (*SatR*, April 12, 1952), and George Mayberry (*NR*, April 21, 1952).

The book was given lavish praise by many white reviewers, but almost always present was an undercurrent, not quite condescending, of Ellison's having written a remarkably good novel—for a Negro. Orville Prescott (*New York Times*, April 16, 1952) exclaimed that *Invisible Man* was "the most impressive work of fiction by an American Negro that I have ever read," a view shared by several other reviewers (Harvey Curtis Webster [*SatR*, April 12, 1952] and William Barrett [*American Mercury*, June 1952]). Few were as unequivocal as Saul Bellow, who flatly stated that *Invisible Man* is a "book of the first order, a superb book." Closely allied to this notion was the feeling that the real value of Ellison's novel was, in Anthony West's words, that "it is about being colored in a white society and yet manages not to be a grievance book."

When Ellison received the 1952 National Book Award in 1953, he stated in his acceptance speech that he felt the true significance of *Invisible Man* to be its experimental attitude, its searching after a new form for the novel. Ironically, it was his experimentation, specifically his style, which generated most of the criticism by white reviewers who in every other regard praised the novel. Although the novel impressed Orville Prescott, he found it flawed by "hysterical reveries which are frequently highly obscure," by passages of gross exaggeration, repetition, and overwriting. Webster Schott noted that it was "a complex overly Joycean piece of writing, burdened with cloudy passages and harmed by occasional inconsistencies," and James Yaffe censured the book for "crude writing and monotonous overearnestness" (*YR*, Summer 1952). And even though Delmore Schwartz said that "the language of literary criticism seems shallow and patronizing when one has to speak of a book like this," he managed to fault the novel for its "tendency to melodrama, to declamation, to screaming, to apocalyptic hallucination" (*PR*, May–June 1952). Robert Langbaum delivered a scathing attack, calling the writing "positively irritating" and Ellison's "flirtations with surrealistic effects . . . capricious so as to give an air of literary affectation to the whole shock effect" (*Furioso*, Fall 1952). Saul Bellow's was the lone voice to note that the novel was important for its "significant kind of independence in writing."

Going beyond those reviewers who found value in the novel but questioned the style were those white reviewers who simply disliked the novel. Sterling North (New York *World Telegram and Sun*, April 16, 1952) called it less a novel than a "flaming manifesto"—"The white man has much on his conscience. But his respect and affection will never be won by such novels as this one, which is virtually a battle call to civil war." Fred P. Oestreicher (Columbus [Ohio] *Sunday Dispatch*, April 27, 1952) concurred and said that with regard to the position of the black in American life, "Mr. Ellison's novel will shed considerable heat on the subject but little light."

Reaction among the black community was, overall, not as favorable, although, significantly, Henry F. Winslow (*The Crisis*, June–July 1952), Alain Locke (*Phylon*, First Quarter 1953), and Langston Hughes (*New York Age*, February 28, 1953), gave the book high praise. Winslow cited Ellison's "rare gift of weaving with masterful story-telling ability the rich texture of atmospheric reality" and added, "Indeed, in the metaphor of violence mounted upon fluid prose he has effected a transcendence of irony in elevating the literature of liberty above the bitter data of direct protest."

The feeling of several black reviewers was that the novel was disappointing, not as good as it should have been. J. Saunders Redding (*Afro-American* [Washington, D.C.], May 6, 1952) lamented Ellison's waste of power when he said that "The book's fault is that a writer of power has put all his power into describing the diurnal life of gnats." Gertrude Martin (*Chicago Defender,* April 19, 1952) and Roi Ottley (*Chicago Sunday Tribune,* May 11, 1952) echoed Redding's disappointment.

The most vociferous attacks by far were put forth by three leftist writers—Lloyd L. Brown (*Masses and Mainstream,* June 1952), Abner W. Berry (*Daily Worker,* June 1, 1952), and John O. Killens (*Freedom,* June 1952). A quotation from Berry expresses the sentiments of all three: "In effect, it is 439 pages of contempt for humanity, written in an affected, pretentious and otherworldly style to suit the king-pins of world white supremacy." Killens put it more bluntly: "The Negro people need Ralph Ellison's *Invisible Man* like we need a hole in the head or a stab in the back. It is a vicious distortion of Negro life."

Folklore   A major theme that runs throughout the essays and interviews collected in *Shadow and Act* is the belief in the richness and fullness of black life in America and the importance of black folk tradition in defining the black person. In "That Same Pain, That Same Pleasure" (*December Magazine,* Winter 1961; reprinted in *Shadow and Act* [New York: Random House, 1964]), Ellison says, "I felt it important to explore the full range of American Negro humanity and to affirm those qualities which are of value beyond any question of segregation, economics or previous condition of servitude. The obligation was always there and there is much to affirm." In another interview, "The Art of Fiction" (*Paris Review,* Spring 1955; reprinted in *Shadow and Act*), Ellison laments the fact that "Too many books by Negro writers are addressed to a white audience" and that by so doing the authors run the risk of pleading the black humanity, when what they should be doing is trying to discover "the specific *forms* of that humanity, and what in our own background is worth preserving or abandoning. The clue to this," Ellison continued, "can be found in folklore, which offers the first drawings of any group's character."

Stanley Edgar Hyman wrote one of the earliest essays on the importance of folklore in *Invisible Man*, "The Negro Writer in America: An Exchange" (*PR,* Spring 1958). Hyman calls the novel "the fullest development I know of the darky act in fiction . . . where on investigation every important character turns out to be engaged in some facet of the smart-man-playing-dumb routine." Ellison's reactions to Hyman's ideas are expressed in "Change the Joke and Slip the Yoke" (*PR*, Spring 1958; reprinted in *Shadow and Act*). Ellison acknowledges the importance of folkloric elements in fiction and in his own novel in particular, but feels that when Hyman "turns to specific works of literature he tends to distort their content to fit his theory." Specifically, Ellison quarrels with Hyman's notion of the "darky" act and the trickster as Hyman applied them to the grandfather and Rinehart. "The identity of fictional characters is determined," Ellison insists, "by the implicit realism of the form, not by their relation to tradition." Black folklore, he continues, is "precious as a result of an act of literary discovery. Taken as a whole, its spirituals along with its blues, jazz and folk tales, it has, as Hyman suggests, much to tell us of the faith, humor and adaptability to reality necessary to live in a world which has taken on much of the insecurity and blues-like absurdity known to those who brought it into being."

Several excellent articles have been written using folkloric elements as a basis for discussing *Invisible Man*. Praising Ellison for defining "the ideological and technical possibilities of American Negro materials more accurately and effectively than any work in our literary history," Gene Bluestein, in "The Blues as a Literary Theme" (*MR*, Autumn 1967), explores in great detail Ellison's use of folklore "to create a distinctly national expression which yet speaks in broadly human rather than racial or regional terms"—in short, to provide a portrait of the American. Bluestein speaks for many critics when he says, "The dynamic of the novel stems from the hero's struggle with himself to acknowledge the legitimacy of his heritage in the face of constant attacks by the white community or its allies in the society of Negroes." Once the narrator can accept his past and all that it implies in terms of a folk tradition, he can begin to discover his identity as an American and as a human being in the broadest sense of that term.

Out of what he says are the novel's "fifty or perhaps seventy-five other motifs," Floyd R. Horowitz in "Ralph Ellison's Modern Version of Br'er Bear and Br'er Rabbit in *Invisible Man*" (*MASJ*, Fall 1963), chose to examine the folklore motif of Br'er Rabbit and Br'er Bear, with the protagonist cast always as the Bear and the Rabbit taking the form of characters from Trueblood to Lucius Brockway to Brother Jack.

In a more general essay, "Folkloric and Mythic Elements in *Invisible Man*" (*CLAJ*, March 1970), Lawrence Clipper uses the motif of the universal folktale as a frame of reference for outlining the action of the novel, relying heavily on Ellison's own reference to having read Lord Raglan's *The Hero*. The medieval Dance of Death is central to George Knox's "The Totentanz in Ellison's *Invisible Man*" (*Fabula*, 1971). Archie D. Saunders, in "Odysseus in Black: An Analysis of the Structure of *Invisible Man*" (*CLAJ*, March 1970), Leonard Lutwack, in *The Epic Tradition and American Novels of the Twentieth Century* (Carbondale: Southern Illinois University Press, 1971), and most recently John Stark, in "Invisible Man: Ellison's Black Odyssey" (*NALF*, Summer 1973), hear echoes of Homer's *Odyssey* in the novel.

Blues   One of Ellison's most famous quotations comes from a review of Richard Wright's *Black Boy*, "Richard Wright's Blues" (*AR*, June 1945; reprinted in *Shadow and Act*). Ellison was describing what he felt was the specific folk art form which helped shape Wright's "attitude toward life and which embodied the impulse that contributes much to the quality and tone of his autobiography"—the blues:

> The blues is an impulse to keep the painful details and episodes of a brutal experience alive in one's aching consciousness, to finger its jagged grain, and to transcend it, not by the consolation of philosophy but by squeezing from it a near-tragic, near-comic lyricism.

This quotation, along with the fact that Ellison was a musician/composer with a strong interest in jazz long before he became a writer, has produced some of the finest and most interesting articles written on *Invisible Man*.

Making use of Ellison's essay on Wright in an excellent article, "Ralph Ellison's Blues" (*JBlS*, December 1976), Shelby Steele uses Ellison's concept of the blues to discuss Invisible Man as a blues singer, with his story, his confession, serving as his song. By confronting his pain and imbuing it with the elements of blues—which include both tragedy and comedy—Invisible Man is able to achieve the goal of the blues singer by managing to transcend the pain of his existence. Steele then takes this idea one step further to suggest that Ellison uses the blues as a basis for his own brand of existentialism. According to Steele, a sense of the blues results in a realization of "infinite possibility" and in the recognition that each man is responsible for shaping his own possibility and destiny.

"Some Notes on the Blues, Style and Space: Ellison, Gordone and Tolson" by Ronald Walcott (*BlackW*, December 1972) also contains a clear explication of what Ellison means when he talks about the blues. This intriguing essay suggests that *Invisible Man* is a novel whose "hero" occupies a peculiar position in time and space—that is to say, *out* of time and space—and that the pain of that suspension is alleviated only by his shaping of a style, here called a sense of the blues. Style is all the narrator has, and from that point Walcott concludes that he will never surface. The narrator is finally an artist with style, but art and style are "what belongs to losers, to the powerless, to those who reside, however fitfully or cunningly, outside of time."

Gene Bluestein, in the previously mentioned essay, offers a detailed discussion of the blues as a folk form used "to create striking and impressive imagery" as well as a form "that makes possible the catharsis we usually associate with tragedy." Bluestein moves from the blues to jazz which, as "a literary theme," he feels "is one of [Ellison's] most impressive accomplishments." He suggests that jazz, specifically the jam session, functions as a metaphor for man in society:

> Jazz values improvisation, personal vision, an assault on the conventional modes of musical expression, but it will not allow the individual to forget what he owes to tradition—not the tradition of a great man, but the legacy shaped by a whole people.

In an equally fine essay in *Anger and Beyond*, edited by Herbert Hill (New York: Harper & Row, 1966), Robert Bone covers many of the same points in his discussion of the blues and jazz, and states that Ellison's fondness for ambiguity and paradox stems from his sense of the blues. Bone also relates the changing prose styles of the novel to the principle of modulation in jazz. In *The Negro Novel in America*, rev. ed. (New Haven, Conn.: Yale University Press, 1965), Bone suggests that jazz forms influenced the "composition" of the novel in that Ellison writes a "melody" (thematic line) and then "orchestrates" it. In another excellent essay, "Ralph Ellison's Blues and *Invisible Man*" (*WSCL*, Summer 1966), Raymond Olderman considers the blues the core of the novel.

Calling jazz and the blues the "aesthetic mainspring" of Ellison's writing, Edward Margolies, in *Native Sons: A Critical Study of Twentieth-Century Negro American Authors* (Philadelphia: Lippincott, 1968), says that each episode of the novel serves as an extended blues verse, with the narrator as the singer. The blues record past wrongs, pains, and defeats, and the narrator is a singer with this history. In this sense he is a black Everyman whose cries of pain are the history of a people as the narrator moves from the South, to college, and then on to the North. Margolies also suggests that the blues define a philosophy of history which undercuts any possible system of history.

Comic Elements Although Ellison himself frequently mentions that he finds *Invisible Man* a very funny novel, critics have been slow to examine the nature and function of those comic elements. Thus, it is startling and refreshing that Earl Rovit opens his very important essay with "The most obvious comment one can make about Ralph Ellison's *Invisible Man* is that it is a profoundly comic work" ("Ralph Ellison and the American Comic Tradition" [*WSCL*, Fall 1960]). By showing Ellison's commitment to what Henry James termed "the American joke" and what Ellison himself has defined as "the ironic awareness of the joke that always lies between appearance and reality," Rovit begins the most detailed examination of the comic elements of *Invisible Man* as they reflect the major theme of the novel, the narrator's search for identity. Rovit maintains that the joke between appearance and reality inevitably leads one to probe the masks of identity in search of some deeper, buried reality, all the while accepting the mask and realizing the impossibility of ever getting beneath it: "That is to say, this comic stance will accept with the same triumphant gesture both the basic absurdity of all attempts to impose meaning on the chaos of life, and the necessary converse of this, the ultimate significance of the absurdity itself." Thus, it is with true comic spirit that the narrator accepts his invisibility at the close of the novel.

Closely allied to Rovit's thesis is Sharon Weinstein's "Comedy and the Absurd in Ralph Ellison's *Invisible Man*" (*SBL*, Autumn 1972), which considers the novel as the protagonist's education in laughter. More recently, Alfred Kazin, in his *Bright Book of Life: American Novelists from Hemingway to Mailer* (Boston: Little, Brown, 1973), considers the monologue form of the novel, as that form has become "the favorite free form for comic fiction about the world's irrationality." Kazin is fascinated by the narrator's voice "in that specific tradition of anecdote, rhapsody, sermonizing, yarn-spilling" and the tragicomic nature of the tale.

In "Irony from Underground—Satiric Elements in *Invisible Man*" (*SNL*, Fall 1969), William Schafer also works from the same thematic standpoint as Rovit. Stating that satiric irony is a basic device in the novel, Schafer analyzes more closely how Ellison achieves his comic effects. He examines four sources of satiric irony: folk humor, objects of everyday life, the white world seen through black eyes, and a prose style based on jazz and the blues. W. M. Frohock's "The Edge of Laughter: Some Modern Fiction and the Grotesque" (in *Veins of Humor*, edited by Harry Levin [Cambridge, Mass.: Harvard University Press, 1972]) shows how Ellison manages to work "the shadowy area between the grotesque and the laughable, not only controlling perspective so as to avoid unwelcome effects, but also by manipulating it for purposes carefully contrived." He concentrates specifically on the race riot and the character of Ras. In "Negro Literature and Classic Form" (*ConL*, Summer 1969), a very carefully worked essay, Nancy M. Tischler discusses the novel as a classical comedy and Ellison's use of three kinds of humor: verbal, character, and situation. Thomas A. Vogler later (*ConL*, Winter 1970) wrote "An Ellison Controversy," a scathing attack on Tischler's thesis, which was followed immediately by Tischler's defense of her essay.

Literary Debts and Analogies In his acceptance speech for the National Book Award, Ellison acknowledged his debt to America's nineteenth-century classical novelists; and throughout the many interviews he has granted, he has repeated the same names—Henry James, Joseph Conrad, Feodor Dostoevsky, André Malraux, Mark Twain, William Faulkner, Ernest Hemingway, and T. S. Eliot—of authors who have influenced his writing. Therefore, it is not surprising that so many articles have been written tracing these literary influences on his novel.

Robert Bone, in *The Negro Novel in America,* briefly considers Herman Melville, Twain, Faulkner, and Eliot, but saves his detailed analogy for Dostoevsky's *Notes from the Underground.* In his essay in *Anger and Beyond,* Bone emphasizes the influence on Ellison of nineteenth-century transcendentalism as espoused by Ralph Waldo Emerson, Henry David Thoreau, and Walt Whitman, and twentieth-century man's insistence on existential freedom, stemming from Gertrude Stein, Ernest Hemingway, William Butler Yeats, and James Joyce, among others. In "The Image of Man Portrayed by Ralph Ellison" (*CLAJ,* June 1967), Therman B. O'Daniel compares and contrasts the backgrounds and writing of Ellison and Richard Wright, whereas Addison Gayle, Jr., in *The Way of the World,* seems to have found the perfect gloss for *Invisible Man* in W. E. B. Du Bois's *The Souls of Black Folk.*

Michael Allen's "Some Examples of Faulknerian Rhetoric in Ellison's *Invisible Man*" in *The Black American Writer,* edited by C. W. E. Bigsby (Deland, Fla.: Everett/Edwards, 1970), is one of the most carefully done essays on this subject. Going beyond other critics, Allen examines the ways in which Ellison uses Faulknerian rhetoric to show how the narrator shares "certain characteristic modes of feeling if not a common vision with the Southern whites." Earl Rovit, in his previously cited essay (*WSCL,* Fall 1960); Leonard J. Deutsch, in "Ralph Waldo Ellison and Ralph Waldo Emerson: A Shared Moral Vision" (*CLAJ,* December 1972); and William W. Nichols, in "Ralph Ellison's Black American Scholar" (*Phylon,* Spring 1970), all concentrate on Ellison's indebtedness to Emerson.

Specific comparative studies have been done as well. William R. Mueller's "Ralph Ellison: A Portrait of the Negro as a Young Man" compares and contrasts *Invisible Man* with James Joyce's *A Portrait of the Artist as a Young Man* in Mueller's *Celebration of Life* (New York: Sheed & Ward, 1972). Barbara Fass draws some interesting parallels between Ellison's novel and Nathaniel Hawthorne's story in "Rejection of Paternalism: Hawthorne's 'My Kinsman, Major Molineux' and Ellison's *Invisible Man*" (*CLAJ,* March 1971), and in "The *Adventures of Huckleberry Finn* and *Invisible Man:* Thematic and Structural Comparisons" (*NALF,* July 1970), Stewart Rodnon carefully studies the many links between Ellison's novel and Mark Twain's. Marvin E. Mengeling's "Whitman & Ellison: Older Symbols in a Modern Mainstream" (*WWR,* September 1966) points out Ellison's use of Whitman's "When Lilacs Last in the Dooryard Bloom'd" in the Homer Barbee speech. Houston A. Baker, Jr., in an article in the *Virginia Quarterly Review* (Summer 1973), attempts to put *Invisible Man* in the continuum of black fiction dating from the mid-1800s, and concentrates on its affinities with James Weldon Johnson's *The Autobiography of an Ex-Colored Man*. In a very different type of article, "Ralph Ellison's Use of *The Aeneid* in *Invisible Man*" (*CLAJ*, March 1974), Charles Scruggs compares Ellison's work to Virgil's epic; his thesis is that the aim of both works is the reunification of a people and that the means of achieving this end in both cases is myth.

Ellison's work is compared to Richard Wright's in two very different types of articles. William Goede, in "On Lower Frequencies: The Buried Men in Wright and Ellison" (*MFS*, Winter 1969–1970), concludes that a comparison of Ellison's Invisible Man and Wright's Underground Man suggests not similarities, but rather Ellison's triumph in transcending Wright's naturalistic art. Jerry Wasserman maintains in "Embracing the Negative: *Native Son* and *Invisible Man*" (*Studies in American Fiction*, Spring 1976) that both Bigger Thomas and Invisible Man come to existential conclusions in their search for identity. Both characters, according to Wasserman, choose to live on the white man's terms by adopting the stereotyped image of "blackness." In so doing both discover "freedom, identity, and a control previously lacking in their lives." A brief comparison of Wright's Underground Man and Invisible Man is taken up by Earl A. Cash in "The Narrators in *Invisible Man* and *Notes from the Underground*: Brothers in Spirit" (*CLAJ*, June 1973).

Although no studies have been devoted to a comparison of Ellison and a contemporary American author, Richard Pearce, in "The Walker: Modern American Hero" (*MR*, Summer 1964), R. W. B. Lewis, in *A Time of Harvest*, edited by R. E. Spiller (New York: Hill & Wang, 1962), and C. W. E. Bigsby, in "From Protest to Paradox: The Black Writer at Mid Century" (in *The Fifties*, edited by Warren French [Deland, Fla.: Everett/Edwards, 1970]), look briefly at the associations between Ellison and Saul Bellow.

Search for Identity In the 1955 *Paris Review* interview with Alfred Chester and Vilma Howard (reprinted in *Shadow and Act*), Ellison outlined the three-part division of his novel, the function of each part, and the novel's overriding theme: "After all, it's a novel about innocence and human error, a struggle through illusion to reality." *Invisible Man* is about the narrator's search for identity, which Ellison says is "*the* American theme."

In "Choice—Ironic Alternatives in the World of the Contemporary Novel" in *American Dreams, American Nightmares*, edited by David Madden (Carbondale: Southern Illinois University Press, 1970), Alvin Greenberg explores the theme of the American dream gone awry and the awakening of twentieth-century man to a nightmare world, a mean-

ingless world, in the midst of which he stands alone, the solitary individual. How is man to give meaning and form to his existence? Using
Ellison's *Invisible Man,* Greenberg posits three alternatives—conformity,
destruction, or withdrawal.

Marcus Klein, in his book *After Alienation: American Novels in Mid-Century* (New York: World, 1962), speaks of the narrator's search for "[a]
primarily existential sense of himself," a search which Klein says ends
in failure. Jeffrey Steinbrink, in "Toward a Vision of Infinite Possibility—A Reading of *Invisible Man*" (*SBL,* Autumn 1976), would agree
with Klein, but only so far. According to Steinbrink, Invisible Man does
not know who he is by the end of the novel, but he does know who he
isn't and he has achieved a certain fix on reality by cutting through
illusion. His next move is to decide what his appropriate action will be
when he emerges. Along these same lines, Jerry Wasserman, in "Embracing the Negative: *Native Son* and *Invisible Man*" (*Studies in American
Fiction*, Spring 1976), suggests that while Invisible Man finds a temporary existential solution to the problem of his identity by embracing his
invisibility, he will soon be forced to redefine himself when he decides
to reenter the world. With some modification, Richard Lehan's "Man
and his Fictions: Ellison, Pynchon, Heller, and Barth (in Lehan's *A
Dangerous Crossing—French Literary Existentialism and the Modern American
Novel* [Carbondale: Southern Illinois University Press, 1973]) agrees
with both Steinbrink and Wasserman. While Lehan concurs that the
narrator finds out who he is *not*, he also says that Invisible Man has
come to believe that "the final source of order is within himself." Lehan
calls this a not-strictly-existential ending because thought is not leading
to action. According to Lehan, the narrator has jumped ahead of history and will not act until history catches up to him. Lehan had considered the existential nature of the narrator's search in an earlier
essay, "Existentialism in Recent American Fiction: The Demonic
Quest" (*TSLL,* Summer 1959). Esther M. Jackson, in "The American
Negro and the Image of the Absurd" (*Phylon*, Winter 1962), also views
the search in existential terms and compares Ellison with Albert Camus, Jean-Paul Sartre, Feodor Dostoevsky, and André Malraux.

Leonard Lutwack's *The Epic Tradition and American Novels of the Twentieth Century*, in likening the narrator's journey to the Ulysses's Odyssey,
sees the novel in terms of death–rebirth images in which the narrator is
doomed never to achieve an identity. Louis Mitchell, in "Invisibility—
Permanent or Resurrective?" (*CLAJ,* March 1974), also concentrates on
the death and rebirth images, but his conclusion is the opposite of
Lutwack's. According to Mitchell, the narrator achieves his permanent
identity, and the ending is an affirmation of Ellison's own hope for
man's ability to come to grips with possibility. A fine essay by Tony

Tanner, "The Music of Invisibility," in Tanner's *City of Words* (New York: Harper & Row, 1971), deals with the nature-of-identity theme and the reality which the narrator as artist must create for himself if he is to survive. Taking this idea one step further, "Writing as Celebration: The Epilogue of *Invisible Man*" (*Renascence*, Spring 1974) by P. A. Parrish contrasts the prologue and epilogue of the novel to reveal how the very act of writing can simultaneously become an act of celebration. "Having written it all down" allows the narrator both "to respond to reality and to affirm its possibilities"; the writing becomes a triumph of love which makes possible the resolution of all ambiguities. In direct contrast is Roger Rosenblatt's section on *Invisible Man* in his *Black Fiction* (Cambridge, Mass.: Harvard University Press, 1974). Rosenblatt sees celebration in the novel, but it is the "celebration of disappearance, of nothingness." The hero who has tried to "think" his way to identity is finally no more than an illusion of which there will be no memory. Grosvenor E. Powell, in "Role and Identity in Ralph Ellison's *Invisible Man*" in *Private Dealings*, by Powell et al. (Stockholm: Almqvist & Wiskell, 1970), describes the narrator as "the man whom society has deprived of a role, and, hence, in a very real sense, deprived of the feeling that his existence has reality." In "Invisibility of the American Negro: Ralph Ellison's *Invisible Man*" J. M. Waghmare (*Quest*, Autumn 1968) states the narrator's problem well when he says that he is

> essentially a humanist . . . he has of course two identities—the racial and the American. One is lost and the other denied. His racial identity is lost because he is a progressive assimilationist. His American identity is denied because he is not a white man. Historically, he is uprooted, socially, he is segregated, and psychologically, he is alienated. Yet his utopian optimism crowns his tragic destiny.

Ellin Horowitz, in "The Rebirth of the Artist" in *On Contemporary Literature,* edited by Richard Kostelanetz (New York: Avon, 1964), examines the initiation rites and formal rituals that lead the narrator each time to a new identity, until at the end he discovers his freedom and is reborn as an artist. In "The Uncompleted Initiation of the Invisible Man" (*SBL,* Spring 1975), Isaac Sequeira also works with the concept of initiation. Sequeira sets forth his own definition of the term, considering initiation "an existential encounter with life," then applies his concept to the narrator's initiation into reality. Eugenia W. Collier, in "The Nightmare Truth of an Invisible Man" (*BlackW,* December 1970), focuses on the narrator's dreams and semiconscious states, which she says "contain the very truth which he is trying so desperately to find." In a much broader treatment of the novel, William Walling's "Ralph Ellison's *Invisible Man*: 'It Goes a Long Way Back, Some Twenty Years' " (*Phylon,* March 1973) works with three major motifs— the past, perception in a world of illusion, and the true source of power in society—as each relates to the black man's search for identity in the United States.

Two recent articles work within ideological frameworks to put Invisible Man's search for identity in perspective. Using Martin Buber's dialogical concepts, Ardner R. Cheshire, Jr., in "Invisible Man and the Life of Dialogue" (*CLAJ*, Sept. 1976), maintains that "Invisible Man" becomes a "unified self, a Single One" at the novel's end. By reaching out to a "Thou" through his art he attempts to affirm his own humanity and to be successful, the reader must join him in a dialogue. E. M. Kist's "A Laingian Analysis of Blackness in Ralph Ellison's *Invisible Man*" (*SBL*, Spring 1976) points to a marked similarity between Ellison's idea of the black man's invisibility and R. D. Laing's notion of ontological insecurity. Kist does a careful job of explaining and defining Laing's *schizoid* and then relating that definition to Invisible Man. In Kist's terms the novel is a psychoanalytical process for the narrator, who is trying to escape from the dead end to which his struggle with identity has led him.

The list of critical studies that use a variety of motifs in attempts to reveal the numerous ways Ellison plays upon this theme is extensive. Notable among them are Phyllis R. Klotman's "The Running Man as Metaphor in Ellison's *Invisible Man*" (*CLAJ*, March 1970; reprinted and revised in Klotman's *Another Man Gone: The Black Runner in Contemporary Afro-American Literature* [Port Washington, N.Y.: Kennikat Press, 1977]), which examines the running-man metaphor, and Todd M. Lieber's excellent discussion of invisibility in "Ralph Ellison and the Metaphor of Invisibility in Black Literary Tradition" (*AQ*, March 1972).

Miscellany The number of critical articles written on *Invisible Man* in the years since its publication runs into the hundreds, and although the preceding sections may suggest the dominant methods used to evaluate the novel, they must necessarily omit many articles that do not fit into specific categories, but which do contribute to an appreciation and understanding of *Invisible Man*.

Four essays have been devoted exclusively to the symbolism of sight. Charles I. Glicksberg (*SWR*, Summer 1954) maintains that the symbolism of vision, which takes the forms of light, color, perception, sight, and insight, "provides the dynamism and momentum of action, the motivational insight, the resolution of conflict" because "To see: that is the preliminary and indispensable step on the part of the Negro people. Then they can set about liberating themselves from all the blind and mindless forces that keep them in dark bondage." Darwin T. Turner (*CLAJ*, March 1970) takes this idea one step further by stating that what the narrator will see when he emerges from the underground is dependent upon what readers have learned to see through their reading of *Invisible Man*. Alice Bloch (*EJ*, November 1966) and

Thomas LeClair (*CLAJ*, March 1970) deal with the same ideas in briefer essays.

Selma Fraiberg's "Two Modern Incest Heroes" (*PR*, September–October 1961) considers the incest theme in the Trueblood incident, and Peter L. Hays's "The Incest Theme in *Invisible Man*" (*WHR*, Autumn 1969) shows how incest becomes "a shaping and controlling metaphor for interpersonal and interracial relations in the novel." In "The Journey Towards Castration: Interracial Sexual Stereotypes in Ellison's *Invisible Man*" (*JAmS*, February 1971), Frederick L. Radford suggests that "the imprisonment of the natural sexual individuality of the black male within the confines of [the] white stereotype" creates problems for the black writer, and that Ellison's attempts to deal with sex in his own novel result in unevenness. Carolyn Sylvander's "Ralph Ellison's *Invisible Man* and Female Stereotypes" (*NALF*, Fall 1975) also blasts away at Ellison's stereotypes, but this time the target is his women. In "Twentieth Century Fiction and the Black Mask of Humanity," an essay in *Shadow and Act*, Ellison deplores the depiction of the Negro as "an oversimplified clown, a beast or an angel." He goes on to say, "Seldom is he drawn as that sensitively focused process of opposites, of good and evil, or instinct and intellect, of passion and spirituality, which great literary art has projected as the image of man." Using that quotation, Sylvander accuses Ellison of doing to his female characters what he says has been done to Negro characters in other works. The minor female characters function only as symbols according to Sylvander, whereas the minor male characters function as characters in their own right as well as symbols.

Using a historical approach, Allen Guttman's "Focus on Ralph Ellison's *Invisible Man*: American Nightmare," in *American Dreams, American Nightmares*, briefly suggests how "in his odyssey, the narrator acts out the stages of Negro history from the Emancipation to the present." In "The Politics of Ellison's Booker: Invisible Man as Symbolic History" (*ChiR*, No. 2 [1967]), a much more detailed analysis, Richard Kostelanetz very carefully reveals the narrator's attempt first to live by the ideology of Booker T. Washington, and his subsequent disillusionment; then his attraction to the lure of radical politics and black nationalism, and again the resulting disenchantment. This same theme is taken up in greater detail by Russell Fischer in "*Invisible Man* as History" (*CLAJ*, March 1974). Fischer breaks the movement of the novel into three parts, the first focusing on Booker T. Washington, the second on the migration North and the Negro's encounter with industrial urban society, and the third on the Negro's involvement with the Communist party. The narrator must find his identity within this historical context, and he realizes at the conclusion that his only escape is to burn the symbols of his past.

"Black Entities: Names as Symbols in Afro-American Literature" (*SBL*, Spring 1970), by Lloyd W. Brown, discusses the importance of names and uses *Invisible Man* to demonstrate the ways in which names can be "interrelated to form a framework of symbolic references." Brown considers the many possibilities suggested by the names Rinehart, Bledsoe, Supercargo, and Norton. In "Ralph Ellison's Exhorters: The Role of Rhetoric in *Invisible Man*" (*CLAJ*, March 1970), he discusses the theme of communication in the novel and emphasizes and examines the importance of the narrator's changing rhetoric.

A very suggestive and far-reaching article by Stephen B. Bennett and William W. Nichols, "Violence in Afro-American Fiction: An Hypothesis" (*MFS*, Summer 1971), postulates that there is a significant difference between the violence of Afro-American literature and the violence of American literature and that the difference may be a distinguishing characteristic of black literature; they discuss the Tod Clifton death scene in this context.

In a very different kind of article, "Leadership Mirages as Antagonists in *Invisible Man*" (*ArQ*, Summer 1966), M. K. Singleton studies the image of Negro leadership in *Invisible Man* and Ellison's satiric treatment of the "stereotyped and stagnant forms of twentieth-century Negro leadership." Elsewhere, Donald B. Gibson's "Ralph Ellison and James Baldwin" (in *The Politics of Twentieth-Century Novelists*, edited by George A. Panichas [New York: Hawthorn, 1971]) discusses *Invisible Man* as a political novel, Ellison's own statements to the contrary notwithstanding.

Robert Bone glancingly reviews Fritz Gysin's *The Grotesque in American Negro Fiction: Jean Toomer, Richard Wright, Ralph Ellison* (Bern, Switzerland: Francke Verlag, 1975) in *American Literature* (May 1976). Bone states that Gysin writes from a linguistic point of view combined with his theory of the grotesque. The section on *Invisible Man*, according to Bone, "leaves no reader without enrichment who will pursue the long and thoughtful chapter."

SHADOW AND ACT

Ellison's *Shadow and Act*, published by Random House in 1964, was hardly the long-awaited second novel for which critics had wished. An anonymous reviewer for *Kirkus* (August 15, 1964) called the collection "a rather modest affair," lacking Baldwin's "electrical displays." Granville Hicks (*SR*, October 24, 1964) labeled the book a "disappointing substitute" for a second novel, but worthwhile for what it tells about Ellison and *Invisible Man*, an opinion shared by Reed Whittemore (*NR*, November 14, 1964). Describing the essays as "awkwardly composed, marred by pompous locutions, clumsy transitions, and sometimes even bad syntax," Norman Podhoretz (*NYHTBW,* October 25, 1964) felt that Ellison had "never mastered the art of the essay enough for his best qualities to find expression in it." And a reviewer for *Choice* (March 1965) claimed that Ellison's literary criticism was "jejeune and absurd."

However, an overwhelming majority of the reviewers were enthusiastic about the collection. In place of a second novel, these essays "will serve splendidly to placate and reassure us," said the reviewer for *Newsweek* (October 26, 1964). Ellison's longtime friend Stanley Edgar Hyman hailed Ellison as "the profoundest cultural critic we have, and his hard doctrine of freedom, responsibility, and fraternity" as indicative of a "wisdom rare in our time" (*NL,* October 26, 1964). John Barkham (New York *World Telegram and Sun,* November 5, 1964) called *Shadow and Act* "a remarkable collection, . . . the credo of a thoughtful, determined, consecrated and courageous man."

The thematic content of *Shadow and Act* was of primary importance in the favorable reviews. In general, more attention was paid to the question of the role of the Negro artist (the Ellison–Howe debate), represented by the essay "The World and the Jug," than to Ellison's ideas about the importance and unique quality of Negro folk culture. Peter de Lissovoy (*The Nation,* November 9, 1964) described the essays as hanging together "as upon a profound theme, around [Ellison's] attempt to find humanity beneath the categories, abstractions and legends through which our thought forms,—indeed, beneath our silences." Commenting on the "gentleness" and "graciousness" of the essays, Bell Gale Chevigny (*Village Voice,* November 19, 1964) compared and contrasted the ideas in *Shadow and Act* and *Invisible Man* while at the same time providing one of the most careful summaries of the contents of the collection. Another well-executed essay, by R. W. B. Lewis (*NYRB,* January 28, 1965), praised Ellison for his "demonstration of his identity . . . Ellison is not only a self-identifier but the source of self-definition in others."

Describing the essays as "astute commentaries on literature, music and society," Robert Penn Warren (*Commentary,* May 1965) went into great detail and quoted extensively from *Shadow and Act* in an effort to convey Ellison's idea of the "basic unity of experience" as well as the idea of the novel as protest and as art. Morris Janowitz (*AJS,* May 1965) focused on Ellison's review of Gunnar Myrdal's *An American Dilemma,* and argued that Ellison is more of a sociologist than he thinks. In an article that reviewed three books about Negro folk music, Roger D. Abrahams (*JAF,* July–September 1966) included *Shadow and Act* for its "magnificent essay-review of Jones's book" (*Blues People: Negro Music in White America,* by LeRoi Jones [Amiri Baraka]) and because as a jazz musician and writer Ellison "makes some of the most pregnant remarks about the Negro as a creative musician that this reviewer has ever encountered."

SHORT STORIES AND ESSAYS

Although Ellison has written a number of short stories and vignettes, they have yet to be collected in one volume, and it is perhaps for this reason that critics have generally ignored this material along with Ellison's early book reviews and essays. Marcus Klein, in *After Alienation: American Novels in Mid-Century* (New York: World, 1962), has written one of the few extensive essays focusing on Ellison's early work. Although Klein's major objective is to examine the thematic concerns in the short stories and to show how these themes appear in final form in *Invisible Man,* he provides a good basic overview of the kinds of writing Ellison was doing for *New Challenge, New Masses,* and *The Negro Quarterly* in the period between 1937 and 1940. In considering pieces like "The Birthmark," which Klein describes as "marred by the smudge of left-wing politics," and "Mister Toussan," which reveals Ellison's growing preoccupation with the "making of a folk hero for the masses," Klein traces Ellison's evolution in perspective on the Negro condition from a restricted economic interpretation, to a psychological interpretation, and finally to his belief in the importance of folklore and the necessity of finding a new definition of Negro culture. Klein's essay is also important for his consideration, however brief, of "That I Had Wings" and "A Coupla Scalped Indians," in which he follows the characters of Buster and Riley, who were first introduced in "Mister Toussan." As an examination of the Negro's relationship to America revealed during World War II, Klein takes a look at "In a Strange Country" and "Flying Home." He ends this section of his discussion with "King of the Bingo Game," calling it "a brief gloss on [Ellison's] entire career, beginning with the ethic of protest against obvious injustice, proceeding to a confusion that is not ethical but metaphysical."

Working from a very different orientation, Ernest Kaiser covers approximately the same ground in his bibliographical essay (*BlackW,* December 1970). Kaiser calls the period from 1938 to 1942, when Ellison was writing for *New Masses,* "the healthiest and best period in his writing career," and regrets Ellison's movement away from his early economic theories. When, under the spell of Richard Wright, Kenneth Burke, and the New Critics, Ellison came to learn about technique, he committed himself to a kind of writing that was "unemotional, uncommitted, uninvolved in people's problems," according to Kaiser. Further, Kaiser levels strong criticism against "Flying Home" for emphasizing the powerlessness of blacks vis-à-vis the powerfulness of whites, and against Ellison's "Richard Wright's Blues" for overpraising and overinterpreting Wright's autobiography. He also censures "It Always Breaks Out" for being an "implausible, unbelievable story," and tears mercilessly into Ellison's interviews and such later essays as "Tell It Like It Is" and "What America Would Be Like Without Blacks."

"Ellison's Early Fiction" by Leonard J. Deutsch (*NALF,* Summer 1973) rejects Kaiser's notion of Ellison's having sold out and puts more faith in Ellison's own insistence on the importance of craftsmanship. Deutsch's article runs along the same lines as Marcus Klein's, but his analysis of Ellison's early short stories is much more detailed and his emphasis on what he calls the affirmative in Ellison's writing serves as a strong link between the early writing and *Invisible Man.* Edith Schor's dissertation, "The Early Fiction of Ralph Ellison: The Genesis of *Invisible Man*" (*DAI,* November 1973), also concentrates on Ellison's growth as a stylist from his early writings through *Invisible Man.* The only other dissertation to focus exclusively on Ellison is Deutsch's "Affirmation in the Work of Ralph (Waldo) Ellison" (*DAI,* December 1972). In a less detailed discussion, Theodore Gross, in *The Heroic Ideal in American Literature* (New York: Free Press, 1971), considers "Flying Home" and "King of the Bingo Game" important for reflecting Ellison's thinking about racial issues just prior to writing *Invisible Man.* Joseph Trimmer's "Ralph Ellison's 'Flying Home' " (*SSF,* Spring 1972) examines that story on the racial and mythic levels. And Edward Guereschi's "Anticipations of *Invisible Man*: Ralph Ellison's 'King of the Bingo Game' " (*NALF,* Winter 1972) suggests several interesting comparisons between that short story and *Invisible Man.*

Patricia Chaffee's "Slippery Ground: Ralph Ellison's Bingo Player" (*NALF,* Spring 1976), dealing with that same story, focuses on the hero's "slippery sanity" and suggests that Ellison's view in "King of the Bingo Game" is much more "grimly negative" than in *Invisible Man.* According to Chaffee, "Slipperiness lies in the stage, the hill, and the brink, and in escape. The security implied in power and freedom is an illusion. The impotence, ignorance, and blind submission of the figures on the movie screen are conditions for sane survival." In "Symbolism in Ralph Ellison's 'King of the Bingo Game' " (*CLAJ,* September 1976), Pearl I. Saunders sees that story as reflecting the suppression of black people in an "indifferent white America."

In "In Need of Folk: The Alienated Protagonists of Ralph Ellison's Short Fiction" (*CLAJ,* December 1975), Mary Ellen Doyle takes time to examine Ellison's short-fiction protagonists closely, specifically Riley in "Mister Toussan," "A Coupla Scalped Indians," and "That I Had Wings"; Mr. Parker in "In a Strange Country"; Todd in "Flying Home"; and the nameless protagonist in "King of the Bingo Game." Her theory is that each protagonist finds himself "alienated in some degree from himself, his own race and white controlled society; he either does not know or cannot accept who he is." Doyle then shows how the characters "find human connection with the world primarily and inevitably through the folk."

A NEW NOVEL

Critics look forward to the publication of Ellison's new novel, excerpts of which have appeared at various times in periodicals such as *Noble Savage* and *The Iowa Review*. Rumor has it that the manuscript pages run into the thousands and that the novel will eventually be published in three volumes. Until that time, critics might consider Ellison's early fiction and nonfiction more fully, although at present they seem content to continue working with the many possibilities of *Invisible Man*.

JAMES BALDWIN

DARYL DANCE

James Baldwin is one of America's best known and most controversial writers. If there is some figurative truth in his declarations "Nobody Knows My Name" and "No Name in the Street," on a realistic level practically everyone knows his name, from people on the street to scholars in the most prestigious universities—and they all respond to him. Those responses are as diverse and as antithetical as the respondents. Indeed, there is little unanimity in the criticism of James Baldwin: some view him as a prophet preaching love and salvation, others as a soothsayer forecasting death and destruction; some see him as a civil-rights advocate writing protest literature, others as an artist imaginatively portraying the plight of the black American or the alienated man. This essay considers many of these varied responses to James Baldwin, the man; James Baldwin, the spokesman for the black people; James Baldwin, the essayist; and James Baldwin, the novelist.

Bibliography

The most helpful and complete bibliographies of Baldwin have appeared in the *Bulletin of Bibliography*. Kathleen A. Kindt's "James Baldwin: A Checklist: 1947–1962" (*BB*, January–April 1965) and Russell G. Fischer's "James Baldwin: A Bibliography, 1947–1962" (*BB*, January–April 1965) cover the same years and should be used together inasmuch as the items not included in one are generally found in the other; together they represent a reasonably accurate and complete bibliography through 1962. Fred L. Standley's "James Baldwin: A Checklist 1963–1967" (*BB*, August 1968) is designed to supplement the two previously cited bibliographies. Standley's work, however, is not as thorough and accurate a compilation of Baldwin materials as the checklists by Kindt and Fischer. He omits numerous reviews and articles by and about Baldwin that appeared in such publications as *Phylon, Freedomways,* and *Negro Digest*; and his checklist has a few errors in dates and titles. All three of these bibliographies contain listings of novels, plays, short stories, articles, and essays by Baldwin as well as reviews, criticisms, and articles about Baldwin.

A much less accurate bibliography is Mary E. Jones's "James Baldwin," which was prepared as a class project at Atlanta University. It was published by the Center for African and African–American Studies (*CAAS*) of Atlanta University as *CAAS Bibliography No. 5.* Some of the entries are incomplete; parts of titles and names of periodicals are sometimes omitted, and there are several errors in this work; but it may be worth consulting because it includes at least one item published prior to 1947 which is not included in the other bibliographies and because it also contains a listing of Baldwin manuscripts in the Trevor–Arnett Library at Atlanta University.

Shorter Baldwin bibliographies have appeared in other longer works. Darwin T. Turner includes a limited but helpful sixty-four-item listing of Baldwin biography and criticism in his *Afro-American Writers* (New York: Appleton, 1970). *Articles on American Literature, 1950–1967,* compiled by Lewis Leary (Durham, N.C.: Duke University Press, 1970), contains a helpful and reasonably complete listing of articles about Baldwin that appeared during the years covered. Stanley Macebuh includes a "Selected Bibliography" in his *James Baldwin: A Critical Study* (New York: Third Press–Joseph Okpaku, 1973), but the basis for his selections is not clear. He chooses, for example, the checklists mentioned above by Fischer and Kindt, but omits the more recent one by Standley. Further, although he omits *Nothing Personal,* as well as other items dealing directly with Baldwin, he includes several works which treat Baldwin only peripherally and some which do not deal with him at all. He frequently gives only the volume number of periodicals without indicating the date or pages, information that would be most helpful in locating articles. Finally, his bibliography is not always a model of accuracy. The first item, for example, contains two mistakes: the author's name is misspelled and the volume number of the periodical is incorrect. Other errors include the confusing of the years of publication of *Another Country* and *The Fire Next Time.* Keneth Kinnamon includes a very short but nonetheless helpful bibliography in *James Baldwin: A Collection of Critical Essays* (Englewood Cliffs, N.J.: Prentice-Hall, 1974). All forty-one items listed are directly relevant to Baldwin, and a few more recent publications are included that cannot be found in any of the other bibliographies. Some of the omissions are glaring, however, such as the exclusion of Robert Bone's significant study, "The Novels of James Baldwin," in *The Negro Novel in America,* rev. ed. (New Haven, Conn.: Yale University Press, 1965). Donald B. Gibson also includes a reasonably good Baldwin bibliography in his *Five Black Writers* (New York: New York University Press, 1970). Another satisfactory guide to Baldwin materials is *Blacks in America: Bibliographical Essays,* edited by James M. McPherson et al. (Garden City, N.Y.: Doubleday, 1971), although it is certainly not convenient or handy, because entries for Baldwin appear in several different places.

Several anthologies of black American literature include brief Baldwin bibliographies. However, some of them are quite limited, such as the one in Ruth Miller's *Blackamerican Literature: 1760–Present* (Beverly Hills, Calif.: Glencoe Press, 1971), which lists only three works about Baldwin. On the other hand, *Black Writers of America: A Comprehensive Anthology*, by Richard Barksdale and Keneth Kinnamon (New York: Macmillan, 1972), contains an excellent Baldwin bibliography.

Editions

FULL-LENGTH WORKS

With the exception of *Nothing Personal* (1964, with Richard Avedon), all of Baldwin's full-length works are now in print; and all, except *The Amen Corner* (1968), *One Day When I Was Lost* (1973), and *The Devil Finds Work* (1976), are available in paperback. With the exception of *Notes of a Native Son* (1955), available in paperback from Bantam and Beacon; *A Dialogue* (1973), from Lippincott; and *If Beale Street Could Talk* (1974), from the New American Library, Baldwin's paperback works are published by Dell in New York, with *Go Tell It on the Mountain* also available in a Classroom Library Series in paperback, with teacher notes, from Noble.

All hardback editions of Baldwin's works now in print are from Dial, with the exception of *A Rap on Race* (with Margaret Mead, 1971) and *A Dialogue,* both of which are available from Lippincott. In addition, a large-type edition of *The Fire Next Time* is published by Franklin Watts.

SHORT STORIES

Most of Baldwin's short stories have been collected in *Going to Meet the Man* (New York: Dial, 1965), or have appeared as chapters in his novels. His "Death of the Prophet" (*Commentary,* March 1950) is a notable exception; nonetheless, it is a fictionalized account of Johnnie's visit to his father's deathbed, obviously based upon and closely paralleling the account of Baldwin's visit to his father's deathbed in "Notes of a Native Son" (*Notes of a Native Son* [New York: Beacon, 1955]). "Exodus" (*American Mercury,* August 1952) and "Roy's Wound" (*New World Writing,* November 1952) are incorporated into *Go Tell It on the Mountain* (New York: Dial, 1953). "Any Day Now" (*PR,* Spring 1960) and "Easy Rider" (*The Dial: An Annual of Fiction* [New York: Dial, 1962]) are incorporated into *Another Country* (New York: Dial, 1962). "The Amen Corner" (*Zero,* July 1954) appears as Act I of the complete work *The Amen Corner* (New York: Dial, 1968).

ESSAYS

Several of Baldwin's essays have been collected and appear in his four volumes of essays as well as in numerous other collections both in the United States and abroad. Many others have not appeared in his own collections, however, although they demand attention from the Baldwin scholar because they give additional information about his views on world events, his contemporaries, and art and the artist, and supply biographical data. A brief chronological scanning here will give an impression of the variety of subjects that have concerned him over the years.

Baldwin's frequently quoted review of Langston Hughes's *Selected Poems*, "Sermons and Blues" (*NYTBR*, March 29, 1959), for example, suggests a changing attitude toward protest literature. "A Word From Writer Directly to Reader" in *Fiction of the Fifties: A Decade of American Writing*, (edited by Herbert Gold [Garden City, N.Y.: Doubleday, 1959]) is a very slight piece, a mere two paragraphs, but Baldwin comments there about the difficulty of remaining in touch with the private life that is the key to his achievements as a writer. He comments again on the artist's dilemma in "Mass Culture and the Creative Artist: Some Personal Notes" (*Daedalus*, Spring 1960). "They Can't Turn Back" (*Mademoiselle*, August 1960) recounts his visit to Florida A&M University during the school integration crisis and includes some revealing accounts of his reaction to the South and the effects of segregation on American education. "The Dangerous Road Before Martin Luther King" (*Harper's Magazine*, February 1961) recalls his first meeting with and his reactions to King. "The New Lost Generation" (*Esquire*, July 1961) discusses the quest for identity of American expatriates in Europe. This essay contains one of Baldwin's early rejections of the possibilities of love; here he notes that during a discussion in which it was stated that there were few decent people in the world, a friend asked him what about love, and he replied, "Love! You'd better forget about that, my friend. That train has gone." (It may also be significant that this young friend of twenty-four committed suicide by jumping from the George Washington Bridge.)

In "As Much Truth as One Can Bear" (*NYTBR*, January 14, 1962), Baldwin discusses the importance of the novelist's being truthful. Again, in "The Artist's Struggle for Integrity" (*Liberation*, March 1963), he speaks of the difficulties of being an artist in the United States. "Color" (*Esquire*, December 1962) is a rather mundane article which may nonetheless be of interest for Baldwin's view of the meaning of *color* and *colored* and his comparison of the pursuit of happiness by blacks and whites. "At the Root of the Negro Problem" (*Time*, May 17, 1963) details Baldwin's views on race relations in the United States and his thesis that the Negro problem stems from the myths created by whites. "Letters from a Journey" (*Harper's Magazine,* May 1963) records his despair as he tried to complete *Another Country* and "Down at the Cross." Here he also reveals his thoughts on the Israeli–Arab conflict, and this in turn evokes some of his views on religion and the suppression of man by man. Very important in a consideration of Baldwin the man is the idea expressed in this essay of homelessness and the quest for a home, motivated by his visit to Europe; although perhaps more relevant to him personally is the revelation of his many thoughts on his forthcoming visit to Africa and all that it signifies to him in terms of the quest for a home. In "We Can Change the Country" (*Liberation,* October 1963), Baldwin again attacks racism in the United States and urges revolution—not armed, but economic. "A Talk to Teachers" (*SatR,* December 21, 1963; reprinted in *Education and Social Crisis: Perspectives on Teaching Disadvantaged Youths,* edited by Robert Fulton and W. E. Gardner [New York: Wiley, 1967]) speaks of the lack of a true sense of identity among Americans, particularly blacks, and Baldwin challenges teachers to educate children to examine society and to try to change it, despite the risks involved. "What Price Freedom?" (*Freedomways,* Spring 1964) is a plea for freedom in the United States following the murders of President John F. Kennedy, Medgar Evers, and the Birmingham Sunday school girls. Here, as elsewhere, Baldwin emphasizes the need for whites to learn to regard blacks as human beings.

"Theatre: The Negro In and Out" (*ND,* April 1966) presents Baldwin's argument that the theater reflects the American confusion, which in turn results from the effort to avoid dealing with the Negro as a person. He comments extensively about the fact that black actors must play roles that are not true, and are thus forced to perpetuate the popular image of the Negro. Baldwin also talks at some length about Edward Albee's *The Death of Bessie Smith* and *The American Dream,* both of which he feels left something to be desired despite their great promise.

Several instances of police brutality in Harlem are cited by Baldwin in "To Whom It May Concern: A Report from Occupied Territory" (*The Nation,* July 11, 1966; reprinted in *Law and Resistance: American Attitudes Toward Authority,* edited by Laurence Veysey [New York: Harper & Row, 1970]); here he describes the anguish of helpless blacks at the mercy of cruel policemen and the resulting lack of respect for the law. He returns to the plight of the artist in "The Creative Dilemma" (*SatR,* February 8, 1967), where he details the role of the artist (obviously the role he has assumed), declaring that the artist has the responsibility to "never cease warring with [society] for its sake and for his own."

Baldwin comments on the controversial subject of Negro–Jewish relationships in "Negroes Are Anti-Semitic Because They're Anti-

White" (*New York Times Magazine,* April 9, 1967; reprinted in *Black Anti-Semitism and Jewish Racism,* introduction by Nat Hentoff [New York: Richard W. Baron, 1969]). He explains that anti-Semitism among black people is really a result of their hatred of whites, noting that Jews have been a part (a visible part in the role of landlords, merchants, and the like) in the exploitation of blacks. He utterly rejects efforts to compare the Jews' plight or suffering with that of the black man in America.

"The War Crimes Tribunal" (*Freedomways,* Summer 1967) is an explanation of (and something of an apology for) his signing Lord Bertrand Russell's War Crimes Tribunal. He apologizes for its possible use by Europeans to condemn America and ignore their own guilt in the war in Vietnam and in South Africa or Rhodesia; but he explains that he had to register his reaction against a totally indefensible American participation in the Vietnamese war. In "From Dreams of Love to Dreams of Terror" (in *Natural Enemies? Youth and the Clash of Generations,* edited by Alexander Klein [Philadelphia: Lippincott, 1969]), Baldwin attempts to explain, using Stokely Carmichael as a point of reference, how young blacks dreamed of love during the civil rights movement, but how and why they moved toward a new militancy that terrified the country.

Baldwin returns to a favorite thesis—that history is present in all of us and in all we do—in "Unnameable Objects, Unspeakable Crimes" (in *Black on Black: Commentaries by Negro Americans,* edited by Arnold Adoff [New York: Macmillan, 1968]). He contends that the United States and the world are menaced because white Americans have been unable to accept their history and continue to defend themselves against it. He speaks also of his personal difficulty—by extension the difficulty of black Americans—in wrestling with his history and accepting it in order to find his identity. Elsewhere, Baldwin attacks Western Christianity as being racist and hypocritical and as failing to live up to its own principles, ("White Racism or World Community?" [*Ecumenical Review,* October 1968; reprinted in *Information Service,* February 22, 1969, and *Religious Education,* September–October 1969]). This essay is the text of an address delivered by Baldwin at the Fourth Assembly of the World Council of Churches in Uppsala, Sweden, in the summer of 1968. Later, upon the occasion of Lorraine Hansberry's death, Baldwin reminisces rather sentimentally about his friendship with her in "Sweet Lorraine" (*Esquire,* November 1969) and briefly considers the effects of her works on black people.

Baldwin's own growing militancy is reflected in "An Open Letter to My Sister, Miss Angela Davis" (*Black Creation,* April 1972), as he pictures the same kind of adulation for militant blacks as he once registered for the Martin Luther Kings. The letter, addressed to the then-imprisoned Angela Davis, treats her plight in terms of the general racial situation in America and glories in the generation of Angela, Huey Newton, and George Jackson, "a whole new generation of people [who] have assessed and absorbed their history, and, in that tremendous action, have freed themselves of it and will never be victims again." Although he admits being of another generation, he asserts that his destiny is inextricably interwoven with that of the Angela Davises; and he concludes with the memorable passage from which Angela Davis borrowed the title of her later book, *If They Come in the Morning:*

> then we must fight for your life as though it were our own—which it is—and render impassable with our bodies the corridor to the gas chamber. For, if they take you in the morning, they will be coming for us that night.

INTERVIEWS AND DISCUSSIONS

Because Baldwin has become a figure of wide public popularity and even notoriety, he has appeared frequently on television and radio shows and has been interviewed by numerous popular magazines, where the interest was as much in his social and political views as in his literary works. In addition to *A Rap on Race,* a discussion with Margaret Mead (Philadelphia: Lippincott, 1971), and *A Dialogue,* with Nikki Giovanni (Philadelphia: Lippincott, 1973), numerous discussions and interviews have been published in various periodicals.

Baldwin participated in a symposium at Hofstra University in Hempstead, New York, in May 1961 with Ben Shabra and Darius Milhaud, moderated by Malcolm Preston, which has been published as "The Image: Three Views" (*Opera News,* December 8, 1962). In this symposium, Baldwin talks about the disorder in the world, the individual's quest for identity, and the need for the individual to understand his history in order to know who he is.

"The Negro in American Culture" (*Cross Currents,* Summer 1961; reprinted in Mathew H. Ahmann, *The New Negro* [Notre Dame, Ind.: Fides, 1961]; *ND,* March 1962; and *The Black American Writer, Volume I: Fiction,* edited by C. W. E. Bigsby, [Deland, Fla.: Everett/Edwards, 1969]) records a discussion originally broadcast over Pacifica Radio (WBAI–FM) in 1961 among Baldwin, Alfred Kazin, Lorraine Hansberry, Emile Capouya, and Langston Hughes, moderated by Nat Hentoff. The participants discuss the conflict between the social and artistic responsibilities of black writers, prejudices facing black artists, and white portrayals of black characters (particularly those of William Faulkner), and comment generally about black–white relationships and the future of America.

In his interview with Baldwin ("James Baldwin Talks with Kenneth Clark," in *The Negro Protest* [Boston: Beacon, 1963]), Kenneth Clark elicits some interesting information about the subject's youth, his family and its southern background, his education, the contemporary racial situation, and his views of Martin Luther King and Malcolm X.

Anyone interested in Baldwin the man will find the interview conducted by Eve Auchincloss and Nancy Lynch, "Disturber of the Peace: James Baldwin" (*Mademoiselle*, May 1963; reprinted in Bigsby, *The Black American Writer*, Vol. I), most helpful. Although the interview does not deal specifically with any of his books, it touches very directly on many ideas he treats and that are of great personal interest to him, and the author speaks of them very honestly and eloquently. He comments on white liberals, his travels through the South, school desegregation, the role of sex in white people's reactions to blacks, his view of himself, and homosexuality.

The racial situation in America is discussed in "Pour Libérer les Blancs" [To Liberate White People] (*Preuves*, October 1963). In a debate held at Cambridge University and published as "The American Dream and the American Negro" (*New York Times Magazine*, March 7, 1965), Baldwin and William F. Buckley, Jr., debate the thesis, "The American Dream is at the expense of the American Negro." In a discussion with James Mossman and Colin MacInnes, televised and recorded by the British Broadcasting Corporation (B.B.C.) and published as "Race, Hate, Sex, and Colour: A Conversation" (*Encounter*, July 1965), Baldwin speaks of religion and human relationships and interactions, particularly between blacks and whites in America. He also comments on his hatred of his father and his early hatred of whites (noting that such hatred is destructive) and rejects the teachings of Malcolm X. Later, Baldwin talks of his need to write, and the necessity of being away from America in order to write, in an interview first published in *CEP Dergisi* (Istanbul) and reprinted in *Atlas* (March 1967), "James Baldwin Breaks His Silence." He also comments on Black Power, the war in Vietnam, and Christianity, expressing views similar to those he has expressed elsewhere on these subjects.

In an interview published as "How Can We Get the Black People to Cool It?" (*Esquire*, July 1968), Baldwin enumerates the causes of the street riots that had recently occurred, and bitterly attacks policemen and politics in America, although he still expresses hope for the United States and advises young blacks not to hate white people. On March 18, 1968, he appeared with Betty Shabazz at a hearing held in New York City before the House of Representatives' Select Subcommittee On Labor on the subject of establishing a National Commission on Negro History and Culture. He supported the establishment of the commission, but cautioned that blacks cannot be taught their culture until American history is truthfully taught and until textbooks are changed, so that the view of American history will no longer destroy the morals of black children by distorting their past. The transcript of this testimony is published as "The Nigger We Invent" (*Integrated Education*, March and April 1969).

In "Conversation: Ida Lewis and James Baldwin" (*Essence*, October 1970), Baldwin explains why he had to leave America. He claims that his role of spokesman, which he never wanted, is over now. In a later interview with David Frost, "Are We on the Edge of Civil War?" (in David Frost, *The Americans* [New York: Stein & Day, 1970]), Baldwin speaks bitterly about race relations in America and discusses the revolutionary impulse among black militants.

The interview with Herbert R. Lottman, "To Be James Baldwin" (*Intellectual Digest*, July 1972), records the growing bitterness Baldwin reflected in his then recently published *No Name in the Street* (New York: Dial, 1972). He notes that his attitude toward the world has changed: "I'm much sadder now," and contends that he sees a holocaust approaching; he says that *No Name in the Street* is about this holocaust. Although the book documents the civil rights movement up to the death of Martin Luther King, Baldwin declares "It's not a documentary. It's a personal book—my own testimony." In a bitter, premonitory tone he explains what he means by *holocaust*: "Americans who have managed to learn nothing are now about to learn a great deal."

A sometimes frustrating record of the fiery debate between Peregrine Worsthorne and James Baldwin may be found in *Encounter* ("Let Me Finish, Let Me Finish . . . " [September 1972]). This unedited transcript is often unclear and confusing because key words are frequently omitted. In this heated debate, chaired by Bryan Magee and broadcast as part of Thames Television's *Something to Say* series, Worsthorne contends that American blacks are largely responsible for their own fate because they have not taken advantage of opportunities the way other minorities have. As Baldwin vehemently rejects this assertion, there is a great deal of screaming but little communication between the two, because Worsthorne cannot understand Baldwin's historical perspective, which allows him to allude to all blacks, slaves, and those in similar conditions as "I," and to refer to all whites, slaveholders, and their like as "you."

A series of interviews with Joe Walker ("Exclusive Interview with James Baldwin" [*Muhammad Speaks*, September 8, 15, 22, 29, 1972]), found Baldwin speaking about the lack of representation of blacks in the government, the renaissance in black American literature, and black films. The next year, in an unpublished television interview on the Dick Cavett Show (September 5, 1973), Baldwin spoke about his forthcoming *If Beale Street Could Talk* (New York: Dial, 1974) and insisted that he had found himself: "Certain battles I've been fighting in myself are beginning to end." "*The Black Scholar* Interviews: James

Baldwin" (*BlackSch,* December–January 1974) is an interesting discussion of many subjects on which Baldwin has commented elsewhere, including the present world political scene and Lorraine Hansberry. Baldwin also emphasizes here the importance of a strong and loving black family for survival.

A recent interview with inmates at Riker's Island prison in New York (*Essence,* June 1976) is notable for its calmness. Baldwin appeals to the women "to save our children," and speaks poignantly of his father, "without [whom] I might be dead." Though he still predicts the fall of Western civilization, his prophesies are couched in the mildest language.

Manuscripts and Letters

Locating Baldwin manuscripts and letters is a frustrating task, partly because Baldwin has little interest in retaining and preserving his manuscripts, according to two of his friends with whom I spoke (Sam Floyd, at Atlanta University, Atlanta, Georgia, in March 1972; and Alex Haley, at Virginia Commonwealth University, Richmond, Virginia, on September 30, 1974) and according to some of his own comments. In a letter to Harold Jackman (1956) Baldwin gave his permission for the manuscript of *Giovanni's Room* to be given to Atlanta University, noting that he'd "just as soon never lay eyes on it again." Further, Fern Eckman has noted that the manuscript of an unpublished novel, *Ignorant Armies,* is "now reposing in a duffle bag in his mother's apartment" (*The Furious Passage of James Baldwin* [Philadelphia: Lippincott, 1966]).

Nothing is cited for Baldwin in Lorenzo Greene's "Negro Manuscript Collections in Libraries" (*NHB,* March 1967); in Philip M. Hamer's *A Guide to Archives and Manuscripts in the United States* (New Haven, Conn: Yale University Press, 1961); or in *American Literary Manuscripts* (Austin: University of Texas Press, 1960), compiled by the Modern Language Association of America, American Literature Group, Committee on Manuscript Holdings. The United States Library of Congress's *National Union Catalog of Manuscript Collections* mentions only the manuscripts at Atlanta University, which will be cited shortly.

Walter Schath's *Directory of Afro-American Resources* (New York: Bowker, 1970) is the only reference that lists several Baldwin manuscripts, but all of these cannot at this time be located. Schath indicates that the American Academy of Arts and Letters Library in New York City has about twenty items. A request for a description of these items was answered by Hortense Zera, the librarian (in a letter dated October 10, 1974), who indicated that they had two typed letters, one "concerning invitations he [Baldwin] wanted sent to family members for the ceremonial at which he was given his grant in 1956" and the other "to W. H. Auden, chairman of the committee, thanking him for the grant."

Schath also indicates that the Museum of African American History at 3806 South Michigan Avenue, Chicago, Illinois, holds taped speeches, interviews, and the like; but there is not now such a museum at that address, nor is a museum by that name listed in the Chicago telephone directory. Finally, Schath indicates that there are tapes Baldwin made for radio broadcast at SCLC Radio in New York City; that radio station is not now at the address listed by Schath, nor is it listed in the telephone directory.

Apparently, the only significant collection of Baldwin manuscripts is at the Trevor–Arnett Library at Atlanta University. These manuscripts were secured through the Harold Jackman Memorial Committee, of which Baldwin is a member. Because the manuscripts in the Countee Cullen Memorial Collections at the Trevor–Arnett Library constitute practically all of this discussion on manuscripts and because they are so fascinating to the Baldwin scholar, a detailed description of them seems appropriate. They include:

1. A holograph note explaining the purpose of *Giovanni's Room*—to show "the near impossibility of love in our time—between men, or between men and women"—and outlining the plan of the book, with additional notes on technique.
2. Several other pages of notes regarding *Giovanni's Room*, concerning matters such as the placement of the description of the room so as to achieve the greatest symbolic significance, and a consideration of the effects Baldwin wishes to achieve in particular scenes and episodes.
3. Several typed versions of *Giovanni's Room*.
4. Notes on the chronology of *Giovanni's Room*.
5. Letter to Harold Jackman from Paris, written in 1956, but undated.
6. Another undated letter to Jackman (previously cited) from Corsica, in 1956, giving Baldwin's permission for the manuscript of *Giovanni's Room* to be given to Atlanta University, with the notation that he would "just as soon never lay eyes on it [the manuscript] again."
7. Letter to James A. Hulbert, librarian at Atlanta University.
8. Several versions of unfinished novels.
    a. One novel with a notation "*earliest* version" and dated 1944 has never been published, but parts of it may have been used in *Another Country*.
    b. A synopsis of a novel to be titled *So Long at the Fair*, portions of which apparently were used in *Tell Me How Long the Train's Been Gone*. It includes suggestions of conflicts, themes, and problems that Baldwin was to treat in all his novels.

    c. "Tentative Plan for *Backwater,* a novel," which begins with a consideration of the problem of relating this tale in the first person. This work obviously was a genesis of *Giovanni's Room.*

    d. Holograph plan of a work to be titled *The Only Pretty Ring Time.*

There is a copy of the typewritten "Autobiographical Notes" Baldwin sent to Alfred A. Knopf in the Barrett Room of the University of Virginia; and Sam Floyd, a friend of Baldwin's, presently has the manuscript of *The Fire Next Time.*

Biography

The fullest and most interesting biographical material concerning Baldwin may be gained from reading his own work. Indeed, one would be hard pressed to find an author whose works are more highly auto-biographical than Baldwin's. Even his fiction is largely autobiographical, and it would not be difficult to discuss his novels and short stories as a telling and retelling of the author's own troubled life. Fern Eckman has noted that "Baldwin broods over the notion that he is fated to live his novels before he can write them" (*The Furious Passage of James Baldwin*). Baldwin himself noted early, "One writes out of one thing only—one's own experience" ("Autobiographical Notes," in *Notes of a Native Son*), and later he asserted, "All art is a kind of confession. . . . All artists, if they are to survive, are forced, at last, to tell the whole story, to vomit the anguish up" ("The Precarious Vogue of Ingmar Bergman" [*Esquire,* April 1960]; collected in *Nobody Knows My Name* as "The Northern Protestant"). Thus it is that in his fictional and nonfictional works Baldwin returns again and again to his own life, particularly to certain events that undoubtedly have greatly affected him, notably his relationship with his father, his embarrassment as an adolescent boy by policemen who humiliated him and speculated about his sexual prowess, his religious conversion, his exile in Europe, and his trips to the South. And each time he returns to these events he gives some new perspective, some added insights, some additional details which suggest not only their effect on him as a man and as a writer at a particular period in his development, but also his wrestling with the confession until he tells "the whole story," until he "vomit[s] the anguish up" completely.

Several of Baldwin's nonfictional works provide biographical information. In "Letter from a Region in My Mind" (*NY,* November 17, 1962; reprinted as "Down at the Cross" in *The Fire Next Time*), Baldwin recounts in eloquent detail the adolescent crisis he faced during the summer when he was fourteen, his religious conversion, and his experience as a preacher, as well as his meeting with Elijah Muhammad. "Notes for a Hypothetical Novel" (delivered as an address at the third annual *Esquire* magazine symposium as "The Role of the Writer in America" at San Francisco State College, October 22, 1960, and published in *Nobody Knows My Name*) furnishes data on his childhood. The previously cited "Autobiographical Notes" covers his childhood, reading, early writing, fellowships, and influences. "Notes of a Native Son" includes an account of his father's death, reminiscences of his relationship with his father, and a description of his experiences living and working in New Jersey.

The "Notes" in *The Amen Corner* tell of his need to leave the United States, his exile in Paris, and his need to return. "Equal in Paris" gives an account of his arrest and imprisonment in Paris in December 1949 (*Commentary*, March 1955; reprinted in *Notes of a Native Son* and in *New Partisan Reader 1945–1953*, edited by William Phillips and Philip Rahv [New York: Harcourt Brace Jovanovich, 1953]). "The Discovery of What It Means to Be an American" again discusses his exile in Paris and his quest for himself (*NYTBR* January 25,1959; reprinted in *Essays Today*, Vol. IV, edited by Richard Ludwig [New York: Harcourt Brace Jovanovich, 1960]; and *Nobody Knows My Name*). "Stranger in the Village" relates some of his experiences during his visits to Switzerland (*Harper's Magazine*, October 1953; reprinted in *Notes of a Native Son; Preuves*, June 1956; Leslie Fiedler's *The Art of the Essay* [New York: T.Y. Crowell, 1958]; *What Country Have I? Political Writings by Black Americans*, edited by Herbert J. Storing [New York: St. Martin's, 1970]; and under the title "The Search for Identity, 1953" in *American Principles and Issues: The National Purpose*, edited by Oscar Handlin [New York: Holt, Rinehart & Winston, 1961]).

"The Hard Kind of Courage" (*Harper's Magazine*, October 1958; reprinted as "A Fly in the Buttermilk" in *Nobody Knows My Name*); "Letter from the South: Nobody Knows My Name" (*PR*, Winter 1959; reprinted in *Nobody Knows My Name*); and "They Can't Turn Back" (*Mademoiselle*, August 1960) recount his trips to the South during the integration crisis. "Alas, Poor Richard" (in *Nobody Knows My Name*) covers his relationship with Richard Wright, and "Letters from a Journey" (*Harper's Magazine*, May 1963) covers his trip to Israel. "Take Me to the Water" (in *No Name in the Street*) is a lengthy and detailed autobiographical selection treating his family, his childhood, his exile in Paris, and his many attempts to return to America to live, as well as his travels through the South. "To Be Baptized" (in *No Name in the Street*) treats his sojourn with his brother and sister in London in 1968, his relationship with Malcolm X, his travels through the United States in 1968, his meetings with Martin Luther King, including the March on Washington, his arguments with Columbia in the effort to film the life of Malcolm X, and his meeting and relationship with Huey Newton.

Although these are some of the most notable essays by Baldwin which are largely autobiographical, many others not only contain facts and details about his life, but also reveal a great deal about Baldwin the man. Even when he is writing about history, politics, or another individual—whatever his ostensible subject—we see Baldwin wrestling with his own personal problems, struggling with his ideas and evolving philosophy, emphatically fused into the event; and frequently the outcome is that he reveals more about himself than about his professed subject, as, to cite two glaring examples, in "The Black Boy Looks at the White Boy: Norman Mailer" (*Esquire,* May 1961; reprinted in *Nobody Knows My Name*) and "Gide as Husband and Homosexual" (*NL,* December 13, 1954; reprinted as "The Male Prison" in *Nobody Knows My Name*). In *The Furious Passage of James Baldwin,* Fern Eckman quotes Baldwin commenting on a sentence from the latter essay in which he faults Gide for writing about his own homosexuality, which Baldwin felt he should not have revealed to the public:

> That was meant as a commentary on *myself.* I was accusing myself, perhaps not directly enough, of a certain fear and a certain hypocrisy. I do *think* that his *Protestantism,* you know, accounts for a certain *coldness* in him—in his *work.* But I wasn't trying—it really wasn't meant as a judgement on *Gide.* It was meant as a judgement on *me.*

Nothing approaching a definitive biography of James Baldwin has yet appeared. The one full-length biography, Fern Eckman's *The Furious Passage of James Baldwin,* is a slight endeavor based mainly on interviews with Baldwin and on his autobiographical writing. The lengthy quotations from these interviews are often reproduced in a fragmented and awkward way. Certain events from his life are taken so directly from Baldwin's essays that the reproductions sound more like Baldwin than Eckman. Overall, this book lacks a sense of coherence because it seems more a compilation of quotations from the interviews and paraphrases from the works than an amalgamation of these sources. Further, some of Baldwin's own analyses and observations about his work are repeated here as if they were Eckman's. Finally, Eckman's emphasis on trivial details and behind-the-scenes revelations of the gossip-column variety detract from the legitimacy of the work as a serious biography. Nevertheless, despite its shortcomings, *The Furious Passage of James Baldwin* cannot be ignored by the Baldwin scholar because it does contain some material not available elsewhere about his childhood, education, the production of *Blues for Mister Charlie,* his close friendships, and his meeting with Robert Kennedy. Eckman also goes into some detail to analyze and describe Baldwin's personality and character, minutely delineating the manner in which he greets a friend, reacts to his audiences, moves about, and the like. She spends a great deal of time discussing his father and considering the effect of his relationship with his father on Baldwin. Her conclusions may sometimes be debatable, but they are worth considering. Eckman also includes in this book several samples of Baldwin's early writings.

Some of the articles that appeared in popular magazines, although they are not serious literary biographies, may be of interest to the scholar interested in Baldwin's life. Allan Morrison's "The Angriest Young Man" (*Ebony*, October 1961) attempts to introduce Baldwin to the general public, including a brief autobiographical sketch, a summary of the themes in his works, his ideas and beliefs, and a view of his activities at the time. Morrison includes a detailed account of the nature of a typical day in Baldwin's life, a view of his apartment in Greenwich Village, and a discussion of his method of writing. Notable in this article are the excellent pictures of Baldwin.

Jane Howard recorded Baldwin's speaking tour through the South in 1963, giving a picturesque view of his hectic life and his dedication to the civil rights movement in "Telling Talk from a Negro Writer" (*Life*, May 24, 1963). Her many quotations from Baldwin's speeches, some of them now well known, and the excellent candid photographs help to produce a vivid and moving portrait of Baldwin during this period. Included also are little details about the author which, while they may seem superfluous, nonetheless contribute to the full-dimensional portrait: his behavior and habits in a restaurant, the way he talks on the telephone, and the like. There is, in addition, a brief biographical sketch.

Gloria Steinem includes a rather full biographical sketch of Baldwin in "James Baldwin, An Original" (*Vogue*, July 1964), written as *Blues for Mister Charlie* was being prepared for production. Her interesting personality sketch of Baldwin also contains some very useful comments about the play by its author.

In the introduction to *James Baldwin: A Collection of Critical Essays* (Englewood Cliffs, N.J.: Prentice-Hall, 1974), Keneth Kinnamon includes a short study of Baldwin's life, something of a psychological biography, that considers the influence of certain events on his life and development. Kinnamon also includes a chronology of important dates in this work; but like most of these kinds of listings, it sometimes oversimplifies to the point of misrepresentation. For example, Kinnamon lists "1948–57 Lives in Paris, Switzerland, and the south of France," without any indication of that significant effort to live in America again in 1952 and the months Baldwin spent in America during 1954 and 1955 when he was completing *Giovanni's Room* and *Notes of a Native Son*. Further, the chronology leaves the impression that Baldwin lived in the United States from 1957 to 1965, which again is misleading.

Brief biographical sketches of Baldwin by Ruth Ulman appear in the *Wilson Library Bulletin* (February 1959) and *Current Biography Yearbook* (Bronx, N.Y.: H. W. Wilson, 1959). Other short sketches can be found in *The Negro Almanac*, edited by Harry A. Ploski and Roscoe C. Brown (New York: Bellwether, 1966); *Contemporary Authors: A Bio-Bibliographical Guide to Current Authors and Their Works,* edited by James M. Ethridge and Barbara Kopala (Detroit: Gale Research, 1965); and *Living Black American Authors: A Biographical Directory,* edited by Ann Allen Shockley and Sue P. Chandler (New York: Bowker, 1973). Clarence Major's "James Baldwin: A Fire in the Mind," in Major's *The Dark and Feeling: Black American Writers and Their Work* (New York: Third Press–Joseph Okpaku, 1974), is a concise sketch of Baldwin's writing career through the publication of *Tell Me How Long the Train's Been Gone.*

Criticism

STUDIES OF INDIVIDUAL WORKS

Go Tell It on the Mountain Baldwin's first novel, *Go Tell It on the Mountain* (1953), enjoyed the warmest reception by critics of any of his novels. Critics praised it as a novel of distinction by an author of exceptional promise. The reviewer for *Time* (May 18, 1953) considered the church scenes "as compelling as anything that has turned up in a U.S. novel this year." Harvey Curtis Webster (*SatR,* May 16, 1953) revealed a penchant for absolutes in his description of *Go Tell It on the Mountain,* asserting that it was written skillfully and that the flashbacks were handled masterfully. He went on to compare Baldwin favorably with William Faulkner for his moving penetration of the minds of his characters. Granville Hicks ("Go Tell It on the Mountain" [*NL,* June 1, 1953]; reprinted in Hick's *Literary Horizons: A Quarter Century of American Fiction* [New York: New York University Press, 1970]) hailed the novel as proof that Baldwin had not succumbed to the dangers Baldwin himself had warned against in protest literature. Hicks also praised Baldwin's technical skill.

A few dissenting voices were heard among the critics. Henry F. Winslow (*The Crisis,* December 1953) saw "no art and nothing new" in the book. He felt that Aunt Florence overshadowed John and that Gabriel served merely as her foil. The anonymous reviewer for *The New Yorker* (June 10, 1953) found "a Harlem without laughter . . . incredible," and went on to insist that this lack of humor in the novel made it "less penetrating." He or she therefore found it lacking compared to Ralph Ellison's *Invisible Man,* but felt with the favorable critics that the novel showed "exceptional promise," despite considering it wooden and without vitality.

One of the earliest critical studies, "The American Negro in Search of Identity: Three Novelists: Richard Wright, Ralph Ellison, James Baldwin," by Steven Marcus (*Commentary,* November 1953), is full of both absurdities and insightful observations. In his discussion of *Invisible Man, The Outsider,* and *Go Tell It on the Mountain,* Marcus makes some highly questionable generalizations: in more than one instance he asserts that Africa is without culture or relevant history; on another occasion he avers, "Negroes themselves believe . . . in their own savagery." Despite these warped views, which would presumably preclude his understanding and interpretation of writings by black authors, Marcus does make some important observations about the theme of the quest for identity among these writers. His assessment of the conversion scene in *Go Tell It on the Mountain* is, however, the weakest part of his essay. He concludes that John's conversion means "his dreams and desires are never to be fulfilled," and he asserts that Baldwin's use of contrasting religious language and ironic voice in this scene suggests that the author is not sure of what he wants to say; obviously Baldwin is very much in command of what he wishes to say here, and these two voices forcefully suggest both the spiritual and the secular implications of this experience.

A similar theme is treated in another comparative study, Caroline Bloomfield's "Religion and Alienation in James Baldwin, Bernard Malamud, and James F. Powers" (*Religious Education,* March 1962). Bloomfield compares the heroes in their works in terms of their alienation and their embracing of life despite its hardships in such a way as to liberate themselves.

In "The Question of Moral Energy in James Baldwin's *Go Tell It on the Mountain*" (*CLAJ,* March 1964), Wallace Graves argues that a major flaw in the novel is the sentimentality with which Baldwin paints Elizabeth and Richard because Baldwin is unable to maintain an artistic distance between the narrator and Richard. Unfortunately, at times the critic goes to ridiculous extremes to support his perfectly valid thesis, such as, for example, his labeling as "mawkish and excessive" diction the very common usage of an old folk expression and Baldwin's humorous comment on it in this passage:

> But her good aunt swore she would "move Heaven and earth" before she would let her sister's daughter grow up with such a man. Without, however, so much as looking at Heaven, and without troubling any more of the earth than that part of it which held the courthouse, she won the day.

Michel Fabre's "Fathers and Sons in James Baldwin's *Go Tell It on the Mountain*" (*EA,* January–March 1970; also collected by M. G. Cooke in *Modern Black Novelists: A Collection of Critical Essays* [Englewood Cliffs, N.J.: Prentice-Hall, 1971]) is a valuable study in which Fabre enumerates and analyzes the numerous father–son combinations in the novel. He also draws interesting and detailed parallels between the life of the author and the events in the novel, discussing at some length Baldwin's projection of Wright into the image of spiritual father and his belief that Wright rejected him. Fabre concludes with the assertion that Baldwin remains an Ishmael in search of a father and this search continues to crop up in his work.

James R. Giles compares the novel with John Rechy's *City of Night* in "Religious Alienation and 'Homosexual Consciousness' in *City of Night* and *Go Tell It on the Mountain*" (*CE,* November 1974), observing that both are homosexual novels which "focus upon the role of a dehumanizing religion in the development of a gay consciousness." Giles observes that Baldwin exhibits a discomfort with his own sexuality in his work, while Rechy transcends any discomfort.

Other studies that deserve attention are John R. May's "Ellison, Baldwin and Wright: Vestiges of Christian Apocalypse" in May's *Toward a New Earth: Apocalypse in the American Novel* (Notre Dame, Ind.: University of Notre Dame Press, 1972), in which the author considers the mood and images of apocalypse in *Go Tell It on the Mountain* and the works of Ellison and Wright; Wilfred Cartey's comparison of *Go Tell It on the Mountain* with three novels by black authors from South Africa, the British West Indies, and São Paulo, Brazil, in "The Realities of Four Negro Writers" (*Columbia University Forum,* Summer 1966); and the slight treatment in Albert Gerard's "Humanism and Negritude: Notes on the Contemporary Afro-American Novel" (*Diogenes,* Spring 1962).

Notes of a Native Son   Baldwin's second full-length publication and his first collection of essays, *Notes of a Native Son* (1955), was generally well received, though not widely reviewed. Dachine Rainer (*Commonweal,* January 13, 1956) calls it a "superlatively written and phenomenally intelligent collection." She describes Baldwin's style of writing as "evocative and illuminating," and says that the virtues of the book are so great that its weaknesses (such as a lack of humor and his repudiation of blackness in "Many Thousands Gone") are negligible.

Although Langston Hughes's reaction (*NYTBR,* February 26, 1956) is less than glowing, he does suggest that Baldwin shows great promise as a writer, and he asserts that "Few American writers handle words more effectively in the essay form than James Baldwin." He suggests also that when Baldwin is able to find himself, to free the American and the Afro-American in him, he will be an exceptional commentator on the problems of the world. Robert W. Flint (*Commentary,* May 1956), however, does not consider the book an important contribution to social or political thought, although he does consider it important autobiography.

Anthony Wills's "The Use of Coincidence in 'Notes of a Native Son,'" (*NALF*, Fall 1974) analyzes the effect achieved by Baldwin's juxtaposition of coincidental events in "Notes of a Native Son." Wills illustrates the manner in which the use of coincidence contributes to the development of the theme of the essay—Baldwin's determination to keep his heart free of hatred. The author's insistence that the essayist cannot tamper with facts suggests that he is unaware that Baldwin made minor adjustments in dates to achieve the effect he desired.

Giovanni's Room Baldwin's second novel, *Giovanni's Room* (1956), did not receive the enthusiastic critical acclaim conferred upon his first; nor have literary scholars given it the individual attention accorded to *Go Tell It on the Mountain* and *The Amen Corner*. Most reviewers conceded that the author had a striking style, but found the subject matter of the book highly objectionable and the characters inadequately realized. J. F. Sullivan's characterization of David as "disgusting" (*Commonweal*, December 12, 1956) was generally representative of the reactions to this character. Anthony West (*NY*, November 10, 1956) satirically relates the plot and describes the story as a "riffle on the surface of life, that completely lacks the validity of actual experience." He expresses the hope that Baldwin "will soon return to the American subjects he dealt with so promisingly and with so much real understanding" in the earlier books. Charles J. Rolo (*AtM*, December 1956) praises Baldwin for his "narrative skill, poetic intensity of feeling, and . . . sensitive command of the language," but objects to the content of the plot.

Although William Esty (*NR*, December 17, 1956) finds several faults in the book (the ending is "lame"; the plot is a bit melodramatic; the descriptions are sometimes too sentimental; the hero is not fully realized), he praises Baldwin's avoidance of cliché literary attitudes as well as his not emphasizing the grotesque; Esty calls the book "the best American novel dealing with homosexuality I have read." A few other critics likewise praised Baldwin's handling of homosexuality. David Karp (*SatR*, December 1, 1956) notes that Baldwin treats the theme of homosexuality "with great artistry and restraint." Granville Hicks (*NYTBR*, October 14, 1956; collected in *Literary Horizons*) praises Baldwin's candor, dignity, and intensity in relating the tale.

Nobody Knows My Name: More Notes of a Native Son *Nobody Knows My Name: More Notes of a Native Son* (1961) sparked both high praise and bitter condemnation. While some critics raved about the eloquence of Baldwin's presentation of social problems and the lucidity of his arguments, others bitterly attacked him for his racism and his lack of logic, particularly those who reacted violently to Baldwin's attacks upon subjects about which they were personally highly sensitive—the white liberals, the white racists, the Faulkner lovers, southerners, and black teachers. A few critics were interested in elucidating the book, but most reacted to isolated passages or essays in which Baldwin rubbed them the wrong way.

One of the more illuminating reviews is Stanley Edgar Hyman's "Blacks, Whites and Grays" (*NL*, July 31, 1961; reprinted in Hyman's *Standards: A Chronicle of Books for Our Time* [New York: Horizon, 1966]), in which Hyman comments perceptively on the impact of the blues on the title, content, and style of the book, and considers that the work reveals Baldwin's problems with identity. Hyman prefers the literary essays in the collection, although he admits that the racial essays are "often shrewd, tough-minded, and eloquent."

Nick Aaron Ford, in "Search for Identity: A Critical Survey of Significant Belles-Lettres By and About Negroes Published in 1961" (*Phylon*, Summer 1962), also comments on the theme of the search for identity which he sees as the thread unifying the thirteen essays. Although Ford's essay is replete with praise, he does take issue with Baldwin's "gullibility" about black teachers when he attacks them for not caring about what they teach and for having themselves reached a dead end. Although Charles J. Rolo (*AtM*, July 1961) alludes to weak spots (he never specifies them), his review is overwhelmingly complimentary, calling the work "informed by a deep seriousness and a major literary talent" that are so preponderant as to preclude any necessity for discussing weaknesses. Alfred Kazin, in "The Essays of James Baldwin" (*Reporter*, August 17, 1961; reprinted in Kazin's *Contemporaries* [Boston: Little, Brown, 1962]), praises Baldwin for giving "voice to all his insights and longings and despairs without losing control," and goes on to note that Baldwin "is radiantly intelligent as he seizes the endless implications in the oppression of man by man." James Finn (*Commonweal*, December 1961) criticizes the essays as "uneven" and "slight," but praises Baldwin's "passion, insight and intelligence" as well as his moral arguments.

Julian Mayfield (*NR*, August 7, 1961), who describes Baldwin as one of America's most perceptive and penetrating thinkers, comments on the essays individually. Of "East River, Downtown: Postscript to a Letter from Harlem," he says, "This is not the strident voice of a flaming radical. It is an eloquent plea. He objects to several essays: "A Fly in Buttermilk" and "Princes and Powers" are too pedestrian; "Alas, Poor Richard" and "The Black Boy Looks at the White Boy" are too personal. Granville Hicks ("Nobody Knows My Name," [*SatR*, July 1, 1961; reprinted in Hicks's *Literary Horizons*]) also finds a few of the essays too pedestrian, but he considers most of them well done, describing the essays on the American Negro as "eloquent, uncompromising, and . . . unanswerable."

Although J. Saunders Redding (*New York Herald Tribune*, June 25, 1961) praises the personal essays in part two, he asserts that "The intellectual quality of [the essays in part one] does not begin to match the emotional quality of them," and wryly observes, "Most of the pieces in Part One can be dismissed, I think, with the observation that, after all, Baldwin had to make a book." Donald Malcolm (*NY*, November 25, 1961) begins his critique with a sarcastic discussion of the recent vogue of "the problem of identity," and goes on to write off those essays in which Baldwin treats the problem of identity as lacking a truly personal tone, intelligence, and selectivity. However, in the essays in which Baldwin comments on various events that shed light on the status of the black, Baldwin proves himself to be, Malcolm asserts, "an extremely valuable member of a small body of literary observers who write with vigor, sense and utter candor about things that matter greatly to this country."

Phillip Bonosky's "The Negro Writer and Commitment" (*Mainstream*, February 1962) is really more of a rebuttal than a review. He attacks as anathema for the black people's struggle for freedom what he sees as Baldwin's thesis: "The Negro tragedy is mankind's general tragedy or original sin, against which it is essentially hopeless to rage or to combat. Victory lies in defeat." In a very sarcastic tone, he ridicules Baldwin's attacks on *Uncle Tom's Cabin* and *Native Son* as well as on W. E. B. Du Bois. Although Bonosky builds a strong case against some of Baldwin's assertions, he is guilty of treating only those ideas in *Nobody Knows My Name* with which he disagrees, and at times he interprets those much too simplistically, thereby failing to suggest the broader implications and interpretations of Baldwin's argument. In "James Baldwin: Voice of a Revolution" (*PR*, Summer 1963), Stephen Spender concedes that Baldwin is a powerful essayist, but attacks him as an overzealous spokesman, given to exaggeration and too often guided by emotions. Spender attacks many of Baldwin's arguments and conclusions, especially his criticism of white Americans and his sense of the superiority of American blacks.

Dan Jacobson ("James Baldwin as Spokesman" [*Commentary*, December 1961]), who obviously imagines he is writing a generous review, constantly praises Baldwin's talents and comments upon the evils of racism in the manner of the unconscious racist posing as liberal. He suggests, moreover, that the impact of the book is weakened by its numerous examples of "rhetoric, of exhortation, of uplift, of reproach," and he goes on to advance his own theories regarding race relations. He prefaces one of his remarks with the statement, "Mr. Baldwin would possibly regard this as no more than a further example of the liberal complacency and self-righteousness he so often inveighs against." It is doubtful that Baldwin would honor Jacobson with the title of liberal (even with all its negative implications) after reading this critic's responses to his arguments, such as "Now it is certain that conditions in South Africa are thoroughly bad; . . . Yet it remains true, too, that the happiest people one sees in the streets of South Africa today are the black people."

Melvin E. Bradford, in "Faulkner, James Baldwin, and the South" (*GaR,* Winter 1965), eloquently defends the alleged assertion by Faulkner that he would move from the middle of the road, where he had been trying to help Negroes, and start shooting in the event of a racial revolution, an assertion which Baldwin attacked in "Faulkner and Desegregation." Bradford's criticism of Baldwin is not lacking in what Bradford would see as generosity: "In fairness," he writes, "we must admit that we had no reason to expect the Negro novelist to be particularly perceptive in his comments on the squire of Oxford." Bradford proceeds to expound the southern concept of community and the "definite order of status, function, and place" which were so important to Faulkner and the South, and which Baldwin (born in Harlem, which "is not community") cannot understand. The critic then enumerates inconsistencies in Baldwin "and the white liberals North and South who helped create him."

Another Country The publication of *Another Country* in 1962 produced howls of rebuke, indignation, and pity that so fine a talent as James Baldwin was producing such unrepresentative work. The negative reception, which all but overshadowed the critical acclaim, was so overwhelming that numerous later scholars have felt inclined to respond to the harsh attacks with lengthy explanations and defenses. Much fuller coverage of the initial reaction than is given here may be found in Mike Thelwell's "*Another Country:* Baldwin's New York Novel," in *The Black American Writer, Volume I: Fiction,* edited by C. W. E. Bigsby (Deland, Fla.: Everett/Edwards, 1969); and in Norman Podhoretz's "In Defense of James Baldwin," in *Doings and Undoings* (New York: Farrar, Straus & Giroux, 1964; reprinted in Donald B. Gibson's *Five Black Writers* [New York: New York University Press, 1970]).

Saul Maloff (*The Nation,* July 14, 1962) decides after reading *Another Country* that there are two Baldwins, one an essayist who writes with "poise and clarity and reverberant feeling," and the other the novelist who has no control of his work. Maloff concludes that the novel has no redeeming features. In "Wrong Pulpit" (*NY,* August 4, 1962), Whitney Balliett likewise attacks the novel as a "turgid melodrama" whose one redeeming feature is Baldwin's power with words. In similar manner, Paul Goodman (*NYTBR,* June 24, 1962) asserts that the characters exist in a vacuum and concludes, "It is mediocre. It is unworthy of its author's lovely abilities. Given his awareness (which he cannot escape), he must write something more poetic and surprising." Although Stanley Edgar Hyman (*NewL,* June 25, 1962) notes some moments of great power, he finds little to praise and much to attack: he insists that the writing is frequently bad, the use of flashbacks confusing and slipshod, and the sex scenes poorly done. He quotes selected scenes at some length to illustrate their "disagreeable sentimental sensuality" (a phrase Hyman borrows from Yeats). James Finn (*Commonweal,* October 26, 1962) finds some remarkable passages in the novel and believes Baldwin has a great future as a writer; however, he expresses great disappointment in this endeavor, which he considers contrived; he notes that the author's imagination "flags and falters," the characters are often unreal, and the conversation is wooden.

William Barrett (*AtM,* July 1962) and Edgar Friedenberg (*NR,* August 27, 1962) continue to weigh the flaws and merits of the novel, but here the balance seems to be shifting slightly in favor of the book's redeeming virtues, even though the latter critic claims his review is not complimentary. The most positive review is Granville Hicks's "Outcast in a Caldron" (*SatR,* July 7, 1962; reprinted as "Another Country" in Hicks's *Literary Horizons: A Quarter Century of American Fiction* [New York: New York University Press, 1970]). Although admitting occasional weaknesses in the book, he nonetheless acclaims *Another Country* as "one of the most powerful novels of our time." He further maintains that although the plot seems to move haphazardly, "the novel is shaped with rigorous care."

The numerous studies in the years following have largely been in response to some of the criticism raised during the novel's initial reception. Norman Podhoretz assails the critics for their attack on the novel in "In Defense of James Baldwin" (cited above), accusing them of being shocked by the militancy and cruelty of the novel's view of life—by its violence—and contending that the author was attempting to show "that the only significant realities are individuals and love." Podhoretz offers no defense of the stylistic problems in the novel, but simply argues that despite its faults it is forceful, intense, and truthful enough to sustain itself as a worthwhile work.

Eugenia Collier's "The Phrase Unbearably Repeated" (*Phylon,* Fall 1964) remains one of the most perceptive and illuminating comments. She considers the tenderness and the "hurting compassion" that dwell beneath the violence and brutality of the novel and the individual's lonely and futile quest for love. There is a full, enlightening study of Baldwin's use of music to reveal the dimensions and tragedy of Lucas, whom she interprets as a tragic victim rather than a villain. Her essay is especially helpful for its lucid explication of the theme, the function of music, and the character of Lucas.

C. B. Cox and A. R. Jones, in "After the Tranquilized Fifties: Notes on Sylvia Plath and James Baldwin" (*Critical Quarterly,* Summer 1964), agree with earlier critics regarding the sex scenes, noting that "Baldwin's obsession with sex at times seems adolescent"; but they defend his characterization and praise his understanding depiction of "the violent emotions by which his people are beset." Their main point in this study is to compare *Another County* with the works of Sylvia Plath in terms of the extremely serious and personal emotional experiences.

Trevor Blount's discovery of "A Slight Error in Continuity in James Baldwin's *Another Country*" (*N&Q,* March 1966), in which Vivaldo removes his shoes, then ten pages later Baldwin forgets and has Eric remove Vivaldo's shoes, hardly seems to justify the introductory sentence—"The reputation of the American novelist, James Baldwin, has soared recently, and when reviewers and publicists are so ready to use the word 'genius' in connection with his work the rest of us ought perhaps to examine with care what he writes"—though it does indeed suggest Blount's meticulousness.

In "The Lesson of the Master" (*YR,* October 1966), Charles Newman, after making some generalizations about the Baldwin canon, presents a detailed and interesting study of *Another Country,* which he compares with the novels of Henry James, particularly *The American* and *The Portrait of a Lady.* Addison Gayle, Jr., in *The Black Situation* (New York: Horizon, 1970), uses the novel to illustrate his thesis that although Baldwin "has a clear insight into contemporary man's alienation, . . . he has failed to defend the plight of the urban Black man in America." The problem, Gayle insists, is that Baldwin "wavers between the philosophy of assimilation and that of nationalism." In *"Another Country:* Baldwin's New York Novel" (cited above), Mike Thelwell accuses the critics of being unable to accept a black person's analysis of American culture. His study is noteworthy for its lengthy and detailed overview of the critical responses to *Another Country* and for its thorough analysis of the characters in the novel.

Elliott M. Schrero's *"Another Country* and the Sense of Self" (*BARev,* Spring-Summer 1971) is a most engaging comparison of *Another Country* and Faulkner's *Absalom, Absalom!* in terms of the authors' concern with the sense of the past in the individual's quest for identity. He notes that the characters in both novels suffer from extremes: Faulkner's southerners are mired in a sense of the past that results in a destructive excess of formality; Baldwin's characters suffer a loneliness and despair that stem from a lack of form caused by the absence of any sense of past and tradition. Schrero's otherwise forceful development seems somewhat mitigated at the end, for after denying the possibility of discussing the dilemma in Baldwin's book in terms of race (because both his blacks and his whites face the same problems of identity), Schrero concludes with a quotation from *Tell Me How Long the Train's Been Gone* that definitely deals with race: Leo, discussing the derogatory history of blacks which whites have created, suggests the need to "read one's history and . . . step out of the book."

Another very helpful study is Fred L. Standley's "Another Country, Another Time" (*SNNTS*, Fall 1972), which contains a noteworthy explanation of the structure of the novel, divided by Standley into four principal narrative strands. This essay also includes a detailed discussion of the meaning and implications of the title.

The Fire Next Time Before publication of *The Fire Next Time* in 1963, the original essay in the book, "Down at the Cross," had already created a furor when it appeared as "Letter from a Region in My Mind" (*NY*, November 17, 1962). Harry Golden's "A Comment on James Baldwin's Letter" (*The Crisis*, March 1963) accuses Baldwin of the same kind of self-pity he evidenced in *Another Country*. He takes issue with Baldwin's thesis that love and forgiveness are the means by which racial problems can be ended, and argues that politics and law are the answer. R. J. Dwyer responds vehemently to Baldwin's "Letter" and Dwight Macdonald's "Our Invisible Poor" in his "I Know About the Negroes and the Poor" (*National Review*, December 17, 1963), insisting that having lived among blacks he knows as much about them and their emotional relationship to society as does Baldwin, whose experience he labels "conspicuously atypical." He contends that Baldwin errs in arguing that something must be *given* to blacks and the poor, insisting that "most poor people in America today are poor because they want to be. They make themselves the way they are by being lazy, uneducated, sick, undependable." After attacking welfare recipients and giving his own facts about poor blacks, Dwyer insists that Baldwin "twists the facts to fit his pessimism."

The critics who responded to *The Fire Next Time* (which in addition to "Down at the Cross" includes "My Dungeon Shook") spend more time attacking and expressing indignation at certain of Baldwin's views of life than in considering the overall work. James Finn (*Commonweal*, July 26, 1963) is greatly perturbed by what he sees as Baldwin's rejection of "our" Judeo-Christian heritage, which he defends vigorously, noting that "Western civilization and Christianity . . . are precisely those sources from which all Americans must draw sustenance in the fight for equal rights." Finn's attack drew a counterattack from John McCudden, "James Baldwin's Vision" (*Commonweal*, October 11, 1963), followed by a further defense of his position by Finn ("Reply" [*Commonweal*, October 11, 1963]). Dorothy Foote, in "James Baldwin's 'Holler Books'" (*CEA Critic*, May 1963), is greatly disturbed by what she labels Baldwin's "curiously reversed stereotyped beliefs." Among these are what she describes as Baldwin's "smug pride" in Negro sexual superiority, his assertion that only the Negro has soul, his accusation that whites feel superior, his depiction of whites as "emotionally inferior and immature," and his pride in the Negroes' musical superiority. She proceeds to refute several of these as misconceptions. For example, she painstakingly substantiates the Negroes' "musical debt to the white man," which includes the use of the white man's discarded instruments.

The anonymous reviewer for *Christian Century* ("Baldwin: Gray Flannel Muslim?" [June 12, 1963]) criticizes Baldwin for incongruities in his arguments regarding America and racism, particularly his attacks on liberals, concluding, "Baldwin will pass his test when he can tell those of us who want to do something *not* that we should but *what* we should."

Stephen Spender, in "James Baldwin: Voice of a Revolution" (*PR*, Summer 1963), seems most disturbed that "Mr. Baldwin . . . makes . . . generalizations about the emasculation, joylessness, lack of sensuality, etc., of white Americans to prove their inferiority to the joyous, spiritual, good, warm Negroes." Garry Wills's "What Color Is God?" (*National Review*, May 21, 1963) gives more of an overview of the complete work, summarizing the main points and commenting on the sense of background music in all Baldwin's works. But Wills, too, is disturbed by Baldwin's attack on American whites and their institutions. After analyzing in some detail the aggressiveness of Ida in *Another Country*, this critic suggests that in *The Fire Next Time* Baldwin is "launched on the self-lacerating task that Ida set herself—deliberately provoking and yet daring anyone to attack." Conceding that Baldwin's charges are moving and beautifully stated, he contends that the main question is, are they true? He proceeds to attack Baldwin's implications that whites are depraved and inferior and his assertions that the suffering of blacks cannot be overstated and that Christianity has done nothing for black people. Wills then stresses the importance of Western civilization and of preserving its truths, particularly Christianity, which Baldwin seems intent on destroying.

After praising Baldwin's style in *Notes of a Native Son*, F. W. Dupee, in "James Baldwin and 'the Man' " (*NYRB*, February 1963; reprinted in Dupee's *"The King of the Cats," and Other Remarks on Writers and Writing* [New York: Farrar, Straus & Giroux, 1965]), criticizes *The Fire Next Time* as an exchange of "prophecy for criticism, exhortation for analysis," which weakens Baldwin's style and his theme. Dupee believes the book will inflame racists and confuse Negroes. In a review in *Critic* (April–May 1963), Andrew M. Greeley observes Baldwin's ignorance about theology, history, and sociology and calls attention to his prejudice and his hatred of whites; yet he suggests that these flaws all result from the author's experience in white America. He asserts that it is good that whites are being forced to listen to Baldwin, and concludes with the hope that saner voices, preaching gradualism and love, will arise from the black community.

If white reviewers roasted *The Fire Next Time*, black reviewers did not pour any water on the flames. J. Saunders Redding (*NYHTBW*, April 7, 1963) added more fuel, accusing Baldwin of offending truth and logic and sacrificing thought to catch-phrases, and concludes, "A brilliant display of stylistic virtuosity, 'The Fire Next Time' would have been better with less manner and more matter." Jean Carey Bond (*Freedomways*, Spring 1953) characterizes it as "almost without organization, occasionally incoherent and contradictory." Noting that the essay's biggest problem is superficiality, Bond observes that it is full of exciting but undeveloped ideas. She accuses Baldwin of being primarily concerned with winning the attention and praise of white American readers. Nick Aaron Ford was a bit more receptive in "The Fire Next Time? A Critical Survey of Belles Lettres By and About Negroes Published in 1963" (*Phylon*, Summer 1964), lauding the book as influential, significant, "artistically satisfying," and "profoundly philosophical." He contends, however, that it offers no new solution to the race problem, for the solution offered—love—is as old as the Ten Commandments. John Henrik Clarke's rambling essay "The Alienation of James Baldwin" (*Journal of Human Relations*, December 1963; reprinted in Clarke's *Harlem, U.S.A.* [New York: Macmillan, 1971]; and in *Black Expression: Essays By and About Black Americans in the Creative Arts*, edited by Addison Gayle, Jr. [New York: Weybright & Talley, 1969]), emphasizes *The Fire Next Time,* but it is mainly an attack on Baldwin as a spokesman, noting that the word *struggle* (which is "inseparable from the existence of the Negro people") rarely appears in Baldwin's works and that none of his characters attain stature in the struggle against their condition.

Nothing Personal *Nothing Personal* (1964), with photographs by Richard Avedon and commentary by James Baldwin, received almost unanimously scathing reviews upon its publication, and has been all but forgotten by Baldwin scholars, many of whom do not even bother to mention it or list it among his works. In his review (*NYRB*, December 17, 1964), Robert Brustein praises the direct and biting criticism of Baldwin's earlier works, but asserts, "*Nothing Personal* shows us an honorable tradition of revolt gone sour," and concludes, "Baldwin's participation in this 'charade' . . . signifies the further degeneration of a once courageous and beautiful dissent." The anonymous reviewer in *Time* (November 6, 1964) writes, "Baldwin's brief text is oddly irrelevant, obviously hasty, too often drawn by his sheer flow of language into shrill overstatement." While the anonymous reviewer of the London *Times Literary Supplement* (December 10, 1964) calls *Nothing Personal* a "terrifying and deeply moving book," he concludes that it is a dishonest work, portraying the United States as a vast wasteland with only a few radicals showing any integrity. *Newsweek* (October 26, 1964) makes very little comment on the book, but does reproduce photographs from it.

Blues for Mister Charlie Baldwin fared little better with the reviewers of his next work, his first published play, *Blues for Mister Charlie* (New York: Dial, 1964). Eric Moon (*LJ*, May 15, 1964) describes the characterization as "paper thin" and the dialogue as "almost pedestrian," and expresses the hope that the author will "quickly return to the essay and the novel." Robert Brustein, in "Everybody's Protest Play: *Blues for Mr. Charlie*" (*NR*, May 16, 1964; reprinted in Brustein's *Seasons of Discontent: Dramatic Opinions, 1959–1965* [New York: Simon & Schuster, 1965]), uses Baldwin's own criticism of protest fiction to attack *Blues,* which he attempts to show embodies everything Baldwin earlier deplored. Brustein also criticizes the use of racial stereotypes and what he calls "Baldwin's curious insistence on the superiority of Negro sexuality." Richard Kluger (*NYHTBW*, May 31, 1964) proclaims that the play is not art, the tone is too shrill, the dialogue is stilted, and the characterization is particularly poor. T. G. Foote ("Thérapeutique de la Haine" [*Preuves,* January 1965]), in an article on the therapy of hatred, accuses Baldwin of no longer being able to write objectively of the black problem, which he had previously described with such sensibility and forcefulness. In *"Blues for Mister Charlie,"* Granville Hicks (*SatR,* May 2, 1964; reprinted in Hicks's *Literary Horizons*) notes Baldwin's movement from *Go Tell It on the Mountain* toward the protest tradition. He argues that *Blues for Mister Charlie,* which he does not consider a major literary work, is propaganda to the extent that Baldwin attempts to produce a specific effect on his audience, but is not propaganda in the sense of a distortion of truth. Although he noted certain shortcomings, Harold Clurman ("*Blues for Mister Charlie,* 1964," in his *The Naked Image: Observations on the Modern Theatre* [New York: Macmillan, 1966]) found that these flaws were usually mitigated by other strengths, and enjoined readers to see the play, which he praised for the direction and acting.

Not very many scholars have treated the play individually. Lofton Mitchell includes a very brief mention of *Blues* in *Black Drama: The Story of the American Negro in the Theatre* (New York: Hawthorn, 1967), with a defense of Baldwin's characterization. C. W. E. Bigsby, who treats it in chapter seven of his *Confrontation and Commitment: A Study of Contemporary American Drama 1959–1966* (Columbia: University of Missouri Press, 1968), accuses Baldwin of writing the kind of protest fiction that he earlier rejected. He notes that the chief fault in the play is not Baldwin's inability to draw valid pictures of whites, whom he dehumanizes, but of blacks, whom he sentimentalizes. Bigsby, who mistakenly calls Emmett Till "another Civil Rights worker," compares *Blues for Mister Charlie* to Albert Camus's *The Plague* in terms of its depiction of the necessity for revolt; he suggests that the dilemma in the drama is whether to be victim or hangman.

Going to Meet the Man The reviews of Baldwin's collection of short stories, *Going to Meet the Man* (1965), ranged from glowing praise to harsh criticism. Augusta Strong (*Freedomways,* Winter 1966) declares that

"In all [the stories] the craftsmanship is superb." She calls "Going to Meet the Man" the best story in the collection and claims that Baldwin's best portrait of a woman is found in "Come Out of the Wilderness."

Although Joseph Featherstone (*NR*, November 27, 1965) praises "The Outing" and suggests that "Sonny's Blues" is "close to a success," he finds "Going to Meet the Man" comparable to *Blues for Mister Charlie* in its failure to enter the white mind adequately and in its attack on the sexual ability of whites. He concludes that "Baldwin is at his best as himself. His finest work is self-revelatory: the fictional selves who walk the troubled regions of his mind." Lamenting the fact—he calls it a tragedy—that Baldwin so frequently mixes racial and homosexual rebellions, Daniel Stern (*SatR*, November 6, 1965) is pleased to find that the collection is basically free of the sensationalism that marred earlier books. He praises the stories generally, particularly "Sonny's Blues" and "This Morning, This Evening, So Soon," but he considers "The Man Child" (which he characterizes as "unbelievable") and "Going to Meet the Man" (in which he accuses Baldwin of equating lust with hate) failures. He concludes that when Baldwin is free of racial and sexual pleading "he is a rare creature." Oscar Handlin (*AtM*, November 1965) found the collection disappointing, lacking in all of the superior qualities of *Go Tell It on the Mountain*.

There have been a few noteworthy studies of individual stories in this collection. John V. Hagopian's "James Baldwin: The Black and the Red-White-and-Blue" (*CLAJ*, September 1963) is the definitive study of "This Morning, This Evening, So Soon." In his detailed analysis of the structure of the story (which he describes as being "full of subtle and surprising complexities"), Hagopian suggests that the three sections of the narrative might well be subtitled "Family," "Friend," and "Strangers," because the story moves from the intimate center of the narrator's experiences outward into public life and society.

"Sonny's Blues" has been given more critical attention that any of the other stories. Despite a misleading introduction which suggests that his study is going to deal with the debate on whether Baldwin is an essayist or a novelist, John M. Reilly's " 'Sonny's Blues': James Baldwin: Image of Black Community" (*NALF*, July 1970) turns out to be a very perceptive study of the development of the theme of the discovery of identity in "Sonny's Blues." After a rather detailed explication of the aesthetics of the blues, Reilly carefully traces the steps by which Sonny leads his brother, by way of the blues, "to a discovery of self in community." Treating much the same subject, E. R. Ognibene, in "Black Literature Revisited: Sonny's Blues" (*EJ*, January 1971), discusses the story as being mainly about the narrator and his need to reconcile himself to his racial heritage. Further, he points out that Sonny and his music are tools that help the narrator to accept his past and thereby find himself.

Like Reilly and Ognibene, in "James Baldwin's Blues" (*NConL,* September 1972) M. Thomas Inge places his emphasis on the narrator and his distance from his brother and his race. Inge, who makes some observations on the use of music as a controlling metaphor in this story, emphasizing the narrator's isolation from his race, his history, and his heritage, stresses the universal theme of brotherly love in "Sonny's Blues." Elsewhere, Suzy B. Goldman, in "James Baldwin's 'Sonny's Blues': A Message in Music" (*NALF,* Fall 1974), emphasizes the theme of communication and the use of music as an instrument in achieving communication. She concludes that Sonny's blues "belong to all of us for they symbolize the darkness which surrounds all those who fail to listen to and remain unheard by their fellow men."

Tell Me How Long the Train's Been Gone Baldwin received very little critical acclaim from the reviewers of *Tell Me How Long the Train's Been Gone* (1968). Granville Hicks's critique in *Saturday Review* (June 1, 1968; reprinted in Hicks's *Literary Horizons*) charges that the novel lacks the strength of Baldwin's earlier works, that the protagonist is not believable, and that the work is "simply flat and commonplace." Although Wilfred Sheed (in "Novel-time for Mr. Baldwin" [*Book World,* June 2, 1968]; reprinted as "James Baldwin: Tell Me How Long the Train's Been Gone," in Sheed's *The Morning After: Selected Essays and Reviews* [New York: Farrar, Straus & Giroux, 1971]), praises Baldwin for his convincing evocation of Harlem life, especially the scenes involving Leo and his family, he considers most of the novel "careless" and "mechanical." In similar manner, Saul Maloff (*Newsweek,* June 3, 1968) acknowledges a few passages which remind the reader that Baldwin is a talented writer, but considers the novel as a whole unsatisfactory. Maloff satirizes the plot and criticizes the characterization and the prose style. Robert E. Long (*The Nation,* June 10, 1968) could obviously find nothing redeeming in this novel to blunt his criticism, so he praises Baldwin's essays before assailing the weak characterization, the awkwardly handled flashbacks, the lusterless prose, the inconsistent diction, and the blurred insights in *Tell Me How Long the Train's Been Gone.*

Although Mario Puzo (*NYTBR,* June 23, 1968) is able to soften his attack with praise for the portrayal of Leo's father and his brother Caleb and the descriptions of the family life in Harlem, he too goes back to praise the essays, before lampooning the plot covering Leo's move into the world of the theater and Greenwich Village and white associates. Puzo seems most dissatisfied with the character of Barbara, exclaiming, "We are asked to believe that the only man in the whole world she can love forever is a Negro homosexual actor." He summarizes the book as "a simpleminded, one-dimensional novel with mostly cardboard characters, a polemical rather than narrative tone, weak invention, and poor selection of incident."

One of the most intelligent and objective (with one exception) attacks on this novel is Irving Howe's "James Baldwin: At Ease in Apocalypse" (*Harper's Magazine,* September 1968). Howe discusses the difficulties of the Negro writer's efforts to escape the role of protest writer, and suggests that Baldwin's inability to find his own identity is reflected in the failure of *Tell Me How Long the Train's Been Gone* and in his character Leo Proudhammer. While Howe, too, has praise for the descriptions of Harlem, he attacks the sentimental descriptions of homosexual encounters, the falseness of the characterizations, Baldwin's language, and the logic of several statements made by the characters. While most of these criticisms are rather fully substantiated with supporting evidence from the work, giving credence and strength to his argument, Howe seems to lose his critical objectivity in dealing with Baldwin's growing militancy and his black militant character. For example, Howe attacks the logic of the militant's statement that the Christians were also outnumbered, citing a lengthy historical explanation to prove the character wrong. The historical accuracy of the statement, of course, is completely irrelevant; Baldwin has put into the character's mouth the rhetoric of the militant, and historical veracity has nothing to do with the realism of his speech.

The most glowing review (representing the opposite extreme in the reception of the book) is John Thompson's "Baldwin: The Prophet as Artist" (*Commentary,* June 1968), in which Thompson avers, "Like everything Baldwin writes, it is beautifully formed." He goes on to praise the clarity with which the plot is related, the beauty of Baldwin's language, the powerful protest, and the lack of melodrama. He concludes, "*Tell Me How Long the Train's Been Gone* is a masterpiece by one of the best living writers in America."

The Amen Corner   *The Amen Corner* (1968) is the most neglected of Baldwin's works. It was virtually ignored by the critics upon its publication and has received no individual attention from scholars. It is, however, frequently touched upon in the general studies of Baldwin's works.

A Rap on Race   *A Rap on Race* (1971), a record of discussions between Margaret Mead and Baldwin, created no stir in the literary world, provoking only a few comments in scattered periodicals. Phoebe Adams (*AtM,* June 1971) notes that Mead's knowledge of unfamiliar societies all over the world contrasts with Baldwin's "impassioned preoccupation" with Negroes in America; she characterizes the conversations as "blunt, peppery, and spontaneous." Kenneth Zahorski (*CLAJ,* June 1971) observes that although the book is at times "repetitive and disjointed," it abounds in "illuminating insights and penetrating observations," and goes on to characterize it as "a truly remarkable and significant social document . . . a fascinating human drama." R. J. Meaddough, in "Ideas Whose Time Has Passed" (*Freedomways,* Third

Quarter 1971) condescendingly credits Mead and Baldwin with honestly attempting to analyze the racial situation in the United States, but he suggests rather satirically that they are too far removed from the realities of the present to comprehend the situation fully: " . . . it's like watching Louis and Marciano fight to a draw in '71: two old, proud, battered champions past their prime and, at the end, what has been proven? They deserve respect and honor for what they were and what they are, but Muhammad Ali is waiting."

No Name in the Street The reception of the bitterest and most militant of Baldwin's essays, *No Name in the Street* (1972), was surprisingly tempered. Only a few critics rejected it outright, as did Peter Prescott (*Newsweek*, May 29, 1972), who wrote it off as an "embarrassing" effort by Baldwin to prove himself a part of the militant young black generation by accepting their prose and rhetoric. Colin McGlasham (*New Statesman*, April 21, 1972) laments that Baldwin "has . . . lost touch with himself and his language," but concludes that the book is worth reading, for it does include "skillful fragments of autobiography." Mel Watkins (*NYTBR*, May 28, 1972) criticizes the ideological discourse as being too abstract and facile, but concludes that Baldwin seeks to dramatize, not to explicate, and that he does this well. He further notes that the prose is "often mesmerizing."

R. Z. Sheppard (*Time*, May 29, 1972) summarizes the book much more than he appraises it. He does criticize Baldwin the artist for succumbing to Baldwin the propagandist and fantasist. Murray Kempton (*NYRB*, June 29, 1972) reviews *No Name in the Street* along with two other works discussing Afro-Americans and Jews. Asserting that there is some "nonsense" in Baldwin, he also notes his strengths, concluding that "The nonsense that is merely language passes soon enough in Baldwin's book, thank heaven; and only the common sense of feeling endures." Edward Weeks (*AtM*, June 1972) suggests that even though it may be intemperate and lack pity, the book should be read, for it "contains truths not to be denied." He does, however, criticize Baldwin's failure to perceive that there are "thoughful white Americans intent that reconciliation shall work." Jim Walker (*Black Creation*, Summer 1972) criticizes the loose, casual form, the lack of structure, and the repetition in the book, but praises the beauty of the prose and the ideas, which he says are encouraging and uplifting to a black man.

One Day When I Was Lost *One Day When I Was Lost* (1973), a scenario based on *The Autobiography of Malcolm X,* was generally received as another Baldwin "mistake." Bruce Cook (*Commonweal*, October 12, 1973) suggests that it "was probably unwise of Baldwin to publish it, for it adds nothing to Malcolm and can only detract from its author's reputation." He concludes that "it is not much worth reading at all, except for those who have a special interest in Baldwin's career and its curious downward spiral during the last years." Edward Mapp (*LJ*, February 1, 1973) also considers the work a failure, but he asserts that it "deserves recognition if for no other reason than its subject and author." The reviewer of the London *Times Literary Supplement* (November 17, 1972) found the first half of the work "sharp, funny and precise," but was surprised by the "flatness" of the second half.

A Dialogue *A Dialogue* (1973), an exchange between Baldwin and Nikki Giovanni taped in London in 1971, was generally well received in the few periodicals that noted its appearance. Cornelia Holbert (*Best Sellers,* September 1, 1973) suggests that Baldwin turns poet in this conversation, which she labels "a privilege to read." A. R. Shucard (*LJ,* June 1, 1973) terms this dialogue fascinating, and describes Baldwin as "delightfully articulate."

If Beale Street Could Talk The reception of *If Beale Street Could Talk* (1974) was a replay of the responses to every Baldwin novel since *Go Tell It on the Mountain.* The critics, who almost unanimously agree that Baldwin is a talented writer, anticipated that masterpiece they know he is capable of producing and were appalled that he had once again disappointed them. Although Baldwin was fifty years old at the time of the publication of this novel, they still tended to regard him as a remiss boy of promise who had yet to realize his potential.

Martha Duffy (*Time,* June 10, 1974) observes, "It is hard to speculate how a writer of Baldwin's quality succumbed to such timeless bathos." John W. Aldridge (*SatR/World,* June 15, 1974) laments, "It is extremely sad to see a writer of Baldwin's large gifts producing, in all seriousness, such junk." Walter Clemons (*Newsweek,* May 27, 1974) labels the novel "an almost total disaster," but bases his optimism that something better will be produced by Baldwin in the future on the few "scenes that give one hope." These reviewers generally criticize Baldwin's use of Tish as narrator and his sentimentality; they also consider the characters stereotypes who are too idealized—too noble, courageous, loving.

It is rather ironic that this latest novel received the same kind of general criticism that his earlier novels underwent, because here Baldwin seemed to be attempting a very different kind of work that would silence the attacks customarily made on his fiction. There is nowhere evident in *If Beale Street Could Talk* his usual "objectionable" subject matter of homosexual and interracial liaisons; Baldwin returns to Harlem, which is where critics have always agreed he should stay; and he portrays a strong, devoted family headed by a powerful and loving father figure.

If Baldwin wants to make one more effort to satisfy the critics (although he claims, "What other people write about me [is] irrelevant to me" [*Essence,* June 1976]), John Aldridge, in the review cited above, has been kind enough to describe in detail the "one great novel [that Baldwin] may have . . . left within him"—a novel of his own life. Alas, has not poor Baldwin already bared enough of his soul? And if he does write the novel Aldridge suggests, I cannot but fear that Aldridge's prophecy that Baldwin is "destined to drown in the throbbing seas of sentimentality" might indeed be fulfilled.

There were, however, a limited number of critics who found a few redeeming features in the novel. Arthur Curley (*LJ*, April 1, 1974), who considers it "old fashioned" with "stereotypical" characters, nonetheless describes it as a "powerful social document" with a story that is "emotional dynamite." Sterling Plumpp (*BlackBB*, Fall 1975) insists that it "is a good book [though] not a great one."

If Beale Street Could Talk received nothing but praise from Joyce Carol Oates (*NYTBR*, May 19, 1974), who characterized it as a poetical and realistic account of human emotions, "a moving, painful story . . . so vividly human and so obviously based upon reality, that it strikes us as timeless." She notes that even Tish's "flights of poetic fancy . . . are convincing."

The Devil Finds Work Baldwin's latest work, *The Devil Finds Work* (1976), is an essay that analyzes the historical role of blacks in American films, beginning with *Birth of a Nation* and continuing through *Lady Sings the Blues* and *The Exorcist*. Baldwin's general thesis is that there has been very little change in the characterization of blacks in American motion pictures, which always have and continue to misrepresent the black experience.

GENERAL STUDIES

Books The only book-length critical study of Baldwin's work is Stanley Macebuh's *James Baldwin: A Critical Study* (New York: Third Press–Joseph Okpaku, 1973). Macebuh's emphasis is on the novels, in which he traces the author's development from an introspective, personal writer to a radical social writer. He begins with a discussion of the profound effect of the dread of hell, the terror of sin, on Baldwin's vision of life. He notes that Baldwin's need to "exorcise his private dread of hell" inherited from his early church experiences prolonged the discovery of a public voice, but it provided him the basis for his best-constructed works—*Go Tell It on the Mountain* and *Giovanni's Room*. In his early works, Macebuh contends, Baldwin did not connect the psychological problems of his characters with the social origins of the problems. Macebuh traces Baldwin's development as he moves toward an increasing radicalization in *Another Country* and *No Name in the Street*. He notes that Baldwin's growing radicalism affected his competence as an artistic craftsman in *Another Country*, which marked his emergence from isolation. *Tell Me How Long the Train's Been Gone* is, according to Macebuh, the first Baldwin work with a "positively activist mood."

The most disturbing shortcoming of Macebuh's study is his insistence upon painting the broadest possible perspective from which to view his principal (Baldwin), which frequently results in a blurring—and at times even a loss—of his subject. For example, Macebuh views the whole range of criticism of black literature in America in his introduction, citing various writers in this very general discussion, so that any emphasis on Baldwin is lost to the reader. In chapter six, "The Agony of Blackness," Macebuh gives a lengthy discussion of the black aesthetic, tracing what he calls "the development of Black literature in America"; again, this discussion is unduly long and only tenuously related to Baldwin. Admittedly, Macebuh makes a defensible effort to see Baldwin in a historical perspective, but the ultimate effect is to see the larger picture and to forget Baldwin, who obviously should be the focal point of the discussion. Later, in a similar vein, he discusses what he calls "the rhetoric of sexuality in Black fiction in America," and although he does finally get around to Baldwin, the earlier emphasis on Norman Mailer and Eldridge Cleaver minimizes his subject. Considering Macebuh's tendency to paint the broadest picture, his elaborate conclusions at the end of each chapter as well as the concluding chapter, which tie together and emphasize the main points of the study, are extremely helpful to the reader, who might otherwise lose sight of the major area of emphasis in what occasionally appear to be slightly rambling discussions.

Macebuh's study is for the most part carefully researched and accurately presented, although a few minor errors are apparent. One slight misstatement, for example, is made more glaring when Macebuh makes a clear distinction between the "conception" and "birth" of John in *Go Tell It on the Mountain,* then in the following sentence mistakenly calls John's "birth" "the one labour of mutual love in the novel." At another point, Macebuh discusses the sin of bastardy and its impact on John in such a way that he confuses it with the act of masturbation and John's resulting guilt feelings from that; he later clarifies this issue, but the clarification unfortunately follows the confusion. The book includes a bibliography, which was discussed earlier.

A very helpful collection of essays on Baldwin has been assembled by Keneth Kinnamon in *James Baldwin: A Collection of Critical Essays* (Englewood Cliffs, N.J.: Prentice-Hall, 1974). In an excellent introduction, Kinnamon gives a brief overview of Baldwin's life, discusses important themes in his works, and traces the development of his loss of faith in the redemptive possibilities of love. Kinnamon includes some noteworthy essays and reviews in this collection, but the basis for the selection is not always apparent. For example, he includes reviews of *Notes of a Native Son, The Fire Next Time,* and *No Name in the Street;* but it is not clear why he would present reviews of these works and not of *Another Country* and *Go Tell It on the Mountain.*

Therman B. O'Daniel has a book of essays on Baldwin scheduled for publication by Howard University Press, tentatively titled *James Baldwin: A Critical Evaluation,* which will include a bibliography as well.

James Baldwin is a subject of major consideration in Sherley Anne Williams's *Give Birth to Brightness: A Thematic Study in Neo-Black Literature* (New York: Dial, 1972). Her emphasis is on the role of the musician in Baldwin's works. She sees the musician as "the embodiment of alienation and estrangement, which the figure of the artist becomes in much of twentieth century literature." She uses "Sonny's Blues" and *Blues for Mister Charlie* to illustrate her thesis that "Music is the medium through which the musician achieves enough understanding and strength to deal with the past and present hurt." Williams also includes a lengthy defense of *Another Country,* which illustrates what she sees as the tendency of critics to deal more with Baldwin's statements as a spokesman and with his homosexuality than with his literature. Attacking Eldridge Cleaver for comparing the masculinity of Rufus to that of Bigger Thomas, and Richard Wright to Baldwin, she notes that this endeavor leads Cleaver away from the major theme of *Another Country.* One chapter of Williams's book, "The Black Musician: The Black Hero as Light Bearer," appears in Kinnamon's *James Baldwin: A Collection of Critical Essays.*

Howard M. Harper, Jr., in *Desperate Faith: A Study of Bellow, Salinger, Mailer, Baldwin and Updike* (Chapel Hill: University of North Carolina Press, 1967), considers what he calls the two sides to Baldwin—the Negro spokesman and the artist—noting that as a public spokesman Baldwin urges rebellion, whereas as an artist he stresses acceptance. Harper gives a rather general but adequate coverage of the novels, considering the need of the characters in all of them for recognition and acceptance of their own inner nature and noting Baldwin's movement from artist to spokesman. He sees *Another Country* as the beginning of Baldwin's trend toward journalism and propaganda, which reaches its climax in *Blues for Mister Charlie,* which he describes as cheap sentimentality and melodrama and which he suggests indicates that Baldwin "the artist has succumbed to the spokesman." The one unique aspect of this study is an interesting discussion of the use of wind as symbolic of "fatal inevitability" in all the novels. (It should be noted, however, that Robert F. Sayre had previously considered the symbolic use of the wind in *Giovanni's Room* in "James Baldwin's Other Country" in *Contemporary American Novelists,* edited by Harry T. Moore [Carbondale: Southern Illinois University Press, 1964]).

Numerous books on black American literature and the American novel include essays on James Baldwin. Foremost among these are *The Black American Writer, Volume I: Fiction* and *Volume II: Poetry and Drama,* edited by C. W. E. Bigsby (Deland, Fla.: Everett/Edwards, 1969); Donald B. Gibson's *Five Black Writers* (New York: New York University Press, 1970); John Henrik Clarke's *Harlem, U.S.A.* (New York: Macmillan, 1971); and *Contemporary American Novelists,* edited by Harry T. Moore. Baldwin is treated in all the major surveys and thematic studies of black American literature, as well as in several general studies of American literature that have been published within the last ten years.

In the revised edition of *The Negro Novel in America* (New Haven, Conn.: Yale University Press, 1965), Robert Bone includes a chapter on the novels of James Baldwin that has appeared in various other sources (*Tri-Quarterly,* Winter 1965; *Images of the Negro in American Literature,* edited by Seymour L. Gross and John Edward Hardy [Chicago: University of Chicago Press, 1966]; and Robert Hemenway's *The Black Novelist* [Columbus, Ohio: Merrill, 1970]). Bone considers Baldwin's movement from a search for identity in his earlier works toward protest in the polemical works. He includes rather lengthy summaries and discussions of the three novels Baldwin had published at the time, praising *Go Tell It on the Mountain,* which he discusses as an autobiographical work, and considering in some detail the father–son conflict there; attacking *Giovanni's Room* as the weakest novel; and assailing *Another Country* as a "failure on the grand scale."

In *Black on White: A Critical Survey of Writing by American Negroes* (New York: Grossman, 1966), David Littlejohn includes a general survey of Baldwin's works through *Going to Meet the Man.* He emphasizes their autobiographical significance, noting that "Each of James Baldwin's three novels has been written out of some personal necessity." His overall assessment of the novels coincides with Bone's. It is perhaps worth noting that he praises highly four stories in *Going to Meet the Man,* including "The Man Child," which he calls "a highly charged, lyrical, pastoral tragedy," and "Going to Meet the Man," of which he writes, "I found his picture [of a southern bigot] to be credible, intense, and at times almost hypnotically convincing."

Edward Margolies presents an interesting chapter that offers some variety in its approach to Baldwin. In "The Negro Church: James Baldwin and the Christian Vision," in Margolies's *Native Sons: A Critical Study of Twentieth-Century Negro American Authors* (Philadelphia: Lippincott, 1968), he expounds the thesis that "the Messianic strain, the apocalyptic vision, the imagery and the fervor of the church . . . the spirit of evangelism" that permeate black life are reflected in the works of Baldwin. He discusses all of Baldwin's works through 1965 in terms of this thesis, which he expands to include the opposition of the purity of innocence to the evil of experience, and the salvation of the homosexual experience. Margolies sees *Another Country* as the point at which Baldwin divides the role of the Negro from that of the homosexual, with the homosexual persevering as a figure of compassion and the

Negro becoming more militant: "The Negro and the homosexual thus assume two attributes of the godhead—the Negro representing justice, the homosexual, mercy." Margolies's treatment of *Blues for Mister Charlie* is more positive than most. He argues that it is "a propaganda piece with 'real-life' characters," noting that Baldwin's white southern racists are more believable than his northern liberals. He suggests that the vehement reaction to Lyles by most critics may have been a result of Baldwin's implications that whites, whether racists or liberals, are varying versions of Lyles.

In *After Alienation: American Novels in Mid-Century* (New York: World, 1964), Marcus Klein discusses the works of James Baldwin in terms of the heroes' search for identity, manhood, maturity, and recognition (all of which he sees as synonymous). Tracing this quest through the essays and the fiction, Klein concludes that Baldwin "makes his longest reach toward an identifiable identity" with southern blacks and Africans.

Conor Cruise O'Brien includes a very general essay in his *Writers and Politics* (New York: Pantheon, 1965), treating the thesis that Baldwin is the first black American who has made his white countrymen "*see* him as a *man* and see how *he sees* them." Citing a few of Baldwin's essays and interviews (but with no reference to the fiction), the author concludes that Baldwin's truthful portrayal of the American situation has made the white man listen.

In *The Crisis of the Negro Intellectual* (New York: Morrow, 1967), Harold Cruse frequently attacks Baldwin, more often for Baldwin's role of spokesman than author. He comments at some length about Baldwin's failure to defend adequately and substantiate his attack on white liberals, suggesting in a footnote that Parnell James in *Blues for Mister Charlie* is "so sympathetically portrayed as to border on the maudlin, despite the author's professed view of white liberals," an accusation that arises from a faulty reading of the play, since Parnell represents the weakness, ineffectiveness, and unreliability of the liberal. In a lengthy, largely sociological, discussion concerning Baldwin and Jews, Cruse attacks "The Harlem Ghetto" as "a chic piece of magazine journalism" that does not deal with the real issues, and contends that Baldwin in reality loves and defends the Jews, or to use Cruse's term, he is an "apologist for the Jews."

Eldridge Cleaver's "Notes on a Native Son," in his *Soul on Ice* (New York: McGraw-Hill, 1968), praises Baldwin's talents but bitterly attacks what Cleaver considers a self-defacing quirk in Baldwin's vision that is tied up with his homosexuality—Baldwin's "total hatred of . . . blacks" and of himself and his unnatural love of whites. Cleaver enthusiastically defends Richard Wright against the attack Baldwin makes on Wright in "Everybody's Protest Novel" (reprinted in *Notes of a Native Son*), noting that the relationship of Rufus to Bigger is analogous to that of Baldwin to Wright—a weak lover of whites to a rebel and a man. All of this illustrates, Cleaver asserts, Baldwin's "playing out the racial death-wish of Yacub"—his attempt, in other words, to destroy both black masculinity and blacks.

David W. Noble's "The Present: Norman Mailer, James Baldwin, Saul Bellow," in *The Eternal Adam and the New World Garden: The Central Myth in the American Novel Since 1830* (New York: Braziller, 1968), considers Baldwin's efforts to find "new ways to restore the American Garden to beauty and the American Adam to vigor." Richard H. Rupp in *Celebration in Postwar American Fiction, 1945–1967* (Coral Gables, Fla.: University of Miami Press, 1970), presents a novel approach to Baldwin, considering his continual quest for a secular celebration to replace the celebration he left behind in the church. There is a lengthy discussion of *Go Tell It on the Mountain,* which represents, according to Rupp, the one instance of celebration in Baldwin's fiction, containing what Rupp calls "a community celebration." In his later fiction, the author continues, Baldwin has been unable to discover "a social context that will give form and meaning to celebration."

Theodore Gross treats Wright, Ellison, and Baldwin in a chapter of his *The Heroic Ideal in American Literature* (New York: Free Press, 1971). Gross's major concern in his discussion of Baldwin seems to be Baldwin's creation of new myths and stereotypes after the effective exposure of white myths about blacks in his earlier works. Gross accuses Baldwin of creating preternatural black heroes and distortions about the white man. He violently attacks Baldwin's portrayal in *Another County* of white middle-class values as abhorrent and of America as an empty, doomed country, characterizing Baldwin's prophecies of tragedy and doom for America "sentimental nihilism." He asserts that the novel fails because (among other reasons) it attempts to "deify blacks and castigate whites in morally simplistic terms" and because "Baldwin cannot describe white people with anything like complexity." Gross praises Baldwin's early essays as expressing the Negro point of view with intense honesty, and comments on the tension between love and power and the quest for love, which is the essence of all Baldwin's works.

Of less importance in a study of Baldwin, but still meriting attention, are Catherine Juanita Starke's *Black Portraiture in American Fiction: Stock Characters, Archetypes, and Individuals* (New York: Basic Books, 1971), which considers the major characters in Baldwin's fiction; Houston A. Baker, Jr.'s *Long Back Song: Essays in Black American Literature and Culture* (Charlottesville: University Press of Virginia, 1972), which does not treat Baldwin in depth, but makes several significant allusions to his themes and works; Alfred Kazin's *Bright Book of Life: American Novelists from Hemingway to Mailer* (Boston: Little, Brown, 1973), which briefly discusses Baldwin, suggesting that he "writes fiction in order to use up his private difficulties"; and Roger Whitlow's weak and often misleading discussion of Baldwin in *Black American Literature: A Critical History* (Chicago: Nelson Hall, 1973), which contains a sketchy summary of Baldwin's life and a listing of his works through *No Name in the Street* (which Whitlow erroneously lists under fiction in the bibliography).

Articles The debate about protest versus art which has hounded Baldwin since the publication of "Everybody's Protest Novel" is the subject of Maurice Charney's "James Baldwin's Quarrel with Richard Wright" (*AQ*, Spring 1963; reprinted in Gibson's *Five Black Writers*). Charney explains Baldwin's attack on Wright in some detail, but notes that for Baldwin the South is remote and mythical whereas for Wright it was the living reality of his life. Charney observes other contrasts between the two authors, among them the fact that Baldwin refuses to accept Wright's naturalistic philosophy and that Baldwin returned from France to search for his identity. He notes also that although Baldwin treats the bleakness of the human heart (the inability to love, the sense of emptiness and waste), "he ends, not in despair but in tragic paradox"—the possibility of love "makes war on the chaos of despair."

Irving Howe also considers protest versus art in "Black Boys and Native Sons" (*Dissent*, Autumn 1963). Citing Baldwin's early attacks on protest literature, Howe notes the contradictions in Baldwin's later review of Langston Hughes's poetry ("Sermons and Blues" [*NYTBR*, March 29, 1959]) in which he speaks of the Negro as finding the conflict between social and artistic responsibilities practically irreconcilable. Howe suggests that during the intervening years Baldwin had lived through the experiences that had created a Richard Wright. Noting that Baldwin has failed in his desire to portray the diversity and richness of the black world without writing protest, Howe suggests that the writer who has come closest to this achievement is Ralph Ellison in *Invisible Man*.

Again the subject of protest versus art is, if not revived, at least rehashed in Albert Murray's "James Baldwin, Protest Fiction, and the Blues Tradition" (in *The Omni-Americans: New Perspectives on Black Experience and American Culture* [New York: Outerbridge & Dienstfrey, 1970]; presented as a paper at the University of California [Berkeley] seminar on "The Negro Writer in the United States" [Summer 1964]; and reprinted in *Anger and Beyond*, edited by Herbert Hill [New York: Harper & Row, 1966], as "Something Different, Something More"). Murray elaborates Baldwin's attack on protest fiction in some detail and assails his assumptions as false or confused. He proceeds to prove that Baldwin is guilty of all the limitations of which he accused Harriet Beecher Stowe and Richard Wright. The major thesis of this article is that Baldwin did not capitalize on "the rich possibilities available . . . in the blues tradition." Murray goes on to state, "But he never really accounts for the tradition which supports Harlem's hardheaded faith in democracy, its muscular Christianity, its cultural flexibility, nor does he account for its universally celebrated commitment to elegance in motion, to colorful speech idioms, to high style." Although the assumption that an author must "account" for these traditions is in itself highly tenuous, a careful reading of Baldwin certainly suggests that not only has he made much use of these traditions and portrayed these aspects of black life (at least insofar as they *are* aspects of black life), but there are times when he has also very definitely "accounted" for them.

B. K. Mitra's "The Wright–Baldwin Controversy" (*IJAS,* July 1969) is another attempt to assess the dispute between Wright and Baldwin, but this consideration is weakened because all of Mitra's judgments of Wright's point of view come from Baldwin's accounts. She considers the differences in the circumstances and influences that produced the two writers a possible explanation of their different views.

Fred L. Standley, in "James Baldwin: The Artist as Incorrigible Disturber of the Peace" (*SHR,* Winter 1970), defends Baldwin against the accusations that his literature is protest fiction of the type he attacked. He argues that Baldwin sees himself as a literary man with concomitant communal responsibilities and that his art, although it involves protest, is not the type of protest literature he attacked in Wright and Stowe. Standley discusses the fiction as works which "deal with the impact on the individual of the conditions of urban life and society," whose protagonist is a "rebel-victim" in quest of his identity.

Morris Dickstein, in "Wright, Baldwin, Cleaver," in *Richard Wright: Impressions and Perspectives,* edited by David Ray and Robert M. Farnsworth (Ann Arbor: University of Michigan Press, 1973), returns to Baldwin's attack on Wright and discusses the irony of the fact that while Baldwin has attempted to keep abreast of the new mood among younger writers, they tend to reject and attack him in a manner reminiscent of his own attack on Wright, and they tend to feel akin to the militant spirit of Wright. Kichung Kim, in "Wright, the Protest Novel, and Baldwin's Faith" (*CLAJ,* March 1974), also observes the more recent tendency to defend Wright in this controversy and to see Bigger as a realistic character. Kim argues that Baldwin's attack in "Everybody's Protest Novel" was motivated by a faith in the humanity of each man, a faith that Baldwin has since lost.

Although most critics suggest that Baldwin's essays are superior to his fiction, only two notable studies deal exclusively with the essays. David Levin, in "Baldwin's Autobiographical Essays: The Problem of Negro Identity" (*MR,* Winter 1964), considers the essays a quest for identity in which the narrator poses the question to the presumably white American audience: "Who am I?" or "How can I be myself?"

Levin notes that Baldwin considers his mission as a writer synonymous with his obligations as a preacher—to give the reader a sense of an experience (being Negro) that, "like Grace, can only be known at first hand"; the writer, who is the center of identity, is the most important means of opening communication between two worlds. In the other study, "Thematic Patterns in Baldwin's Essays" (*BlackW,* June 1972), Eugenia Collier attempts to determine a basic assumption or theme running throughout and unifying the essays. She suggests that Baldwin attempts in his essays to explain the personal and political chaos that is our lives and to offer solutions to it. The answer he purports is that we must accept with love ourselves and each other.

Several noteworthy essays deal exclusively with Baldwin's novels. Robert F. Sayre's study "James Baldwin's Other Country," in *Contemporary American Novelists,* edited by Harry T. Moore (Carbondale: Southern Illinois University Press, 1964), contemplates the importance of self-knowledge in Baldwin's novels and the fact that this self-knowledge is always a compound of the present and the past. Sayre considers *Another Country* Baldwin's most valuable book in its projection of Baldwin's vision. Therman B. O'Daniel considers the novels in "James Baldwin: An Interpretative Study" (*CLAJ,* September 1963) in terms of their treatment of two unpopular subjects, homosexuality and the problems of blacks. The emphasis in this article is on *Another Country,* which O'Daniel argues is carefully structured, corresponding to Greek tragedy and to the Elizabethan tragedy of revenge, with which he compares it in some detail. John S. Lash, in "Baldwin Beside Himself: A Study in Modern Phallicism" (*CLAJ,* December 1964), notes that Baldwin has a conscious need for a value system to replace Christianity, which he denounced, and that he thinks he has found it in "a modern cult of phallicism, the fear and admiration and worship of the male sex organ." Lash proceeds to discuss *Giovanni's Room* and *Another Country* in terms of this thesis, noting that in these works heterosexual activity is animalistic and the male characters seek spiritual gratification in homosexual acts.

George E. Kent's "Baldwin and the Problem of Being" (*CLAJ,* March 1964; reprinted in Gibson's *Five Black Writers* and in Kent's *Blackness and the Adventure of Western Culture* [Chicago: Third World Press, 1972]) is a superb study of the search for identity in the novels. In addition to outlining the quest for identity, Kent makes illuminating observations on characterization and technical matters of style, plot development, and the like.

In "The 'Stink' of Reality: Mothers and Whores in James Baldwin's Fiction" (*Literature and Psychology,* 22, 1 [1968]; reprinted in Keneth Kinnamon's *James Baldwin: A Collection of Critical Essays* [Englewood Cliffs, N.J.: Prentice-Hall, 1974]), Charlotte Alexander offers a fresh psychological interpretation of love and sex (specifically homosexuality) in Baldwin's works. She points out that both the fascination and the revulsion that most of Baldwin's characters experience for women are based on their childhood experiences with their mothers or surrogate mothers. This results in their maintaining their "virginity" or prostituting themselves, since they fear the "stink" of the reality of love. Alexander's thesis is persuasively developed with extensive supporting evidence. Brian Lee, in "James Baldwin: Caliban to Prospero," in *The Black American Writer, Volume I: Fiction*, edited by C. W. E. Bigsby (Deland, Fla.: Everett/Edwards, 1969), suggests that Baldwin's own feelings about the ironies of a life lived on two levels—that of a black and that of a man—are expressed in the paradoxes confronting his haunted protagonists. Considering the novels, Lee notes that Baldwin treats best the inner experiences of his characters, though occasionally he powerfully evokes the wider society. In his discussion of *Go Tell It on the Mountain*, Lee compares that novel with D. H. Lawrence's *Sons and Lovers*.

David E. Foster's essay " 'Cause My House Fell Down': The Theme of the Fall in Baldwin's Novels" (*Crit*, Winter 1970–1971) attempts to explain how Baldwin uses the theme of man's fall from innocence in his first three novels and why he abandons this theme in *Tell Me How Long the Train's Been Gone*. He suggests that *Go Tell It on the Mountain* is a forceful illustration of John's finding redemption, but that *Giovanni's Room* and *Another Country* fail because Baldwin, having become disillusioned with the Christian theme of redemption, tried to invest the theme of the fall with secular meaning; thus, Baldwin had to abandon this theme altogether. In "Black Women, Black Men" (*Harvard Journal of Afro-American Affairs*, 2, No. 2 [1971]), Felicia George treats the "dynamics of the Black female's relationship with the Black male" in the works of four black writers, including Baldwin. George E. Bell's "The Dilemma of Love in *Go Tell It on the Mountain* and *Giovanni's Room*" (*CLAJ*, March 1974) is an attack on Stanley Macebuh's assertion in *James Baldwin: A Critical Study* (New York: Third Press–Joseph Okpaku, 1973) that both novels fail to provide any answers to the dilemma of love. Bell argues that "Love *is* an attainable goal," *if* man overcomes his "puritanical sense of evil and guilt." He goes on to cite the possibilities in both works: Gabriel and Esther, Richard and Elizabeth, and Elisha and John in *Go Tell It on the Mountain*; and Giovanni in *Giovanni's Room*. Donald B. Gibson, in "Ralph Ellison and James Baldwin," an essay in *The Politics of Twentieth-Century Novelists*, edited by George A. Panichas (New York: Hawthorn, 1971), develops the thesis that Ellison and Baldwin are intentionally nonpolitical writers. Although many may disagree with his description of Baldwin as consciously nonpolitical, Gibson develops his argument forcefully and interestingly, discussing mainly *Go Tell It on the Mountain* and *Another Country*.

Although Walter Meserve's study "James Baldwin's 'Agony Way' " (in *The Black American Writer, Volume II: Poetry and Drama,* edited by Bigsby) mentions certain attitudes and ideas (betrayal of the son by the father, the quest for identity, the need for love) that appear in all Baldwin's works, his major emphasis is on the plays. He presents an interesting and lengthy discussion of Baldwin's efforts in the theater. Meserve considers *The Amen Corner* the most successful of Baldwin's plays, but he cites several flaws in both it and *Blues for Mister Charlie.* A good overview of the plays can be found in Darwin T. Turner's article on Baldwin in *Contemporary Dramatists,* edited by James Vinson (New York: St. Martin's, 1971; second edition 1977).

Several essays treat Baldwin's works generally, touching upon his productions in various genres. Kay Boyle's introduction of Baldwin, given when he spoke at Wesleyan College in 1962 ("Introducing James Baldwin," in *Contemporary American Novelists,* edited by Harry T. Moore), includes a brief but eloquent comment on his major concerns and achievements. Augusta Strong, in "Notes on James Baldwin" (*Freedomways,* Spring 1962), assesses the writer's talent, touches upon his themes, and quotes from several of his works in an essay that is so general as to have little usefulness to the Baldwin scholar.

A more satisfactory general treatment of Baldwin's works is Colin MacInnes's "Dark Angel: The Writings of James Baldwin" (*Encounter,* August 1963; reprinted in Donald B. Gibson's *Five Black Writers* [New York: New York University Press, 1970]). Suggesting that James Baldwin is "a premonitory prophet, a fallible sage, a soothsayer," MacInnes notes that Baldwin addresses himself to white America, appealing to it to solve the racial problem. Rather extensive and intensive discussions of Baldwin's works follow. The one flaw in this fine general study is the author's tendency to pause for lengthy explanations that do little to advance the discussion, such as her explanation of her choice of a topic, the lengthy detailing of various views of homosexuality that precedes her discussion of *Giovanni's Room,* and the defense of zealous militancy.

Harvey Breit's "James Baldwin and Two Footnotes," in *The Creative Present: Notes on Contemporary American Fiction,* edited by Nona Balakian and Charles Simmons (Garden City, N.Y.: Doubleday, 1963), suggests that Baldwin's role as race leader and spokesman for his people has a detrimental effect on his creativity. In his conclusion, Breit expresses concern about Baldwin's future as a creative writer. Theodore Gross voices a similar concern in "The World of James Baldwin" (*Crit,* Winter 1964–1965), lamenting that Baldwin has relinquished his role as observer for that of preacher, and that with his growing popularity he is removing himself from the source of his material as well as the honesty which is so necessary for a good writer: Baldwin is allowing the commercial media to dissipate his energies and is sacrificing his artistic distance and control to play a social role. Beau Fly Jones's "James Baldwin: The Struggle for Identity" (*British Journal of Sociology*, June 1966) abstracts and synthesizes Baldwin's views and extrapolates their relevance to sociology. The essay is painfully sociological in its approach, with such subtitles as "The Problem," "Negro Opportunity-Structures," and "Evaluation."

In "Blood of the Lamb" (in *Amistad 1*, edited by John A. Williams and Charles F. Harris [New York: Vintage, 1970]; first published in *White Papers for White Americans*, edited by Herndon [Garden City, N.Y.: Doubleday, 1966]), Calvin C. Herndon considers Baldwin's "syndromes." The first "syndrome" he discusses is Baldwin's involvement with the father figure. The second—Baldwin's homosexuality—Herndon sees as being resolved in *Giovanni's Room*. The third problem—coming to terms with his blackness—Baldwin attempted to resolve through his return to America. Herndon calls the result a "romance," noting that white Americans love Baldwin as they have loved no other black writer, "because of his lack of 'masculine aggressiveness.' In the psyches of most white people," Herndon asserts, "Baldwin does not symbolize the historic fear of the great, black phallus which lurks to rape and pillage." Although Baldwin is a good writer and an honest man, he still must revolve this third "syndrome," Herndon avers, for he is still crying for love. Herndon concludes this essay, which was written in 1964, with a prediction that is uncanny for its accuracy:

> Baldwin will change. He will be forced to. He will massage the white man's conscience less, and become more militant. His exotic style, his perfumed words, will undergo a metamorphosis, or should I say a turbulent baptism! When this happens, James Baldwin will not be less eloquent but more crude and brute.

In a later essay, "A Fiery Baptism" (also in *Amistad 1*), Herndon suggests that *Blues for Mister Charlie* indicates the accuracy of this prediction. (*No Name In the Street* is, of course, the ultimate realization of the prediction.) Herndon characterizes *Blues for Mister Charlie* as "brute, crude, violent, and bold" and describes Baldwin as "masculine" and "aggressive." For Herndon the play indicates Baldwin's becoming a spokesman for his people, and he notes that it killed the romance between Baldwin and white America, which could not accept a presentation of its sexual feelings about blacks.

Naim Kattan's "Deux Écrivains Américains" (*Écrits du Canada Français*, 17 [1964]) discusses Baldwin's life and treats the general themes in his works. Robert F. Sayre's "James Baldwin's Another Country," cited previously, discusses the early essays, noting that Baldwin's novels are his "other country," through which he has developed his talents, while his nonfiction has broadcast his prophecy and his reports. Raymond

Schroth's "James Baldwin's Search" (*CathW*, December and February 1964) attempts to summarize Baldwin's life and to state the central thesis in his works. Schroth achieves very little in this essay—perhaps because he attempts to achieve so much. Although he praises Baldwin's "intellectual powers" and his ability to make his experiences live for others, there is a slightly derogatory undertone in much of the essay, such as the wry comment, "The fact that he is illogical does not bother him" and the crude summary of *Blues for Mister Charlie* as "a play about a Negro dope addict who comes home to the South from New York to die."

J. Saunders Redding, in "The Problems of the Negro Writer" (*MR*, Autumn–Winter 1964–1965), accuses Baldwin of probing the minds of his white characters while examining the Negro characters only perfunctorily in *Another Country*. He suggests that Baldwin the essayist perceptively articulates the thoughts and feelings of Negroes, but Baldwin the novelist does not lead his audience to understanding. John Rees Moore's criticism of Baldwin in "An Embarrassment of Riches: Baldwin's *Going to Meet the Man*" (*HC*, December 1965) for trying to cram everything into one novel might well be applied to Moore in his efforts to analyze and comment on the stories individually and then to summarize and assess the novels in this one essay. He attempts to tie all this discussion together with the theme of authenticity in Baldwin, noting that Baldwin's authenticity, which is his most valuable quality as a writer, may be found in the autobiographical stories. Edward A. Watson's "The Novels of James Baldwin: Case-Book of a 'Lover's War' with the United States" (*QQ*, Summer 1965; also in *MR*, Summer 1965; and *Marche Romane*, 6 [1965]) studies the works in an effort to illustrate Baldwin's artistry and to prove that Baldwin must be accepted as an artist and not as a civil rights spokesman. Lawrence Langer, in "To Make Freedom Real: James Baldwin and the Conscience of America" (*Americana–Austriaca*, 1966), presents a general overview of Baldwin's writing, noting that his prominence has lain in his ability to speak with both a public and a private voice, and praising his ability to transcend bitterness and reliably report the American scene, until *Blues for Mister Charlie*.

Two other essays published in 1966 give general reviews of Baldwin's works: Mario Matterassi's "James Baldwin, un profèta del nòstro tèmpo (con un brève inedito)" [James Baldwin, a Prophet of Our Times] (*Il Ponte*, March 31, 1966) and Fred L. Standley's "James Baldwin: The Crucial Situation (*SAQ*, Summer 1966).

Fred Peterson's "James Baldwin and Eduardo Mallea: Two Essayists' Search for Identity" (*Discourse*, Winter 1967) discusses Baldwin's works as spiritual autobiography, the theme of which is the search for himself—both his personal self and his social being within American society—and compares Baldwin as a writer of spiritual autobiography in search of his identity with the Argentinian author Eduardo Mallea. Nathan A. Scott, in his general discussion of black literature, "Judgment Marked by a Cellar: The American Negro Writer and the Dialectic of Despair" (in *The Shapeless God: Essays on Modern Fiction,* edited by Harry J. Mooney, Jr., and Thomas F. Staley [Pittsburgh: University of Pittsburgh Press, 1968]), devotes considerable attention to a discussion of Baldwin in terms of the theme of the whole essay, the myth of the wounded Adam. Gregory Mowe and W. Scott Nobles, in "James Baldwin's Message for White America" (*QJS,* April 1972), list Baldwin's rhetorical themes and the various roles he assumes (artist, outraged black, preacher) in his efforts to identify those themes favorably with his white audience. In " 'You Can't Go Home Again': James Baldwin and the South" (*CLAJ,* September 1974), Daryl Dance studies Baldwin's attitude toward the South, considering the role of "the old country" in his quest for a home and an identity.

A final item that may be of assistance is the collection of passages from reviews and studies of Baldwin's books in *A Library of Literary Criticism,* Vol. I, edited by Dorothy N. Curley, Maurice Kramer, and Elaine Kramer (New York: Ungar, 1969).

PERSONAL CRITICISM OF BALDWIN

Harold R. Isaacs's interesting study of the attitudes of leading black American writers toward Africa, in "Five Writers and Their African Ancestors" (*Phylon,* Winter 1960), includes a comprehensive coverage of Baldwin's views of Africa prior to 1960. It is, of course, seriously dated, inasmuch as Baldwin has had a great deal more to say on the subject since then. Robert Cole's "Baldwin's Burden" (*PR,* Summer 1964) is a trite and insignificant comment on Baldwin in which Cole attacks Baldwin for hating whites, predicting the doom of the white man and America, and describing the black children who integrated New Orleans schools as aristocrats. Cole appears to delight in citing quotations from Baldwin out of context to substantiate his attack, and offers in rebuttal highly selective evidence such as a quotation from a black woman who said that white children suffered more attacks than black children during the integration of schools in 1960 and 1961.

Another attack on Baldwin that likewise makes use of isolated quotations (thereby misrepresenting their broader implications) is Sylvester Leaks's "James Baldwin: I Know His Name" (*Freedomways,* Winter 1963), in which Leaks asserts that Baldwin, like Wright, neither loves, admires, nor understands blacks. Leaks is in turn attacked in Calvin C. Herndon's previously cited essay in *Amistad 1* and in Julian Mayfield's "And Then Came Baldwin" (*Freedomways,* Spring 1963; reprinted in

John Henrik Clarke's *Harlem, U.S.A.* [New York: Macmillan, 1971]). Mayfield suggests that such attacks as Leaks mounts are motivated by Baldwin's critical and commercial success and by his homosexuality. He praises Baldwin's talent and comments that unlike most blacks, Baldwin is still trying to continue dialogue with the white world. Robert A. Lee's "James Baldwin and Matthew Arnold: Thoughts on 'Relevance'" (*CLAJ*, May 1971) considers Baldwin's dilemma as contemporary black artist, with the many varied demands made of him by radical blacks and others who call for a new black aesthetic (one which is anti-Western) and who demand that he be among other things, appropriate, unique, and original.

FUTURE NEEDS IN BALDWIN CRITICISM

Although many illuminating and penetrating studies (as well as some vague and confused ones) have been written on Baldwin the man and Baldwin the artist, the definitive study of James Baldwin has not yet appeared. A full assessment of his later works—*No Name in the Street, One Day When I Was Lost, If Beale Street Could Talk*—will obviously demand a reconsideration and a reevaluation of his talents, his philosophy, and even his literary style and techniques. The one thing now certain is that Baldwin, both the man and the artist, is still in the process of development.

This essay was completed with the aid of a grant from the National Endowment for the Humanities. I should like to acknowledge the assistance of Samuel Washington, who provided photocopies of numerous essays and assembled materials for my use at the Library of Congress; William S. Simpson, Jr., of the Richmond Public Library, and the staff of Virginia Union University, who assisted me in locating various materials.

AMIRI BARAKA
(LEROI JONES)

LETITIA DACE

Amiri Baraka (LeRoi Jones) has been cited by many critics as the creator of and foremost writer in the new black arts movement, and he is acknowledged by many other black artists as their inspiration or model. Despite his importance and the comparatively large body of materials published about Baraka, very few critical and scholarly works of stature have yet appeared. The relative absence of thorough and accurate scholarship has exacerbated the difficulties of producing appreciative yet objective criticism of works often published in ephemeral outlets and written by an author whose fame frequently interferes with lucid appraisal.

Born LeRoi Jones in Newark, New Jersey, on October 7, 1934, Baraka changed his name (roughly in the summer of 1968) to Ameer (prince) Baraka (blessedness). Within months he had added the title "Imamu" (spiritual leader). By early 1970 he had adopted the Swahili form "Amiri" in place of the Arabic "Ameer." After his conversion to Marxism in the next decade, he decided to forgo the title Imamu, with its "bourgeois nationalist" implications. Although for a time he was sometimes called "Chairman" or "Comrade," by 1977 he preferred to be addressed as "Amiri." In order to suggest which part of Baraka's career is under discussion, the name Jones is employed to refer to the early period and Baraka is used for the later years.

Bibliography

Because so many of Baraka's works, especially his poems, first appeared in fugitive books, broadsides, and ephemeral periodicals not even included in the *Index to Little Magazines,* it is difficult for critics to compile their own working bibliographies. Readers who aim at thoroughness in their acquaintance with the Baraka canon and its criticism must therefore employ one of the published checklists, but these are not of equal usefulness.

The least helpful bibliography on Baraka is that prepared by Deborah Smith Fouch for a class in the School of Library Science at Atlanta

University and published by that university's Center for African and African-American Studies as its *CAAS Bibliography No. 2: Everett LeRoi Jones (Imamu Ameer Baraka)* in 1970. In seven pages Fouch lists seven "general" books by Baraka, two anthologies, eight appearances of poetry (including four books and two of the periodicals in which he has published), six sources of his plays, four of his articles, fifty entries for secondary sources and interviews, and four citations of bibliographies containing references to his work. That her attempt "to include all works by and about LeRoi Jones as far as they could be identified" has fallen far short of its goal is not, however, the major shortcoming of this listing; its utility is diminished by numerous errors, including mistakes in a book title, periodical titles, a poem title, and dates of publication. In one instance a periodical title is omitted altogether, and in two others plays published in the *Drama Review* are listed as appearing in *Black Theatre*.

Three other bibliographies devoted exclusively to Baraka appeared in 1971. The shortest of these, Stanley Shatt's "LeRoi Jones: A Checklist to Primary and Secondary Sources" (*BB*, April–June 1971), contains a brief (not entirely accurate, but nevertheless useful) alphabetical checklist of work by Baraka—much more helpful than Fouch's endeavor on periodical items—and an annotated list of twenty-eight secondary sources. Theodore R. Hudson's eighteen-page *A LeRoi Jones (Amiri Baraka) Bibliography* (Washington, D.C.: n.p., 1971), although not covering as many years as the bibliography in his *From LeRoi Jones to Amiri Baraka: The Literary Works* (Durham, N.C.: Duke University Press, 1973), is useful because of the keys it provides to the generic classification of the items by Baraka and the major works or areas considered in each of the secondary sources.

The fullest listing of works by and about Baraka appears in Letitia Dace's *LeRoi Jones (Imamu Amiri Baraka): A Checklist of Works by and About Him* (London: Nether Press, 1971). This 196-page book includes a bibliographical description of domestic and foreign books entirely by Baraka (20 titles) and of volumes containing the first book printings of contributions by him (35 titles). These sections, arranged in chronological order, include a title page transcription, descriptions of binding, page height, collation, exact dates of publication and of later impressions, number of copies printed, price, contents or contribution by Baraka, and list of reviews (301). Also included are 287 citations (some multiple) of Baraka's periodical contributions, each with generic key; a list of 63 anthologies that reprint works by Baraka; and a miscellanea referring the reader to 14 Baraka collections, 8 ephemeral publications (broadsides, for example), 16 published interviews, 37 books edited by Baraka, 11 periodicals on which he has held a staff position, 4 albums for which he has written liner notes, 8 recordings of his work, 5 petitions and letters he has signed, 3 films written by him, 9 quotations from his work that appear in book illustrations, and so forth. The secondary bibliography—arranged chronologically within the classifications "General" (267 items), "Political and Racial Views" (417), "As Dramatist" (316), "As Poet" (90), "As Music Critic" (94), and "References in Literary Works" (28)—is coded to inform the user of the size of each item. An author–title index concludes this bibliography.

A more recent Baraka checklist is an updating of his 1971 guide by Theodore R. Hudson in *Black Books Bulletin* (Fall 1974). "An Imamu Amiri Baraka (LeRoi Jones) Bibliography: A Keyed Guide to Selected Works By and About Him" differs little from its earlier version, not even correcting the 1966 date on *Cuba Libre* (actually published in January 1961 by the Fair Play for Cuba Committee). The list of books by Baraka, however, conveniently includes such recent titles as *Afrikan Revolution,* and the secondary list repays examination with some additional critical studies published between 1971 and 1973. The journal's printers have done Hudson a disservice by repeating several items and are doubtless responsible for errors (such as "1971" for "1972" on *Spirit Reach*) not found in the Hudson listings published in 1971 and 1973.

Several larger reference works consider Baraka along with many other writers. Notable among these are Helen H. Palmer and Jane Anne Dyson's *American Drama Criticism* (Hamden, Conn.: Shoe String Press, 1967) and its *Supplement I* (1970), each providing short checklists of criticism on *Dutchman, The Slave,* and *The Toilet;* Marietta Chicorel and Veronica Hall's *Chicorel Theater Index to Plays in Anthologies, Periodicals, Discs and Tapes* (New York: Chicorel Library Publishing, 1970), which lists printed versions of Baraka's plays; and James V. Hatch's *Black Image on the American Stage: A Bibliography of Plays and Musicals 1770–1970* (New York: Drama Book Specialists, 1970), which provides an extensive list of plays written by Baraka and some notations on locations of the published plays.

Although brief references to Baraka are included in a variety of checklists of black writers (for example, Darwin T. Turner's *Afro-American Writers* [New York: Appleton, 1970]), Baraka surprisingly has been omitted in such disparate literary checklists as Dean H. Keller's *Index to Plays in Periodicals* (Metuchen, N.J.: Scarecrow, 1971) and its *Supplement* (1973); Irving Adelman and Rita Dworkin's *Modern Drama: A Checklist of Critical Literature on 20th Century Plays* (Metuchen, N.J.: Scarecrow, 1967); *The Contemporary Novel,* by the same authors and publishers (1972); Donna Gerstenberger and George Hendrick's *The American Novel* (Chicago: Swallow Press, 1970); and Arthur Coleman and Gary R. Tyler's *Drama Criticism: A Checklist of Interpretation Since 1940 of English and American Plays* (Denver, Colo.: Allan Swallow, 1966). What operation of discrimination or inadvertence prevented Baraka's inclusion in these and other reference works is difficult to say, but his stature surely requires rectification of this oversight in future editions of these works.

Editions

Most of the twenty-five volumes entirely by Baraka that had been published by 1975 are still in print, at least in paperback editions, and the others are available in the library collections listed in the Dace bibliography. Diligent scholars should have no trouble locating copies of these books, but they should be warned to keep up with new Jihad publications (such as *Afrikan Revolution,* published in June 1973) inasmuch as these are not listed in *Books in Print.*

Most elusive to the collector are those volumes published by sources ideological rather than literary in purpose, such as the Fair Play for Cuba Committee's 1961 edition of *Cuba Libre* and the Congress of Afrikan People's 1972 *Political Liberation Council Organizing Manual,* and those printed in small impressions, such as the first (1967) edition of *Slave Ship* (500 copies) and *Arm Yrself or Harm Yrself* (500 copies).

Many of Baraka's first publications have appeared in anthologies, in periodicals (including numerous little magazines), and on such ephemera as broadsides and record jackets. Some of his poetry has not been published, but is available on such recordings as the Library of Congress's April 17, 1959, Library Work Order tape no. 2831. Other little-known but interesting tapes made by Baraka include the *Birthday Garland for Ezra Pound,* edited by Paul Blackburn, and the tapes in the collection of the New York Public Library's Schomburg Collection. Baraka critics should also be familiar with such scarce items as his 1961 Paterson Society Statement; his 1962 poem on the dance that appeared in a New York City Center Ballet souvenir program; the nearly unobtainable issues of the *Stirling St. Newspaper,* published in his home by the children on his block in the fall of 1966; and his published and recorded interviews. Even the periodicals in which Baraka has published are often exceedingly difficult to locate, but are indispensable inasmuch as the Dace bibliography index lists 197 of Baraka's works published in English in magazines and newspapers but not reprinted in book form by 1970.

Fifty-seven poems, for example, fall into this category; they were not published in the 1972 collection *Spirit Reach* (Newark, N.J.: Jihad Productions) and have thus far received little or no criticism:

"The A, B, C's"	"Bo Peep"
"April 13"	"Boswell"
"Archie and Them Other Cats"	"Brides of the Captured"
"Axel's Castle"	"Central Park in Winter"

"Chapter"
"Confucius Say"
"The Disguise"
"Dr. Jive"
"DoubleFeel"
"Down Front"
"Engines"
"Exaugural Address"
"The Fire Must Be Permitted to Burn Full Up"
"For Maulana Karenga and Pharoah Saunders"
"The Gift of the Unicorn"
"The Heavy"
"In JW's Rug"
"In Wyoming Territory"
"The Last Roundup"
"Lefty"
"Like Rousseau"
"A Long Poem for Myself"
"March"
"Nana: 1888–1963"
"Nick Charles Meets the Wolf Man"
"No Matter, No Matter, the World Is the World"
"Node"
"The Occident"

"Ode to Laney Poo"
"Oedipus Poem"
"Old Men's Feet"
"A Paramount Picture"
"Parthenos"
"The Pimp"
"A Poem for Myself, The Fool"
"Predicates/Categories"
"Radar"
"Relurk"
"Riding and Shooting"
"Scenario"
"The Scholar"
"Slice of Life"
"The Southpaw"
"Spacepoem for Four Tones"
"Spirit House: Unity Creed"
"Spring and Soforth"
"Sundance"
"Sunspots"
"Theory"
"To a 25 Year Old King"
"West of Dodge"
"Who Will Survive America? Few Americans, Very Few Negroes, No Crackers at All"
"X"

Of the prose works which have been virtually ignored, again because critics have not known of them or have not located copies, perhaps the most interesting, because of its contradiction of a firm Baraka principle, is the review of Langston Hughes's *Tambourines to Glory* in *Jazz Review* (June 1959), in which Jones alleges that Negro writing can at best be folklore; such work fails to achieve the status of true literature because it is written out of racial consciousness, argues the young Jones.

In his informative essay "LeRoi Jones, Secessionist, and Ambiguous Collecting" (*YULG*, January 1972), John Baker argues, in a style both unusual and expressive, that collectors of Baraka are frustrated in their attempts to order books and periodicals by the carelessness of the small presses and the indifference or even outright hostility of black publishers to white buyers: "Corresponding with Jihad [Baraka's publishing house] is like running the barricades of a seceded province." If this is the case, the usual diligence required of a researcher must, for scholars searching out Baraka's works, be mixed with extra portions of patience, tact, and perseverance. Perhaps someday one such paragon, well versed in principles of textual bibliography, will give us a reliable and complete edition of Baraka's works. In the meantime, Baker has made an additional contribution with his useful "Criteria for First Printings of LeRoi Jones" (*YULG,* January 1975).

Manuscripts and Letters

Baraka letters and manuscripts, some of them holograph, exist in considerable numbers and should reward the examination of scholars who are willing to undertake the traveling necessary to examine them. The largest collections are held by the George Arents Research Library at Syracuse University and the Lilly Library of Indiana University. The LeRoi Jones Papers at Syracuse comprise a large assemblage of items once in the possession of Baraka, including letters received by him during 1961 and manuscripts of two issues of *Yugen, The System of Dante's Hell, The Baptism, The Toilet, Dutchman,* and *The Slave,* as well as the poem "The Turncoat" set to music. The Lilly Library's holdings boast a sizable collection of correspondence to and from Baraka in addition to manuscripts for *Preface to a Twenty Volume Suicide Note* and the plays *The Baptism, Dutchman,* and *The Eighth Ditch.*

Another significant collection of Baraka's papers is that in the Special Collections Department of the University Library at Northwestern University; of particular importance is the group of working papers and manuscripts for *The Moderns.* Several libraries hold groups of Baraka's letters: the University of Iowa Library has six letters written by Baraka in 1962; Founders Library at Howard University has correspondence from Baraka to Rosey E. Pool; the Manuscript Division, Washington University Libraries, St. Louis, has ten letters from Baraka to Robert Duncan (March 1962–October 1963) and two to Robert Creeley (Fall 1962), in addition to letters from Duncan and Walter Lowenfels to Baraka; and the Beinecke Rare Book and Manuscript Library at Yale University owns (in its James Weldon Johnson Memorial Collection) letters from Baraka to Ron Loewinsohn and Langston Hughes.

Although it does not contain manuscripts and letters, the Dr. Marvin Sukov Collection of LeRoi Jones will doubtless be used by those fortunate enough to conduct research at the Beinecke Library, because the Sukov Collection is the largest group of materials by and about Baraka in any library.

Other materials available in public collections include proof copies of Baraka's books and duplicated acting scripts of *Dutchman, The Baptism,* and *The Toilet,* all of these found in the collections of several libraries. Among the many private Baraka collections are scattered letters from him and books of his inscribed by him. Of special interest is the holograph of "The New Sheriff" owned by Robert A. Wilson of New York.

Biography

Published biographical materials about Baraka fall into three groups: those that give the "facts" (and frequent inaccuracies); those that publish, usually as newspaper reports, accounts of single incidents; and those that are to one degree or another anecdotal accounts designed to convey an impression of the man. The first group suffers from the perpetuation of mistakes originally recorded in program notes for early productions and the notes on contributors that accompanied the early publications.

The shortest record, contained in *Who's Who in America,* for example, beginning in 1967 records that Baraka graduated from Howard University in 1954. This error (sometimes varied to read 1953) has been copied and recopied to such an extent that it is difficult to find a source that omits or repudiates it. Probably the first published acknowledgment that Baraka did not receive a Howard degree appears in the passing reference to him as a college dropout in Nathan Hare's "Behind the Black College Student Revolt" (*Ebony,* August 1967). The error persists, however, despite the easily available printed list of degree recipients from Howard and confirmation to Professor Diane Dippold of Oberlin College by records of the registrar's office that LeRoi Jones left the university after completing his junior year.

The same mistake about Baraka's education as well as additional errors disfigure the Baraka entries in *The Ebony Success Library: 1,000 Successful Blacks* (Nashville, Tenn.: Southwestern Co., 1973); *Living Black American Authors: A Biographical Directory,* edited by Ann Allen Shockley and Sue P. Chandler (New York: Bowker, 1973); *Black American Writers Past and Present: A Biographical and Bibliographical Dictionary,* Vol. I, edited by Theresa Gunnels Rush, Carol Fairbanks Myers, and Esther Spring Arata (Metuchen, N.J.: Scarecrow, 1975); as well as two somewhat longer listings, those in *A Biographical History of Blacks in America Since 1528* (New York: David McKay, 1971) and *Crowell's Handbook of Contemporary Drama* (New York: T. Y. Crowell, 1971).

Although not free of inaccuracies, the entries most useful for factual information, if only because of their length and detail, are those in the reference works *World Authors: 1950–1970* (Bronx, N.Y.: H. W. Wilson, 1975); *Current Biography* (May 1970; reprinted in the 1971 yearbook issued by the H. W. Wilson Company); and *Contemporary Authors: A Bio-Bibliographical Guide to Current Authors and Their Works,* vols. 21 and 22, edited by James M. Ethridge and Barbara Kopala (Detroit: Gale Research, 1969). Let the reader beware, however; the degree to which the latter is untrustworthy can be illustrated by its assignment of *three* higher degrees to Baraka, not only the usual Howard B.A. but also two M.A.s, one from Columbia University and the other from the New School for Social Research. Furthermore, the writing of this piece becomes so disjointed as to suggest at one point that Baraka was arrested as a result of his 1960 trip to Cuba.

A portrait of Baraka which especially suffers from its dependence on the *Contemporary Authors* entry is that found in *Mug Shots: Who's Who in the New Earth,* by Jay Acton, Alan le Mond, and Parker Hodges (New York: World, 1972). This biography is slanted toward a view of Baraka as representative of "the alternate culture" which forms the volume's subject. Further, nearly half of Deborah Smith Fouch's bibliography of Baraka for Atlanta University consists of an article entitled "Important Events in the Life of LeRoi Jones." Based on information gleaned from only two published sources, this essay presents an undocumented mixture of fact, hearsay, and error in a prose crippled by jarring stylistic infelicities. One must lament not merely the inaccuracies of these articles—and their paucity—but also the absence of diligent inquiry into the facts available in government and institutional records. So much misinformation about Baraka has been disseminated that the previously published admixtures of history and myth should not be taken on faith.

The sources that provide descriptions of single incidents in Baraka's life are much too numerous to review in detail; but it should be noted that they are not the usual materials for a literary biography, inasmuch as they contain accounts of several arrests and of a variety and degree of political activity unusual in the life of a creative writer. When a definitive biography of Baraka is eventually undertaken, the hundreds of reports published in newspapers and magazines of the right, the left, and the center should be carefully culled. It is difficult to single out the high points here, but a few examples perhaps deserve special mention. One of those reporters who at an early date noticed Jones's increasing racial militancy is James W. Sullivan, whose "The Negro 'National Consciousness' of LeRoi Jones" (New York *Herald Tribune,* October 31, 1965) describes Jones's departure from the East Village for the ghetto, his conscious cultivation of bitterness, and his call for Harlem to secede from the United States and become an independent nation. And surely few young poets have received coverage such as Baraka did in the "Week in Review" section of the Sunday *New York Times;* "A Man for Two Seasons" (December 10, 1972) described his actions as community leader and as revolutionary. The many reports of Baraka's arrest and subsequent trials on gun-possession charges contain different—and sometimes contradictory—information. An interesting contrast is provided, for example, by "LeRoi Jones Seized in Newark After Suffering

A Head Wound" (*New York Times,* July 15, 1967) and Paul Boutelle's "LeRoi Jones Convicted in N.J." (*The Militant,* November 13, 1967). Both stories carry the same photograph of the wounded poet in the hospital, but the former reports that Baraka was "hit on the head by a bottle," then treated at City Hospital and only later arrested—a chronology that even police reports repudiate—whereas the latter captions the photograph: "WASN'T BEATEN? This picture of LeRoi Jones, in wheelchair, was taken in the hospital, where he had to be sent after 'not being beaten' by cops."

The Militant subsequently published several articles about the trials, all more or less editorializing in favor of the poet. Elizabeth Barnes's "LeRoi Jones Defense Gains Strong Backing" (February 5, 1968), for example, provides an especially full description of and quotations from the forces rallying behind him. David J. Nelson's "LeRoi Jones Didn't Say Please" (*Liberator,* February 1968) exemplifies other protests over incarceration of a man regarded as not lawless but righteous.

Good coverage of the reasoning behind the reversal of Baraka's conviction by the Appellate Division of Superior Court is offered by "LeRoi Jones Wins Retrial in Jersey" (*New York Times,* December 24, 1968). As Baraka became a political force in Newark, the *Times* devoted a variety of articles to his actions. Michael T. Kaufman's "Jones Asks Votes, Not Rioting, to 'Take' Newark" (April 14, 1968), for instance, recounts the poet's preparations for Newark's black political convention of that year, with an interesting postscript on *The Toilet.* In 1972 the *Times* ran such extended treatments as Joel Dreyfuss's "Baraka's Many Steps: LeRoi Jones a Mellower Man Now" (May 11); Joseph F. Sullivan's "Newark Housing Stirs Hot Debate, but Imperiale Offers Baraka Meeting for Discussion of North Ward Project" (November 11); and "Issue and Debate: Kawaida Towers Confrontation" (December 5). Equally informative on Kawaida Towers are *The New Yorker*'s long "U.S. Journal: Newark" (December 30, 1972) and Owen Moritz's "The Africanization of Newark" ("View" section of New York *Sunday News,* January 21, 1973).

The several anecdotal features on Baraka give diverse views of the man. Several items printed in 1964 treat LeRoi Jones as a Greenwich Village interracial bohemian. The most extensive of these, Isabel Eberstadt's "King of the East Village" ("New York" Sunday magazine of New York *Herald Tribune,* December 13) regards Jones as a cult figure on the Lower East Side, but describes him in terms that in retrospect sound very Euro-American middle class.

A more truly bohemian and personal picture of the poet during the same period emerges in Diane di Prima's "Spring Thoughts for Freddie," not published until June 1968 by *Evergreen Review.* This article takes the form of a letter to the dead dancer Fred Herko. Included in the memoir are occasional references to "Roi" and to her life shared with him. Di Prima quotes a short conversation between him and her daughter Jeanne, and she notes her abortion of a child of his. Much more detail of the Jones–Di Prima relationship is contained in the Diane di Prima papers owned by the Kenneth Spencer Research Library at the University of Kansas. This "diary" consists mostly of carbon copies of letters and runs from 1953 while she was still a student at Swarthmore into the early 1960s. These papers constitute a rare treasure trove of primary materials for Baraka's biographers and give a vivid if sketchy view of his relations with his coeditor of *The Floating Bear,* an underground literary newsletter they appear to have named in allusion to the A. A. Milne story, "In Which Piglet Is Entirely Surrounded by Water"; in that story "The Floating Bear" is the name with which Pooh christens a large honey pot that he uses as a boat during a severe rainstorm. Di Prima refers here also (on November 8, 1960) to an abortion, as well as to Jones's use of drugs, to *Yugen,* to parties at the Jones's apartment, to their personal relations and their work on the *Bear,* and to Jones's personality and his relations with others. Included also are two letters that she wrote to him.

A memory of Baraka at a slightly later period is included in William M. Birenbaum's *Something for Everybody Is Not Enough* (New York: Random House, 1972). Birenbaum, now president of Antioch College, is the man who in the early 1960s, as dean of the New School for Social Research, hired LeRoi Jones to teach creative writing. He describes applicant Jones as lacking credentials and previous teaching experience but still impressive enough that he left Birenbaum's office with the job and an advance on his salary. Jones was the first black faculty member teaching on the graduate level and became popular with students. Birenbaum also tells us that Jones's "first book had yet to be published" and that it was published in 1963; acknowledging Jones's earlier publications would perhaps seem to detract from Birenbaum's self-proclaimed "keen intuition about people, a capacity to judge them." He can be forgiven his self-importance, however, in exchange for his tale about the ladies from the Upper East Side and Westchester giving Jones a party to celebrate the publication of *Blues People: Negro Music in White America.* After contrasting the enjoyment of beer and jazz by Jones's friends from the Village and Harlem with the upper-middle-class Jewish ambiance, Birenbaum recalls Jones's "speech": He paced slowly within the circle of surrounding admirers and announced: "You have just seen a young Negro in action. Now go home in peace."

In November 1965 Nat Hentoff described the high points of a conference at the New School on the Negro writer's vision of America in "Uninventing the Negro" (*EvR*). Hentoff particularly appreciated Jones's performance of his own poems and wished he would make frequent recordings of them. And Hentoff turns mere dialogue into dramatic confrontation between Jones and a white girl and Jones and an elderly black man. Interesting too is the argument he recounts between Jones and Richard Gilman concerning the nature of theater. Throughout his treatment of Jones, Hentoff's respect for the poet is clear.

Another favorable article, this one a sort of biographical apologia for Jones from a black friend, appears in the January and February 1966 issues of *Liberator*. Lawrence P. Neal's "Development of LeRoi Jones" appeared at a stage of the poet's career when his altered racial consciousness and changed life-style were not yet widely known. Neal's article announces that Jones is truly dedicated to the liberation of his people, not merely indulging in some sort of adolescent rebellion against authority. He follows Jones from Howard, where Jones saw blacks trying to escape their color and to assimilate and where he developed in his disapprobation for the black bourgeoisie; through his growing political awareness, fostered even by his white friends and literary associates and modes; to his new clarity of thought as articulated in his essays on music and black nationalism. Jones's talent faces the obstacle of possible estrangement between himself, an intellectual, and his community, concludes Neal, but he will no longer support white culture.

A quite different portrait of Jones is provided in Jack Richardson's "Blues for Mr. Jones" (*Esquire*, June 1966). Here a sensibility far removed from Jones's own describes encounters with the poet (accompanied by his daughters) in Greenwich Village, and with Olabumi Osafemi and Willie James in Harlem; cites some of Jones's opinions with distaste; and decides that Jones can't write. A much more deferential view is presented in Cecil M. Brown's "Apotheosis of a Prodigal Son" (*KR*, November 1968; substantially the same as his "About LeRoi Jones" [*EvR*, February 1970]). Personal recollections of Jones in 1964 and 1968 are mixed with an account of Brown's waiting fruitlessly for him in 1968 and attending, at that later date, productions of *Dutchman* and of *Home on the Range* and *A Black Mass*. Brown finally surmises that a black who has lived white is not as good as a "Home Boy."

In the same year, white recoil from the new Baraka, mixed with a measure of respect, was represented by Stephen Schneck's "LeRoi Jones or, Poetics and Policemen or, Trying Heart, Bleeding Heart" (*Ramparts*, June 29–July 13, 1968). In tracing the details of Baraka's career, Schneck ridicules both the poet who attacked white America and the white Americans who enjoyed it; judges that Baraka has proven to be a racist rather than an opportunist; creates vivid sensory images of slum life while discussing Baraka's move to Newark; and provides an extended account of Baraka's July 14, 1967, arrest and his trial before Judge Leon Kapp. Although he argues that Baraka's appeal of his conviction should be sustained, Schneck alternates between exhibiting disgust and bitterness at Baraka's apparently selling out to white interests in Newark (vis-à-vis the CBS News interview of April 10, 1968) and making excuses for his conduct as being in black interests as well.

The next year a highly appreciative feature on Baraka appeared in *Ebony*. Especially valuable for its excellent photographs, including an uncharacteristic shot of Baraka laughing, David Llorens's "Ameer (Le-Roi Jones) Baraka" (August 1969) explains to black readers the importance of the Imamu (spiritual leader) to black people. Baraka is revered as a man who has helped bring other black writers to prominence and "whose political awareness" is matched by "his artistic gift and his energy." Llorens is more accurate on the facts of Baraka's life since the move to Newark than on the earlier periods. He evokes a sense of enormous energy and dedication in Baraka and describes something of his life-style and values. Baraka's move to Newark is praised as a journey finally to become a leader among his people.

A white viewpont of Baraka in Newark informs Ron Porambo's *No Cause for Indictment: An Autopsy of Newark* (New York: Holt, Rinehart & Winston, 1971). Although providing some information about Baraka's arrest during the Newark riots, this book is not notable for original research on that incident and its aftermath. The book's value to readers of this essay lies instead in its confirmation of Baraka's attitude toward Newark's white administration. Porambo's blistering arraignment of that city covers both its slumlords and slums, its incidences of drug addiction, its medical care, its schools, its racist police, its biased judiciary, and its organized-crime-influenced and inept municipal government on the one hand; and the human events before, during, and after the riots which illustrate the general charges of brutality, deceit, and corruption, especially among the police, on the other. Porambo's indictment is leveled forcefully:

> Despite the words of hundreds of eyewitnesses, formal depositions, complaints, bloodstains, spent bullets, and hospital records, not *one charge* against the Newark police, National Guard, or State Police was conclusive enough— black people were told—to warrant even an admission of guilt, much less punishment.

In contrast, his vignettes on specific lives affected—or ended—by lawless law-enforcement officials are recounted in a relaxed, evocative, narrative style.

Porambo's attitude toward Baraka, sympathetic with respect to his arrest and first trial, cools when he reaches his description of Baraka's complicity in laying the blame for the riots at the door of Communist agents rather than crediting white corruption. Porambo wonders whether Baraka was bought, and asserts positively that Baraka was in possession of the two guns which police officers claimed to have found in his car. He does not offer to substantiate the accusation, but he does trace Baraka's career subsequent to the riots in some detail. Most interesting is his contention that Baraka's arrest taught him to appreciate the value of—even the immunity offered by—political power, and therefore caused his energetic participation in Kenneth Gibson's successful campaign for mayor of Newark in 1970. Porambo's final assessment, nevertheless, is that Baraka is out of touch with much of the community, whose basic needs are still at worst trampled and at best ignored.

Another white writer who assesses the post-riot politics of Newark is L. H. Whittemore, who, in *Together: A Reporter's Journey into the New Black Politics* (New York: Morrow, 1971), registers complaints against the city similar to Porambo's and then focuses on the 1970 runoff election for mayor between incumbent Hugh Addonizio and eventual victor Kenneth Gibson. Only a small portion of the book directly describes Baraka's contributions to the campaign, but Whittemore deals at some length with the tactics of the opposition, designed to terrify white voters about blacks in general and Baraka in particular. Rape and pillage were predicted should a black mayor be elected, and from the rhetoric of the Addonizio camp one would have thought that Baraka, not Gibson, was the incumbent's opponent. Despite this grim atmosphere, an act of courage occurred: John Caufield, a former Addonizio appointee as fire director, after polling only 12,000 votes himself in the May election, endorsed Gibson in the runoff and even actively campaigned for him, at the cost of threats to the lives of his children. Whittemore's description of the Addonizio campaign concludes—as the campaign did—with the violent physical attack on newsmen who were present at the announcement of defeat.

With many of these accounts of events in Baraka's life we are clearly leaving the area of biography proper and moving into evaluation of the man: praise, often from fellow black writers; and blame, generally from white detractors. Much writing on Baraka, in fact, is prompted by his political notoriety rather than by his creative talent. He has received a degree of attention disproportionate to his literary stature from disparate and sometimes unlikely sources.

The editorial staffs of *Freedomways* (Winter 1968), *Publishers Weekly* (January 15, 1968), and *The Nation* (January 22, 1968) write about Baraka to protest the severity of Judge Kapp's sentencing of the poet on the firearms-possession charges following his arrest during the Newark riots; whereas the editors of the *Chicago Tribune*, no admirers of Baraka, protest (on October 4, 1968) his invitation to speak at Northwestern University. An editorial in the *Saturday Evening Post* by Stewart

Alsop entitled "The American Sickness" (July 13, 1968) takes an objective view uncharacteristic of these assessments in deploring not only Baraka's penchant for "violence" but also a similar obsession on the part of his opponent Anthony Imperiale. James Wechsler deplores Baraka's failure to appreciate the whites who are finally joining black civil rights workers (*New York Post,* March 18, 1965).

A number of representations of Baraka as a violent fulminator of antiwhite racism appear from the far right, all apparently based on common originals: a November 30, 1965, Associated Press (*AP*) dispatch and, in most cases, subsequent AP releases dated December 2, 1965, and March 17, 1966, all concerned with Baraka and the Black Arts Repertory Theatre and School (*BART/S*). *U.S. News and World Report* printed the report on December 13, 1965, and the contents of all three AP releases thereafter formed the gist of attacks on Baraka in Phoebe Courtney's *Communist Infiltration of Anti-Poverty War* (New Orleans: Independent American, 1966), Patty Newman's *Pass the Poverty Please!* (Whittier, Calif.: Constructive Action, Inc., 1966), Shirley Scheibla's *Poverty Is Where the Money Is* (New Rochelle, N.Y.: Arlington House, 1968), and a book with particularly wide circulation during Senator Barry Goldwater's unsuccessful bid for the presidency, John A. Stormer's *The Death of a Nation* (Florissant, Mo.: Liberty Bell Press, 1968). The items by Courtney, Newman, and Scheibla attack the Office of Economic Opportunity for partially funding the BART/S through a HARYOU–ACT (Harlem Youth Opportunities Unlimited–Associated Community Teams) grant. Writing after Baraka's conviction on the riot charge but before his subsequent acquittal on appeal, Stormer produces a description of the poet that is notable for its stress on violence and its juxtaposition of sometimes irrelevant details, for example, a statement by Baraka condoning hatred of whites adjacent to a report on the discovery by police of an arsenal at the BART/S, *after* (Stormer neglects to add) Baraka had severed his ties with that organization. The most extensive of this group of diatribes is Gary Allen's "War on Poverty: Billions to Finance Revolution" (*American Opinion,* February 1968). Written from the same perspective but with considerable addition of original ammunition is Bob Francis's "On the Firing Line," issued by the Florida Americanism Committee on August 31, 1968. This entire broadsheet protests the scheduled appearance of Baraka on the campus of St. Petersburg Junior College by citing such evidence of sedition as his appearance at an antifascist rally in 1964 and his criticism of "The Star Spangled Banner" in 1965.

Many other attacks on Baraka, generally charging him with racism, have seen print, some in the form of letters to the editors of the *New York Times, Downbeat,* the *Village Voice,* and other periodicals and some as full-fledged articles. One of the latter, Stanley Kauffmann's "LeRoi

Jones and the Tradition of the Fake" (*Dissent,* Spring 1965) contrasts Jones's white life and his black writing, complaining that he preaches violence against the very society which nurtures him. Kauffmann is accusing Jones of something worse than ingratitude—that is, insincerity, failure to live the life which he demands of other blacks. This is one of those articles about which one must wonder: If LeRoi Jones read it, did he, in partly acquiescent response, then become Amiri Baraka? A less virulent but also less well-written indictment appears as "LeRoi Jones and the Myth of His 'Holy Grail,' " by W. F. Lucas (*News Illustrated,* January 1966). In inflated, sometimes repetitive, sometimes inappropriate diction and occasionally garbled syntax, Lucas accuses Jones of exacerbating an already tense racial confrontation in order to further his own career.

Two other articles discuss Jones not as opportunist but as anti-Semite. Shlomo Katz, in "LeRoi Jones' Teutonic Accent" (*Midstream,* April 1966), regards Jones's "fascism" as so extreme as to have been designed as a parody of black nationalism by Ku Klux Klan caricaturists. "You Don't Have to Be Jewish to Love Leroi Jones" (*Realist,* May 1965), on the other hand, offers a desultory but amusing argument that we would be foolish to label anti-Semitic a man whose wife is Jewish, and that, if Jones is not untainted, well, he did not invent bigotry and many people, Jew and Gentile, return the compliment of prejudice.

Several years later, at a time when Baraka had proven himself a more formidable political opponent than his earlier detractors would have acknowledged, Murray Kempton's "Newark: Keeping up with LeRoi Jones" (*NYRB,* July 2, 1970) appeared. Although writing before the election of Kenneth Gibson as Newark's first black mayor, Kempton concedes that Baraka is now an important force in that city's campaigning, which he describes with élan and some original information. Particularly valuable are his vivid portraits of the principals in the coming contest—Baraka, Gibson, and indicted Mayor Hugh Addonizio.

In still greater contrast to those evaluations of Baraka's racial views that merely reiterate their objections—or shock—is Paul Velde's "LeRoi Jones—II: Pursued by the Furies" (*Commonweal,* June 28, 1968). Velde argues that we must not confuse rhetorical attack with physical assault. Baraka is a writer, not a warrior; in taking him seriously as a racist, critics have sought to deny him the power of poetry. Treating him as a criminal not only subverts our guaranteed freedom of speech but also curtails opportunities for settling the country's racial animosities with the pen instead of the sword. And refreshingly nonjudgmental and informative is Cynthia Jo Rich's "Where's Baraka's Jones?" (*Black Times,* October 1974; reprinted from *Race Relations Reporter,* September 1974), which reviews Baraka's recent political activities on the local, national, and international scenes, providing facts and quotations from Baraka and others.

Two writers who prefer to assess Baraka as revolutionary rather than poet, Harold Cruse and Robert L. Allen, do so in the context of serious sociological analysis. The earlier of these studies, Harold Cruse's *The Crisis of the Negro Intellectual* (New York: Morrow 1967), evaluates Baraka as cultural revolutionary. Cruse excoriates those black writers who fail to create ethnic literature and those intellectual anticapitalist blacks who cooperate with Marxist whites. He devotes much of his chapter on "The Intellectuals and Force and Violence" to Jones, describing his personal observation of the soft-spoken Village poet, of Jones later visiting Cuba (at a time when Cruse considers him to have been especially immature, impressionable, and uncritical), and still later of Jones working within his racially integrated On Guard for Freedom Committee in cooperation with older white and black liberals to assist Robert Williams in his self-defense tactics in Monroe, North Carolina. Cruse sees Jones in the latter period (1961) as confused by Communists and by his prowhite and relatively antinationalist stands. He attributes Jones's developing hatred of whites to his requiring an excuse for segregating activities which must necessarily be exclusively black if they are to deal adequately with the black situation. Ironically, when Jones finally rejected interracialism in 1965, he was in turn spurned by extremists of an anti-intellectual persuasion who preferred terrorism to culture. Cruse himself faults the BART/S, but for accepting federal funds instead of raising support from among the middle class or at least first establishing viable economic and political bases.

Cruse continues to blame Baraka for inadequate theoretical philosophy, lack of organizational expertise, and paucity of programs for implementing social change in three subsequent chapters, predictably those on "Negroes and Jews—The Two Nationalisms and the Blocked Plurality" (where Baraka's rejection of sympathy from Jews should require his dissociation from Abolitionists as well), "Intellectuals and Theatre of the 1960's" (where Baraka is admonished that theater is changed by, rather than a producer of, social change), and "The Harlem Black Arts Theater" (where that institution is admired but Baraka's administrative failures are castigated). All of Cruse's criticisms, but particularly those voiced in this last chapter, suggest that Baraka read them and heeded them before establishing Spirit House, Jihad, and *The Cricket,* before espousing and further developing Maulana Ron Karenga's concepts of Kawaida, and before establishing or helping to establish several impressive and systematically ordered political organizations on the municipal, national, and international levels. Either Baraka learned from Cruse or he drew from some other sources similar conclusions about his previous weaknesses and errors.

Robert L. Allen, in *Black Awakening in Capitalist America: An Analytic History* (Garden City, N.Y.: Doubleday, 1969), although expressing great admiration for Harold Cruse's book, regards Baraka as a political rather than a cultural leader. He describes the political machinery Baraka has erected in Newark but predicts his failure to achieve meaningful progress for blacks in the 1970 municipal elections and fears that white extremists may provoke violence in an attempt to exterminate their black enemies. Allen ultimately argues that cultural nationalism such as that adopted by Baraka must give place to the revolutionary nationalism advocated by Huey Newton. The degree of active discord between these two fervent brands of nationalism can perhaps be measured by the *Black Panther*'s attack on Baraka as "counter-revolutionary," accompanied by the hope that he will fall victim to an assassin's bullet (August 23, 1969).

In early 1972, Mary Ellen Brooks published an article on Baraka's life and philosophy which might well be thought to have exerted an influence on her subject's future career. If Baraka has not been influenced by Brooks, it is at least an interesting coincidence that her article should call for his return to Marxism, a course which Baraka in 1974 determined to follow. "The Pro-Imperialist Career of LeRoi Jones" (*L&I*, Winter 1972), after rehashing oft-printed biographical mistakes, makes an original contribution by taxing Baraka for his failure to join the revolution. Brooks reasons that Baraka's black nationalism is in the interests of capitalism because it does not threaten the bourgeoisie; if he is not a Communist, then he must be supporting imperialism. His black value system is found to be bourgeois in its principles and aspirations, and his art is judged to be so concerned with revealing black consciousness that it fails to further the class struggle.

In the following year, Henry Winston's *Strategy for a Black Agenda* (New York: International Publishers, 1973) further berated Baraka's "separatist fantasies" and "neo-Pan Africanism" as "remote from the realities of racism, massive unemployment, increasing poverty and discrimination in the U.S. as it is from the realities confronting the peoples of Africa." Winston accuses him of cooperating with United States capitalism and likewise castigates his impractical yen for primitivism. Like Brooks, Winston urges Baraka to unite with other races in the cause of dialectical materialism.

By early 1974, no longer "reactionary," Baraka had rejected the democratic system of government in which his own candidates were beginning to lose elections and had reembraced the Communist ideology he had supported back in 1960 when he served as president of the Fair Play for Cuba Committee and wrote of his admiration for the new Cuba; he was even said to have substituted "Chairman" for "Imamu." His espousal of Marxist–Leninist dogma and his rejection of black nationalism as racist have been variously reported, for example in *The New York Times* (December 27 and 29, 1974) and *Jet* (January 16, 1975).

No doubt this shift to Socialist emphasis, which has already provoked a schism in the Congress of Afrikan People and a furious complaint from James Steele ("Maoism and the Youth Movement" [*Political Affairs,* June 1975]) that Baraka's Maoism is really just a disguise for cultural nationalism which dilutes "the purity of Marxism–Leninism," will prompt still further boos and bravos of the sort which represent, to a disproportionate degree, what is really not biography at all.

Criticism

Baraka's literary works meet with the same sort of aggressively partisan approbation and attacks as does their author. It is important for black critics to apply some sort of aesthetic criteria, though not necessarily traditional white standards, to distinguish among the good, the mediocre, and the bad in black literature. It is equally important for white critics to react to black writing with an effort to appreciate its aims. Blind prejudice either for or against black separatist writers is no substitute for literary criticism.

THE PLAYS

Amiri Baraka is best known as a playwright, and his plays have received more attention, from both theater reviewers and literary critics, than have his poems, fiction, or essays. His productions through 1963 had attracted little notice; but in 1964, Jones's big year off-Broadway, Jerry Tallmer announced to readers of the *New York Post* (March 16) that *The Eighth Ditch* (also known as *Dante*—it is part of *The System of Dante's Hell*) possessed "a rhythm and a force unusual on the stage." Tallmer predicted, accurately, that the police would close it. Theatergoers who had missed making the acquaintance of a Jones play in that effort were advised by Tallmer in the March 24 issue of the *Post,* "LeRoi Jones Strikes Again." This review of *The Baptism,* faulting its characters but praising its humor, was followed the next day by a series of startled, and generally admiring, reviews of *Dutchman,* which made one in a triple bill at the Cherry Lane Theatre.

Dutchman Of all Baraka's plays, *Dutchman* was the most favorably reviewed in its first professional production, and it has continued to be acclaimed in critical articles and books as his best play, often as one of the great plays of the contemporary theater. Later criticism has detailed its wit, subtleties, sources, and symbols, but initial reviews concentrated on the powerful impact of the raw racial tensions it dramatizes. For example, John Gruen praised Jones in "Blistering Light on Conflict" (New York *Herald Tribune,* March 25, 1964) as "a writer possessed of a fierce and blazing talent," and Harold Clurman hailed "the emergence of an outstanding dramatist" (*The Nation,* April 13, 1964).

Most interesting of the *Dutchamn* reviews is *Newsweek*'s "Theater: Underground Fury" (April 13, 1964), which offers a similar tribute to the play as "the most impressive work by an American playwright in the last few years," and also provides commentary on the author and the work. After quoting Jones to the effect that he is not a propagandist, the reviewer explains that Lula is "the contemporary Flying Dutchman, condemned to ride forever in pursuit of an impossible quarry, made murderous by her misreading of the world and of others," and he argues that the use of myth and the play's "complex poetic texture" raise it "far above sociology."

Professional production of *Dutchman* on the stage was followed by its filming. The movie received generally good reviews, but fewer screenings and less fuss than it merited. Praise by such critics as Hollis Alpert (*SatR,* March 4, 1967), Brendan Gill (*NY,* March 4, 1967), and Clarence Major (*BlackD,* Winter 1967–1968) was countered by such negative responses as Bosley Crowther's panning (*New York Times,* February 28, 1967) and John Simon's venom (*NewL,* March 13, 1967). Simon not only terms action, characters, and central symbol all equally devoid of credibility but even deplores as "disgusting" evidence of "white liberal masochism" society's continued support of this author in spite of "his almost total lack of talent."

Possibly in response to the filmed version, critics finally began to turn their attention to retrospective analysis of *Dutchman.* The first of these commentaries, Hugh Nelson's "LeRoi Jones' *Dutchman*: A Brief Ride on a Doomed Ship" (*ETJ,* March 1968), briefly notes three sources of the Dutchman myth, suggests several ways in which the subway is an appropriate setting, and then examines those respects in which Clay and Lula each embody the title's legendary cursed captain. Nelson concludes that Lula is the more appropriate choice, and, after passing acknowledgment of the play's racial implications, summarizes the parallels and contrasts between the myth as presented by Wagner and by Jones: each Dutchman seeks redemption, discovers a possible redeemer, recognizes apparent betrayal, and is involved in a violent denouement; but in Jones's version the lovers are separated by, not united in, death. *Dutchman* is then compared briefly to August Strindberg's *Miss Julie,* some of its dialogue and its conclusion are faulted, but most of its action and language are praised.

Tom S. Reck's "Archetypes in LeRoi Jones' *Dutchman*" (*SBL,* Spring 1970) is a short, poorly developed and substantiated, but nevertheless provocative consideration of *Dutchman* as a modernization of the Adam and Eve story, which he concludes is here more representative of racial conflict than of sexual temptation: Clay is innocence corrupted or natural man before the fall. Only in his conclusion does Reck refer to the title character, whom he identifies with Lula (to whom he consistently refers as "Lulu"), and defend Jones's dramatization of her starting at the end to stalk further prey.

George R. Adams, in " 'My Christ' in *Dutchman*" (*CLAJ*, September 1971), varies this interpretation by arguing that Clay, while suggesting Adam, is more importantly symbolic of the New Adam: Christ. Adams explicates both the sacrifice of Clay and some of Lula's enigmatic religious references. He identifies Lula as Satan and the young black at the play's end as Clay's symbolic resurrection. "The Fall of Man Theme in Imamu Amiri Baraka's [LeRoi Jones'] *Dutchman*," by Willene P. Taylor (*NALF*, Winter 1973), rehashes much of Adams's and Reck's interpretations from the questionable premise that critics dismiss the play as mere propaganda. *Dutchman* is defended, therefore, as a work of art about the expulsion of a black from the American "paradise" because he has sampled the forbidden truth; the fall itself is explicated in sexual metaphors. Another religious interpretation that is heavily dependent on Adams's is Jerold J. Savory's "Descent and Baptism in *Native Son, Invisible Man,* and *Dutchman*" (*Christian Scholar's Review*, Fall 1973), which finds Clay more self-assertive than the other black heroes who descend into hell and are baptized by fire.

A radical departure from these attempts to trace the play's metaphor to a foundation in myth or religion is Robert L. Tener's identification of "dutchman" as "the theatrical term meaning a strip of cloth used to hide a defect of some kind" in "Role Playing as a Dutchman" (*SBL*, Autumn 1972). Tener points out that the title omits the definite article we might expect were it a reference to the Flying Dutchman and proceeds to detail the role-playing engaged in by the two "living dead" antagonists. Lula is an author creating a series of characters for herself, including offended white woman, white liberal, a guest at a party, and a romantic temptress; Clay merely conceals his blackness behind the dutchmen of white clothes, intellectual interests, and courteous habits. Because Lula cannot permit him to choose an identity, but insists upon his assuming the roles which she imposes upon him as foils for her own, she rewards his rebellious self-assertion with murder. Incidental to this analysis are several other salient observations which increase the article's value, notably that the subway resembles the "underground railroad" used to transport escaping slaves.

Among the other approaches to this play, Julian C. Rice's "LeRoi Jones' *Dutchman*: A Reading" (*ConL*, Winter 1971) is unusually rich and varied in its analysis. Rice is not advancing a limited thesis; rather, he is illuminating the play scene by scene, sometimes line by line, in a close textual exegesis. Unifying his interpretation is his conviction that *Dutchman* dramatizes concepts on the black race central to *Blues People*. But while following the attempted seduction of an Uncle Tom and eventual genocide by white America, Rice identifies "dutchman" as "a killer whose duties include disposing of the corpse," locates the mythic quality of the play in its contemporary significance rather than in its source, finds symbolic value in several stage props, and skillfully explicates a number of exchanges between Clay and Lula. "Death eating a soda cracker," for example, is clarified by the information that "soda cracker" is black jargon for a white man and that Clay is killing his black identity by his assimilationism. Rice sees hope, finally, in the possibility that the young man whom Lula spies at the play's end may be wiser than Clay and that blacks in the audience will avoid being victimized and prevent whites from becoming dutchmen.

Michael J. Iannarella's "Black and White" (*Studies in English,* Spring 1971) takes the form of an imaginary interview of Baraka conducted by two white liberals on the subject of *Dutchman.* The fictive Baraka mixes racial slurs and eloquent explication of, for example, the title as a reference to explorer Henry Hudson and the characters as each, in part, an embodiment of the stereotypes associated with the other's race. In cadences appropriate to Baraka and to *Dutchman,* this clever "play" by Iannarella builds to not one but two climaxes, the first a murder in imitation of Lula's, the second a murder-suicide clearly expressive of its writer's own nonviolent perspective.

Another treatment of *Dutchman* somewhat sociological in its orientation is John Leonard Tedesco's "The White Image as Second Persona in Black Drama: 1955–1970," a Ph.D. dissertation accepted at the University of Iowa in 1974 (*DAI,* January 1975). Tedesco's concern is with the image of a white "controller" which Lula projects and the criticism of white spectators implicit in such a replica of themselves.

Interested also in images, but in this case those of the black psyche, are Albert Bermel's "*Dutchman,* or the Black Stranger in America" (*ASoc,* Fall–Winter 1972) and Jerome Klinkowitz's "LeRoi Jones [Imamu Amiri Baraka]: *Dutchman* as Drama" (*NALF,* Winter 1973). Both articles give persuasive, close textual readings demonstrating that *Dutchman*'s central concern is with black identity. Klinkowitz praises the symmetry whereby roles assumed in the first scene are reversed in the second, and he links the sexual and racial levels of action, concluding that the "authentic black self cannot survive." Bermel interprets the same materials as evidence of the more affirmative stand that blacks, as an alternative to race war, must adopt a strong self-image and separate from the rest of American society. Among several fresh interpretations offered by Bermel, especially well developed is the analysis of Lula as Clay's conscience, which finds him wanting when he fails truly to shed his whiteness; from this perspective Clay's death becomes self-inflicted.

Despite its somewhat misleading title, John O'Brien's " 'Becoming' Heroes in Black Fiction: Sex, Iconoclasm, and the Immanence of Salvation" (*SBL,* Autumn 1971) chooses for its exemplar of Baraka's work not *The System of Dante's Hell* or *Tales,* but *Dutchman.* O'Brien considers maturation, including sexual fulfillment and experience of violence, in several black protagonists and draws parallels between Clay and his precursors. A bibliographic ghost (a reference to a book which does not exist) in the footnotes and the suggestion that Jones is a graduate of Columbia University detract from what is otherwise a cogent presentation of the view that Clay is in the process of recovering his "manhood and dignity" when he is killed. Clay's rejection on the sexual level of the fantasies offered by Lula corresponds to his decision to get off the white liberal train of freedom and claim his black identity: in both reactions he affirms his manhood. These responses immediately follow the "iconoclastic tirade" requisite to discovering salvation.

O'Brien's views of Clay's psychology are presented clearly in layman's terms. In contrast, Dianne H. Weisgram's "LeRoi Jones' *Dutchman*: Inter-racial Ritual of Sexual Violence" (*AI,* Fall 1972) presents an intricate clinical psychoanalytic reading replete with notations of the primal scene, incest, maternal rejection, oral gratification and loss, separation rage, and phallic aggression, as well as less integral but certainly important observations. For instance, the title refers to the first slave ship to America and the black residents of once-Dutch Harlem as well as to the Flying Dutchmen whose captain is embodied in both Lula and Clay.

Whereas Weisgram feels that Jones has manipulated his materials so as to force our psyches to require revenge for Clay's murder, an opposite view is presented in another study grounded in psychoanalysis, George R. Adams's "Black Militant Drama" (*AI,* Summer 1971). Adams explains the play's rejection (unfortunately not substantiated) by subjecting negative audience responses to analysis. He theorizes that the "psycho-esthetic response" is determined by the "mental structure" of the viewer and by the embodiment of ego, superego, and id in the play. Adams describes *A Raisin in the Sun* as an "ego-play" and *Blues for Mister Charlie* as a "superego-play"; *Dutchman,* on the other hand, "exemplifies the function of the id" in the person of Clay, who is destroyed by Lula—that is, by a neurotic ego's repression of "libidinal demands." Viewers who reject the play do so because its sexuality, violence, and suggestion of black revolution create in them considerable anxiety.

The Toilet and **The Slave**   Adams's explanation of *Dutchman*'s "rejection" would perhaps apply with even more effect to the production of *The Toilet* and *The Slave* late in 1964. On the morning after the double bill's opening, the dailies registered vociferous protests. Those reviews written after a few days' consideration are in some cases more erudite but rarely more thoughtful. The plays are simplified and presented as solely hate-filled; the anger of which Jones is accused is equaled by that of his reviewers.

"Spasms of Fury" (*Time,* December 25, 1964) terms Jones "a man who needs an enemy so badly that the nearest friend will do." Edith Oliver, in "Off-Broadway: Bang! Pow! Nope" (*NY,* December 26, 1964), insists "The wit is curdled by spite, the passion has dwindled into brutality and sexual swagger, the rage sounds prefabricated, the characters are nebulous, and the only surprise is that both plays are so boring." Richard Gilman, in "Evasive Action" (*Newsweek,* December 28, 1964; reprinted in Gilman's *Common and Uncommon Masks* [New York: Random House, 1971]), adds to the charge of dreariness in the plays allegations of "a poverty of ideas and a painfully immature emotional structure" in the playwright. Robert Brustein, in "Three Plays and a Protest" (*NR,* January 23, 1965), regards the plays as "inspired primarily by race hatred." He lashes out at both plays, but reserves his special spite for *The Slave,* which is "out of control," its language "full of semi-literate blather." George Dennison's "The Demagogy of LeRoi Jones" (*Commentary,* February 1965) charges Jones with being a racist as well as a demagogue. Ivan Morris, writing in *Vogue* (February 1, 1965), reveals his positive contempt for the plays; whereas Martin Gottfried in *Women's Wear Daily* (March 12, 1965) says he is simply bored by *The Slave* and twists *The Toilet* into a parable demonstrating the importance of close relations between blacks and Puerto Ricans.

Exceptional reviews, of course, do find matter to praise. Harold Clurman, who very much liked *Dutchman,* offers some cogent reservations (*The Nation,* January 4, 1965) but nevertheless concludes that both plays are important and issue racial warnings that should be heeded. Henry Hewes (*SatR,* January 9, 1965) likewise offers several possible objections, yet counters these with actual interpretations of the plays (unusual amidst so much diatribe masquerading as reviews) and praises *The Toilet* in particular as "a vivid and indelible work of art." Lawrence P. Neal (*Liberator,* February 1965) also admires the plays, and even Langston Hughes speculates, during a largely hostile review (*New York Post,* January 15, 1965), that Jones "might become America's new Eugene O'Neill."

Subsequent critical consideration of these two plays has been meager but more favorable. Paul Witherington's "Exorcism and Baptism in LeRoi Jones's *The Toilet*" (*MD,* September 1972), the first article devoted solely to that play, justifies the brutality as "carefully staged to suggest the acting out of a ritual . . . an adolescent exorcism of the maternal, ironically changing course near the play's end to emphasize Jones's point that maternal values must be incorporated, rather than destroyed." Witherington explains that it is particularly crucial for these black adolescents to make the transition from family to gang because their society is so matriarchal, and he cites as evidence of their rebellion against such a society the game of "the dozens," consisting of ingenious insults to one another's mothers. Witherington argues that

Jones here takes a stand against the gang's insensitivity and in favor of Ray's eventual demonstration of fondness for Karolis.

Robert L. Tener, in "The Corrupted Warrior Heroes: Amiri Baraka's *The Toilet*" (*MD,* June 1974), approves and develops in detail an idea advanced by Witherington concerning the domination of stereotypes about a real man. Tener argues that the gang members in *The Toilet* have internalized a white macho value which corrupts and dehumanizes; only Ray and Karolis retain some of their black dignity, for they still possess the ability to love.

An interpretation more likely to win Baraka's own approval is that advanced by Owen E. Brady in "Cultural Conflict and Cult Ritual in LeRoi Jones's *The Toilet*" (*ETJ,* March 1976). Ray Foots is the embodiment of the tensions between black and white cultures in the United States. The protagonist's conflicted nature—the black-goal-oriented Foots versus the white-goal-oriented Ray—reflects the larger social divisions both in the play's other characters and in the America for which the boys' toilet is a metaphor. Brady delineates Foots's "double consciousness" in detail, specifying the part played by "verbal concepts of blackness and badness," by "the dozens" and "imaginary one-on-one basketball games," and by Foots's sexual desire for Karolis and its counterpart in his attraction to white culture. Brady's cogent scene-by-scene interpretation of Foots's interaction with each of the others as well as the revelation of Foots's own character culminates in the observation, "He loses the respect of his community, yet must be a part of it; he loses Karolis' love by betrayal, yet must mourn and renew his attachment to it."

"The Language of Leroi Jones' 'The Slave' " (*SBL,* Spring 1973), Richard Lederer's article devoted exclusively to that play, contends that *The Slave* is great because it is violent, because the characterizations of the Easleys are unusually fully drawn, and because of "the brilliant and unifying function of dramaturgic language." Much of Lederer's support for the thesis that Jones's language excels appears in the form of long quotations from *The Slave.* His suggestion that what critics have found botched in Walker's speeches is really a valid projection of his conflicts, or his "cultural schizophrenia," could with profit be further elaborated. Another admirer of *The Slave*'s violence is James V. Hatch in his introduction to the play in *Black Theatre, U.S.A.,* edited by Hatch (New York: Free Press, 1974). He dismisses any inconsistencies in the play as irrelevant, inasmuch as it is not really realism but rather "ritual drama of decolonization." Bernard F. Dukore's "Commentary" on *The Slave* in his *Drama and Revolution* (New York: Holt, Rinehart & Winston, 1971) contrasts the enslavement of Easley and Grace to outmoded white liberal ideas with Walker's freeing himself. Dukore praises *The Slave* as "a striking example of social theatre, political theatre, black revolutionary theatre."

A rare attempt at comparison of Baraka with another dramatist is made by Sy Syna in "The Old Prof Takes the Stage" (*Players,* December 1970–January 1971); but the focus is entirely on similarities, and these are of content rather than form: Edward Albee's *Who's Afraid of Virginia Woolf?* and *The Slave* hold the academic community responsible for the decay of society because the professors, who are passive and sterile, are unable to keep alive the humanistic principles upon which civilization depends.

The Slave and Dutchman Several critics explore *The Slave* and *Dutchman* together in a single article or chapter. The earliest of these treatments, that by Miles M. Jackson in "Significant Belles Lettres by and about Negroes Published in 1964" (*Phylon,* Fall 1965), is so simplistic in its plot summaries and interpretation as to give no sense of the plays' drama, either favorable or otherwise. The much more extensive discussion in C. W. E. Bigsby's *Confrontation and Commitment: A Study of Contemporary American Drama 1959–1966* (Columbia: University of Missouri Press, 1968) forms part of a study of humanist existentialists who believe in and dramatize freedom of choice. The book's section on theater of commitment also considers plays by James Baldwin and Lorraine Hansberry. Bigsby prefers Hansberry's affirmation of man's possibilities to Jones's festering rancor. After a brief, muddled dismissal of *The Toilet* and a contrast of Jones and Bertolt Brecht, Bigsby turns to an analysis of violence as the dominant factor in *Dutchman* and *The Slave.* Bigsby interprets the former as focused upon Clay's manhood, which is corrupted by Lula when Clay permits himself to be assimilated into her white society; such a view of the play is in marked contrast, of course, to that of the many critics who consider that Clay has been assimilated long before his confrontation with Lula. Bigsby views *The Slave* as a parable designed "to circumvent what Pirandello, Artaud and Beckett had seen as the fundamental flaw of the theatre—the arbitrary and imprecise nature of language"; again his response is unusual among critics, who generally regard the play as heavily dependent upon language in the form of debate. Bigsby's lack of respect for the dramatist is expressed repeatedly, as in his contention that Jones's plays "are at base, revenge fantasies—public rites of purgation in which the audience is invited to participate." And throughout the chapter Bigsby argues with the ideology that informs the plays. Although he describes Jones's plays as pretentious, brutal, and undisciplined, Bigsby nevertheless finally acknowledges in Jones's drama some mastery of dramatic technique. It is a relief to find that in his later "Black Drama in the Seventies" (*KanQ,* Spring 1971) Bigsby has become less prescriptive and more descriptive.

W. A. D. Riach's discussion of these two plays as black messages to white America is more tolerant if less illuminating than Bigsby's treatment. His " 'Telling It Like It Is': An Examination of Black Theatre as Rhetoric" (*QJS*, April 1970) briefly cites the concern with black manhood in *Dutchman* and *The Slave*, but describes each protagonist as an undesirable character. Yet Riach admits that his white consciousness may be unfit to respond properly to plays intended for blacks.

John Ferguson's "*Dutchman* and *The Slave*" (*MD*, February 1971) bases its interpretations on a staging of these plays at Hampton Institute. This article is a convenient and concise source of many of the interpretations of these plays presented at greater length elsewhere, and his structural criticisms of *The Slave*, as well as his discernment of two analogues to Walker's behavior, are informative. John Lindberg's " 'Dutchman' and 'The Slave': Companions in Revolution" (*BARev*, Spring–Summer 1971) focuses more clearly on a thesis: that the plays compare and contrast with each other in several striking ways, and both dramatize, in the context of race war, the themes of "search" and "sanity." Where other critics have described Walker as Clay's natural extension, Lindberg sees him as the obverse of Clay. It is unfortunate that Lindberg—or the printer—has given us Lula's name as "Lulu," a title redolent of Frank Wedekind's heroine. But Lindberg has quite a lot to say, and he says it effectively.

Catherine Juanita Starke, in *Black Portraiture in American Fiction: Stock Characters, Archetypes, and Individuals* (New York: Basic Books, 1971), though ostensibly considering novels, discusses Clay as a victim of environmental determinism in her section on archetypal patterns. Walker is examined in a later chapter on "individuals"; he has been destroyed because his passion has enslaved him even as it disposed of his past associates.

Slave Ship   With a particularly vehement exception in Walter Kerr ("Is This Their Dream?" [*New York Times*, November 23, 1969]), most critics were impressed with *Slave Ship*; but the reviews differed so much as to suggest that each critic had seen a different play. One stresses the excellent ensemble acting, another the use of sensory media, another the horror engendered, another the message to Baraka's black brothers, while still another struggles to summarize the "plot." Clayton Riley's praise of the play's impact on modern slaves (*Liberator*, December 1969) tells us more about the critic than about the work criticized. Jack Kroll, while admiring the play's artistry and impact, deplores the attitude, insisting, in "Dark Voyage" (*Newsweek*, December 1, 1969), that a play should teach "life, not death," and concluding, "For Jones to set powerful talent in this direction is to design still another slave ship, a ship of fools which will carry all of us to destruction." Again, Kroll tells us more about his attitudes than about the play he saw. From his quite different perspective, John Lahr ("America: The Collapsing Underground" [*Gambit*, 5, No.17, 1971]) commends the theatrical rallying of black opinion against a common enemy of the race.

Writing in retrospect over two years later, Eric Bentley, in "Must I side with Blacks or Whites?" (*New York Times,* January 23, 1972), assures us that even at first viewing he felt that *Slave Ship* evoked a universal protest against capitalist exploitation. He accords the play the accolade of the "strongest piece of theatre I have seen in the past couple of years," an impressive tribute from this distinguished critic.

We must turn to Stefan Brecht's "LeRoi Jones' *Slave Ship*" (*TDR,* Winter 1970) for an extended critical appraisal, although his examination of the play is based quite as much on Gilbert Moses's production as on the text. Brecht is a white man writing from a very black perspective; he assumes the guilt of his race as a personal burden and defends what he sees as the play's advocacy of white genocide as black self-defense. Brecht's conclusion captures the point in a vivid image: "Jones' play is a window onto a scene in which Euro-America is strangling the Black Panther. . . . They come and murder sleeping men. Those men were armed, they say, and dangerous. I wonder why those men had armed?" Besides, Brecht reasons, all whites need not be killed. If that doesn't palliate the offense, he adds that "killing the powerful" is salutary because it reduces blacks' feelings of inferiority. Brecht also indicts capitalist economics as destructive of community and praises *Slave Ship* for rallying blacks to recognition of their superior noncompetitive communal relationships. Yet, he is dissatisfied with the level of dramaturgy, the play's primitivism or "reductionism," the expression of theme almost exclusively by means of spectacle and the attenuated interaction of largely indistinguishable representatives of a group, albeit in specific conflicts and concrete images. Brecht classifies the movement of the action as "a dialectic of identity: deprivation of identity, alienation, retrieval of identity," an insightful analysis that nevertheless ignores the jumps in time which characterize the play's montages.

Other Later Plays   The montage technique has been utilized by Baraka in some of his other recent work, about which only a small body of commentary yet exists. Reviews of productions are few and often unsympathetic. One such is Mel Gussow's review of the Afro-American Studio productions of *Madheart* and *A Black Mass* for the *New York Times* (September 20, 1972), a tangle of weak plot summaries. Reviews of *Great Goodness of Life* divide their consideration among this and the other three parts of *A Black Quartet*. Nothing more noteworthy appears than the venom in John Simon's attack. In "Theater: Quartet, Three-Quarters Jarring" (*New York,* August 11, 1969), Simon asserts, "LeRoi Jones has never seemed to me to have real talent for anything but hatred . . . . His poetry, fiction and plays are the works of an ungifted amateur whom the distemper of the times has turned into an ungifted professional." Simon offers as his assessment of *Great Goodness of Life*: "As political dynamite, this bit of soggy agit-prop is unlikely to explode in anyone's face except the author's; as art, it is beneath criticism." In contrast, Lance Jeffers offers a black writer's estimate of the play in "Bullins, Baraka, and Elder: The Dawn of Grandeur in Black Drama" (*CLAJ*, September 1972). Jeffers recounts how Court Royal denies the potential promised by his royal heritage and murders his son's manhood. Then Jeffers imaginatively describes Baraka's talent, first in terms of liquid and solid mass, then as a Biblical God of wrath "trampling out evil," and finally as outraged religious fire, cleansing a corrupt country.

Most of the other considerations of Baraka as dramatist which focus on his late plays appear as reviews of his *Four Black Revolutionary Plays* (Indianapolis: Bobbs-Merrill, 1969) and provide only a cursory comment on his abilities. The review in *Choice* (June 1970), for example, labels these plays a "catechism of hatred" and fears they sacrifice artistry to message. Irving Wortis (*LJ*, May 15, 1969) hopes that librarians will courageously purchase the book despite its fury because of its relevance to American theater. And Harry J. Cargas, in "What's Behind the Black Rhetoric?" (*National Catholic Reporter*, February 11, 1970), explains the obscenity and violence in the plays as exaggeration typical of the black oratorical tradition.

A book review that devotes somewhat more consideration to one of Baraka's plays is Stanley Crouch's essay on *Black Fire* (New York: Morrow, 1968) in the *Journal of Black Poetry* (Spring 1969). In discussing *Madheart*, Crouch presents a judicious blend of praise—for the humor and force—and objections—to an excess of antiwhite anger, to preachment, and to the "cardboard" hero and heroine. Crouch hopes that Baraka will write a longer play in which he will have room for more developed dramatization.

Further discussion of *Madheart* appears in two articles by Charles D. Peavy. The first, "Satire and Contemporary Black Drama" (*SNL*, Fall 1969), employs *Madheart* as one of several examples of Baraka's Juvenalian satire directed against whites, whom he hates, and against assimilationist blacks. Peavy explains that Baraka's habit is a departure from the more usual black practice of satirizing blacks in the hope of improving them. Peavy's other article, "Myth, Magic and Manhood in LeRoi Jones' *Madheart*" (*SBL*, Summer 1970), is a brilliant and erudite study in depth of the attainment of manhood by the drama's hero. After establishing the connection between white female interference in this maturation process in *Dutchman* and *Madheart* (including suggestion of several expressive derivations for Lula's name), Peavy devotes himself to careful, detailed consideration of the confrontation first of Black Man and Devil Lady, then of Black Man and his mother, sister, and woman. Peavy skillfully explains symbols and literal actions alike for the action in which Black Man encounters and vanquishes the white foe and takes his place beside a now submissive Black Woman. Of particular interest is Peavy's account of Sister's "death" as both psychological transference and the response of a victim to magic wrought with a voodoo doll.

Baraka's first full-length play, *A Recent Killing,* after being submitted to, considered by, and even optioned by several producers in the mid-1960s, was not staged until 1973, when it was finally given its premiere at the New Federal Theater. Although not completed until 1964, the play grew out of Jones's Air Force experiences in the mid-1950s and reflects a world view very different from that of its later quite militant author. The play's rebellion is fomented not by Lennie (the LeRoi character) but by the clever and likable white airman Stanley Laffkowitz. Because the play includes a humorous scene in a toilet and others involving sexual fantasy, as well as the murder of a white man by a black woman (the inverse of *Dutchman*), potential producers had feared that its sensationalism would be offensive. By 1973, however, its materials seemed tame and failed to shock or even hold the attention of reviewers.

Instead, Jerry Tallmer (*New York Post,* January 29,1973) recognized the autobiographical element, complained of the play's length (three and a half hours), and found both writing and acting of mixed merit. *The New York Times* ran two reviews. First came Mel Gussow's examination on January 30,1973, again complaining of the length and wishing Baraka had reconstructed and tightened his plot, but nevertheless commending the script's language and the building dramatic impact and pronouncing it "powerful and stage-worthy." Gussow explains the theme as "the conflict between reality and romanticism," which has its resolution when Lennie recognizes that he must take an activist role and produce changes. On February 4 the *Times* printed a review by Julius Novick, "Perhaps Baraka Needs His Rage." Novick laments the tedium: "has he ever written anything so meandering, so self-indulgent, so clumsy, so simultaneously naive and pretentious, as this?" The opening is poor comedy, the subplot is clichéd melodrama, and the point is much too long in coming. The play, unexpectedly, is not anti-white, but some rage might have given it power and purpose.

Among the play's other reviews, that in *The Nation* (February 12, 1973) by Harold Clurman, who himself had refused to do the play, provides the most direct contrast to Novick's. Clurman recognizes that the script needs polishing but praises its anger and energy. And Jack Kroll, writing in *Newsweek* (February 19, 1973), has not an unfavorable word to say, instead describing Lennie's conflict as one between hatred of hypocrisy and brutality and love of art. It is in explaining the sym-

bols representing Lennie's admiration of culture that Kroll identifies
Sebastian Flyte as a character in Evelyn Waugh's *Brideshead Revisited,*
not as the T. S. Eliot figure recognized by some other critics.

General Discussions   Baraka's plays have been discussed in pairs or
larger combinations by a number of critics. Some of their analyses,
especially those written shortly after Jones was catapulted to fame in
1964, are not of sufficient importance to warrant mention here. The
earliest which need concern us is Hoyt Fuller's brief treatment of *Dutchman, The Toilet,* and *The Slave* as exemplars of drama of hatred in his
"Contemporary Negro Fiction" (*SWR,* Autumn 1965). Fuller's comments are noteworthy both because they epitomize a common attitude
toward Jones as malevolent angry young man and because this view is
not likely to represent that still held by Fuller, editor of *Black World* and
now an admirer of Baraka's. In another early discussion of the dramatist, Waters E. Turpin's "The Contemporary American Negro Playwright" (*CLAJ,* September 1965), Jones is referred to as an angry
young man, but the analyses of *Dutchman, The Slave* and *The Toilet* do
not dwell upon anger. In fact, a faulty chronology which supposes *The
Toilet* to have been written after the other two plays leads Turpin into
the ludicrous prediction that Jones is developing into a mellower playwright, more concerned than before with universality.

A more realistic appreciation of change in the direction taken by
Jones's plays appears in Pierre Dommergues's "Chroniques: LeRoi
Jones au Théâtre" (*LanM,* May–June 1966). Dommergues recounts a
process by which Jones, like Clay in *Dutchman,* has become conscious of
the danger of internalizing white values. His implication, however, in
this relation of life to art, that Jones wrote *Blues People* after moving to
Harlem, is incorrect. And somewhat surprising is Dommergues's explication of the plays as not only political-revolutionary but also spiritual;
he illustrates the latter quality—which he labels a form of traditional
humanism—with *Dutchman* and *The Slave.*

Martin Gottfried, on the other hand, in *A Theater Divided: The Postwar
American Stage* (Boston: Little, Brown, 1967), discerns neither spirituality nor even artistry in Jones's plays. About *Dutchman,* the one play
almost universally admired, Gottfried remarks, "Written in self-defeat-
ing fury (whether real or worked-up), it was a dull and sloppy work,
relying on a stock climax (a murder) for most of its drama." Gottfried
both dislikes the play and misunderstands it; he surmises that Lula
murders Clay because he wants to be white, whereas it is Clay's revelation of his real feelings (his blackness) that betrays him into the hands
of his executioner. Gottfried similarly misinterprets *The Toilet* as a celebration of black and Puerto Rican brotherhood, as he had two years
earlier in his review in *Women's Wear Daily* (March 12, 1965). After

rejecting *The Slave* as untheatrical, he concludes that Jones "has very little talent for the stage."

In 1967 two popularized histories of black drama by black writers provided much more sympathetic discussions of Jones's plays. Loften Mitchell's *Black Drama: The Story of the American Negro in the Theatre* (New York: Hawthorn) contends that the theater has reflected America's suppression of blacks. His history traces the influence of prejudice on the theater and of the theater on prejudice. But Mitchell's vivid evocation of the pioneer black actors and theater troupes is not equaled by his discussion of Jones, which is marred by both inaccuracies and oversimplifications. Of some interest, however, are his comparisons of Jones with Jean-Paul Sartre and George Bernard Shaw and his suggestion that Jones's personal appearances on television be replaced by televised productions of his plays. Langston Hughes and Milton Meltzer, in *Black Magic: A Pictorial History of the Negro in American Entertainment* (Englewood Cliffs, N.J.: Prentice-Hall), undertake somewhat less than Mitchell but accomplish more where Jones is concerned, especially in their short survey of "The Jones Year" (1964). Here they name each of the five plays presented that year and give some sense of both the subject of and the critical response to each.

Although published in 1968, Donald P. Costello's "LeRoi Jones—I: Black Man as Victim" (*Commonweal*, June 28, 1968) likewise limits its consideration to plays produced before 1965. This article is the first significant critical study that includes *The Baptism, The Toilet, Dutchman,* and *The Slave.* For *The Baptism* Costello has little use, but the other three he analyzes as plays about victims. He contrasts *The Toilet* and *Dutchman* as focusing on, respectively, love and hatred. *The Slave,* however, he regards as diatribe rather than art, dramatic only in its depiction of Walker as a victim—"of his own philosophy." *The Slave* is propaganda, revolutionary theater, unsatisfactory alike as drama and as philosophy.

A diametrically opposite viewpoint is presented in Larry Neal's "The Black Arts Movement" (*TDR*, Summer 1968). Neal explains that black art is nationalistic and expresses the concepts of Black Power. It is developing its own aesthetic because the Western aesthetic is decadent. It is antiwhite and it is functional, expressing black ethics. Amiri Baraka's plays are the finest products of the black arts movement. Although Clay and Walker are victims and at a transitional stage, the protagonist of *Jello* has freed himself and takes what he deserves from his stingy employer. Baraka's lyricism and spirituality emerge in *A Black Mass,* which implicitly demonstrates the evil of art for art's sake, as they do in *Slave Ship.*

In 1969, Baraka's importance as a playwright evidently well established, his plays received several analyses that differed markedly in quality and length. Emory Lewis's *Stages: The Fifty-Year Childhood of the*

American Theatre (Englewood Cliffs, N.J.: Prentice-Hall) is superficial in its approach to Baraka and is based on only a fleeting acquaintance with his dramatic works; the discussion is likewise misinformed in parts. Lewis nevertheless admires *Dutchman* enormously. After treating Baraka as savage and violent, he suddenly wrenches the reader's sensibilities by suggesting that this separatist may contribute to healing a divided nation, to encouraging "a communion of black and white."

Gerald Weales's *The Jumping-Off Place: American Drama in the 1960s* (New York: Macmillan, 1969), which surveys American theater for only a decade, also considers Baraka's plays in the context of the larger scene. But Weales much more successfully sheds light on Baraka's abilities, contrasting him favorably with James Baldwin and tracing his rejection of white audiences for black. Although Weales lacks both familiarity and sympathy with most of Baraka's plays produced since 1964, his discussions of the five early plays are perceptive.

A third consideration of Baraka published in 1969 and set in a larger context is Doris E. Abramson's *Negro Playwrights in the American Theatre: 1925–1959* (New York: Columbia University Press). Abramson contrasts the assimilationist attitudes of black playwrights prior to 1960 with those of Baraka, and in addition notes that some foreshadowing of the separatist stance appears in the earlier works. In an epilogue she considers Baraka as a writer with more appeal to the young and unestablished than to the bourgeoisie whose financial support he requires; her concern seems to be with the BART/S, since she does not mention Spirit House. The few specific references to Baraka's plays are not admiring.

More successful criticism appears in the two articles published in 1969 devoted exclusively to Baraka. Maria K. Mootry's "Themes and Symbols in Two Plays by LeRoi Jones" (*ND*, April 1969) avoids most of the superficiality that is frequent in surveys of the plays by concentrating on *The Baptism* and *The Toilet*. The former she views as a play about diverse religious attitudes encompassed within the black church. Her emphasis on racial elements within the play is unique but effectively supported. Mootry explicates *The Toilet* as a more personal dramatization of what in the other play is treated on a social level; the theme of each is the rejection of nonviolence, accompanied by an assertion of black pride. Louis Phillips's "LeRoi Jones and Contemporary Black Drama," contained in *The Black American Writer: Volume II: Poetry and Drama,* edited by C. W. E. Bigsby (Deland, Fla.: Everett/Edwards, 1970) stresses violence and anger in the early plays, focusing especially on the black man's search for identity.

"LeRoi Jones: High Priest of the Black Arts Movement," by Daphne S. Reed (*ETJ*, March 1970), informs—and in some matters misinforms—about Baraka's career, his glorification of black, his anger, and his influence on others in the Black Arts movement. Reed appraises Baraka's drama as a great deal finer than most critics, to her knowledge, have judged it. Another of the many female critics of Baraka's work, Jeanne-Marie A. Miller, in "The Plays of LeRoi Jones" (*CLAJ*, March 1971), largely rehashes what Baraka himself has said about his work; she discusses, in addition to the early plays, *Experimental Death Unit # One, A Black Mass, Great Goodness of Life, Madheart*, and *Slave Ship*. On the other hand, Ruby Cohn, in *Dialogue in American Drama* (Bloomington: Indiana University Press, 1971), interprets *The Eighth Ditch, The Toilet, The Baptism, The Slave*, and *Dutchman*, preferring these, because of her emphasis on language, to the later, less literary, plays.

Of the several reference works on drama published recently, only two consider Baraka. Errol Hill's essay on Baraka in *Contemporary Dramatists*, edited by James Vinson (New York: St. Martin's, 1973), although containing the inaccuracies which seem almost inevitable in Baraka scholarship, delineates expressively the styles and stances of the plays, justifies their violence, and identifies some of their ritual elements. The *McGraw-Hill Encyclopedia of World Drama* (New York: McGraw-Hill, 1972) provides an entry on Baraka that is inaccurate, incomplete, and even contradictory (for example, in its count of seven plays by Baraka in spite of its references to ten plays). That critical discussion of the plays which is included is idiosyncratic, as in its treatment of *The Slave* as merely an indictment of Walker Vessels.

Much more satisfactory (though not error-free) is W. W. Burford's "LeRoi Jones: From Existentialism to Apostle of Black Nationalism" (*Players*, December–January 1972). After brief comments on *The Toilet*—including the inexplicable remark that Karolis is killed—Burford turns to *Dutchman* (explicated with both relish and insight), *The Slave, Experimental Death Unit # One, A Black Mass, Great Goodness of Life*, and *Madheart*. These plays he divides into the earlier, which dramatize the search for identity, and the later, the revolutionary group, which condemn the old order and prepare the way for the new. Moreover, in the post-1964 plays, Baraka's concern with sin, redemption, and salvation qualify him as a dramatist of theological significance.

A consideration of Baraka that is even more steeped in his blackness, although in this case considering the racial character only of early plays, is Sherley Anne Williams's *Give Birth to Brightness: A Thematic Study in Neo-Black Literature* (New York: Dial, 1972). Her book concentrates on *Dutchman, The Slave*, James Baldwin's *Blues for Mr. Charlie*, and Ernest Gaines's *Love and Dust*, focusing in each case on the character of the protagonist. Baraka is discussed as a dramatist who creates about and for blacks, one of those writers striving for "dehonkification," who nevertheless draws his protagonists from the white "tradition of the tormented central character whose doom is foreshadowed by the tragic flaw in his own nature" (whatever that may mean exactly) and who writes for white as well as black audiences. *Dutchman* and *The Slave* are therefore discussed as examples of a "hybrid tradition" important in black fiction for over a hundred years; note the word "fiction," which Williams applies to both novels and plays. So thorough is Baraka's dramatization of racial conflict that other writers are now free to concentrate on the black experience.

After thus considering Baraka in a general way, Williams turns to the failures of Clay and Walker to achieve heroic stature in her chapters entitled, respectively, "The Limitation of a Middle-Class Hero" and "The Limited Solution of Revolution." The implications of *Dutchman*'s title as well as Clay's betrayal of himself are explicated in the former chapter. In the latter, Walker, who has chosen the murder that Clay cannot stomach, nevertheless remains "in psychological bondage to the white man" and uncomfortable in his role as black leader; Walker, like Clay, is really "a white hero in blackface." Williams also comments on the manner in which, in each play, the language, syntax, rhythm, and images of each speaker appropriately convey his character and states of mind.

Two shorter discussions of Baraka's plays which encompass some of the more recent plays as well as the better-known works are Letitia Dace's "LeRoi Jones: *A Négerek Mozgalmának Drámaírója*," translated by Zombori Erzsébet for the Hungarian journal *Nagyvilág* (December 1970), later expanded somewhat and published in English (the title translates as "LeRoi Jones: Black Revolutionary Playwright") in *The Theatre Student: Modern Theatre and Drama* by Letitia Dace and Wallace Dace (New York: Richards Rosen Press, 1973), and Samuel A. Hay's "African-American Drama: 1950–1970" (*NHB*, January 1973). Dace describes Baraka's personal and artistic progressions from white to black orientation and discusses fifteen of the plays, contending that those produced since 1964, although propagandistic in purpose and characterization, are not always verbally polemical, but frequently communicate by the nonverbal means advocated by Antonin Artaud. Samuel Hay's excellent article divides black drama into several useful categories. He places some of Baraka's plays in the "Drama of Accusation" group, contrasting these to other protest plays by observing that Baraka accuses not only white oppressors but also willing black victims. According to this interpretation, *Dutchman* addresses blacks who need to be nudged into performing "the liberating act," and *The Toilet* dramatizes an invidious black affection for one of the white persecutors. Hay offers in defense of the violence in some of Baraka's accusatory plays the precedent of violent Greek plays. More interesting still is Hay's label of "Cultural Nationalist Drama," which participates in nation-building by dramatizing motives and biases in the form of white oppressors, black assimilationists, and black liberators. Praised as exemplars of this dramatic style are *Slave Ship* (teaching black history), *Great Goodness of Life* (dramatizing the assimilationist as social pariah), *Experimental Death Unit # One* (visualizing the extermination of such a traitor), and *Madheart* (depicting blacks showing the way to their erring sisters). Hay accords Baraka special credit in the latter plays for providing lessons for blacks in how to alter their circumstances, for replacing accusations with models for action. In considerable contrast to Hay's appreciation of Baraka is the distaste exhibited by Leonard C. Archer in *Black Images in the American Theatre* (New York: Pageant-Poseidon, 1973). Archer judges the black racism he perceives in Baraka to be no less reprehensible than white racism.

Much more thorough in its analysis of Baraka's dramatic works is Alain Ricard's *Théâtre et Nationalism: Wole Soyinka et LeRoi Jones* (Paris: Présence Africaine, 1972). Ricard notes certain superficial similarities between Soyinka and Baraka: each was born in 1934, each rejected his success in major Western cities to return to his native community, and each was arrested in 1967. Using nine of Baraka's plays written prior to 1969, however, Ricard then contrasts the dramatists on the basis of language, characters, racial and spiritual preoccupations, styles, settings, sexual roles, and personal and political philosophies. The remarks on myth, religion, and ritual in Baraka's plays are especially incisive, and Ricard's comments on Baraka's cultural nationalism especially irreverent.

A recent article that also explores ritual in the plays, Linda G. Zatlin's "Paying His Dues: Ritual in LeRoi Jones' Early Dramas" (*Obsidian*, Spring 1976), explicates the usual social and spiritual functions of ritual and demonstrates that the rituals in these plays reinforce the characters' insecure positions and therefore fail to achieve the usual goals. Zatlin's interesting analysis suffers somewhat from a failure of her own: she perceives a chronological development, but she predicates this upon a faulty dating of the plays. Another recent article which considers several of the plays, Floyd Gaffney's "Black Theatre: The Moral Function of Imamu Amiri Baraka" (*Players*, Summer 1975), considers the didactic rather than the spiritual side of Baraka's dramas and defends his pragmatism as aesthetically satisfying. Gaffney is especially thorough in his explication of *Great Goodness of Life*.

The first full-length study devoted exclusively to Baraka as a dramatist was "Form and Meaning in Some Plays by Imamu Amiri Baraka (LeRoi Jones)," a Ph.D. dissertation submitted by Roland Lee Reed to the University of Nebraska in August 1972 (*DAI*, January 1973). Although he has little to say about Baraka's post-1967 plays, Reed provides appreciative and provocative analyses of seven of the earlier plays: *The Toilet, The Baptism, Dutchman, The Slave, Experimental Death*

Unit # One, A Black Mass, and *Slave Ship.* Reed's concern is primarily with dramatic and literary values rather than with theatrical techniques. His sources are not so much previous critical studies as mythic, religious, and literary analogues to the Baraka dramas. He provides a simple but useful morphology of character functions (as substitutes for full character development) in *Experimental Death Unit # One, A Black Mass,* and *Slave Ship.* Another valuable aspect of Reed's study is his enthusiastic appreciation of the artistry of Baraka's particularly didactic plays; his relish for these provides a salutary contrast to the antipathy harbored by many white critics toward everything Baraka has produced since *Dutchman.* Reed's study is so thorough as to demonstrate amply its contention that Baraka's form and meaning are highly complex. He meticulously considers such factors as character names, settings, language, themes, conflicts, humor, suspense, symbols, and the growing concern with inculcating nationalist principles, all for what they can tell us about the import and style of each play and its place in the development he discerns in Baraka from socially conscious to revolutionary playwright.

Another equally satisfying Ph.D. dissertation on the plays is that submitted by Owen Edward Brady III to the University of Notre Dame in 1973 (*DAI,* January 1974). "This Consciousness Epic: LeRoi Jones's Use of American Myth and Ritual in *The Baptism, The Toilet, Dutchman, The Slave* and *A Recent Killing*" provides a close, careful reading of each play and interprets each as a dramatization of a black's initiation into consciousness of himself in an America rife with cultural conflicts. The chapter on *The Toilet* is essentially Brady's *Educational Theatre Journal* article (March 1976); that on *A Recent Killing* is a valuable explication of that little-known play which considers the manuscript in great detail and concludes that Len, in his embracing of new rituals, has developed a true self-awareness which will enable him to deal with the world in an effective manner that eludes the other protagonists.

THE NONFICTION

Baraka's essays have been evaluated primarily in reviews. Critical response to *Blues People, Home, Black Music,* and *Raise Race Rays Raze* (New York: Morrow, 1963, 1966, 1968; Random House, 1971) has taken the form of reviews that are generally more notable for partisan paeans and proscriptions than for incisive insights, literary or otherwise. One group of articles, however, does examine, not a single book, but that favorite of Baraka's subjects, the proper aesthetic criteria for use in evaluating black literature.

Baraka's Black Aesthetic One of Baraka's special targets is the white critic who presumes to judge the black artifact. Especially galled by Baraka's objections to the "presumption" of criticism offered by whites is C. W. E. Bigsby, who, both in his collection *The Black American Writer* and in "The White Critic in a Black World" (*NALF,* Summer 1972), inveighs against the bias that not only presumes incompetence by race but accords praise and blame to writers on a strictly ideological basis. Thus, aesthetically satisfactory black writing may be rejected by Baraka or other black critics for being insufficiently revolutionary or activist. Bigsby counters these prejudices by arguing that (1) the reputation of a writer like Baraka rests precisely on those works in which he circumvents his own restrictions and emulates the great white authors, producing writing of universal import; (2) ironically, Baraka's views are forcing him to condemn the finest black literature; (3) there is a difference between polemics and literature; (4) a white critic can enter the world of the black writer just as he enters that of the Old English saga or the medieval French tale; and (5) black literature is not yet exclusive, accessible by virtue of its values, aesthetics, language, and market solely to the black reader.

Others who take issue with Baraka's aesthetic of exclusivity are Gerald Weales, in "The Day LeRoi Jones Spoke on the Penn Campus, What Were the Blacks Doing in the Balcony?" (*New York Times Magazine,* May 4, 1969), and Cecil M. Brown, in "Black Literature and LeRoi Jones" (*BlackW,* June 1970). While recording his impressions of a "be black" speech by Baraka and a production by the Spirit House Players and Movers, Weales questions the black members of the audience's segregating themselves and Baraka's ignoring his white auditors. The white students attended expecting to receive an explanation of Baraka's separatism; instead they heard it praised and saw it practiced. And Brown, who elsewhere has lauded Baraka's talent and his separatism and assailed his ever having wandered from the black fold, in this article (written well before its publication) admonishes Baraka that black writing is not the mediocre morass of the poet's description in "The Myth of a Negro Literature." Brown cites Baraka's argument that black literature lacks the stature of black music—that is, the blues—and retorts that the realistic lyrics of the blues constitute literary productions of merit, comparable to their melodic accompaniment in stature. Brown also classifies Baraka's plays as thematic (like essays) rather than literary (like most plays) and argues that they are therefore similar to the very black literary tradition Baraka reviles. Finally, Brown concludes that a black writer's work is not bad merely because it differs from what the black critic himself happens to be writing.

Another consideration of Baraka's black aesthetic appears in Kathryn Jackson's "LeRoi Jones and the New Black Writers of the Sixties" (*Freedomways,* Summer 1969). Although more appreciative of the merits of Baraka's methods of inculcating black pride than are Bigsby, Weales, and Brown, Jackson nevertheless, after summarizing at length the salient points of nine of Baraka's essays as well as those of his poem "Black Art," finally concludes that Baraka's condemnation of whites distracts attention from the real culprit—the American system—and the real aesthetic standards—celebration of love and survival and expression of universal values.

A fifth judgment on black aesthetics—the shortest but the most virulent—is John V. Hagopian's "Mau-Mauing the Literary Establishment" (*SNNTS,* Summer 1971). In addition to deploring the terror Baraka inspires in whites and blacks alike and denouncing Baraka's work as the irrational "rhetoric of violence," Hagopian argues that the whole concept of black art is nonsense: "There is no separate black way of pointing out a bird, or of experiencing sorrow, rage, indignation, injustice, or anything else."

Two more recent articles attempt to appreciate black aesthetics as a viable alternative to traditional Western aesthetics. LouAnne Pearson's "LeRoi Jones and a Black Aesthetic" (*Paunch,* February 1972) explains Baraka's predilections for the process that produces art rather than "art as artifact," for function and content rather than form, for art as interpretation rather than as mirror or lamp, for the communication of a point of view and a sense of lived experience over such criteria as Freudian, mythic, structural, or thematic focuses. Cathy Arehart, in "Pepper's Categories, Dewey's Contextualism, and the Black Aesthetic" (*Paunch,* April 1973), reviews Pearson's article and Baraka's rejection of formism and organicism and decides that he prefers the sort of pragmatism termed by Stephen Pepper "contextualism." Arehart compares the aesthetics of John Dewey in *Art as Experience* and Baraka in *Home.* Both attack Western aesthetics for regarding art and life as separate, and both place greater than usual emphasis on the function of perception and on the importance of the creative process, thereby encouraging the integration of art and life.

Blues People   In contrast to the hullabaloo over Baraka's concept of black art, critical response to *Blues People: Negro Music in White America* has been largely favorable, although nearly every pinch of praise has been leavened with some measure of objections faulting him for errors in musicology; see, for example, Joe Goldberg's "Music, Metaphor, and Men" (*SatR,* January 11, 1964) and Don DeMicheal's review in *Down Beat* (January 2, 1964). The admiring reviews nevertheless praise the book as a history of the development of the blues. The negative responses, on the other hand, denounce the book as sociology masquerading as music criticism; see, for example, Roger D. Abrahams (*JAF,* July–September 1966), Robert Coles (*PR,* Winter 1964), and Richard Howard's "Some Poets in Their Prose" (*Poetry,* March 1965).

Two efforts of appreciation and another negative response, all comprising segments of full-length books, merit special attention. The least favorable of these is Ralph Ellison's essay in *Shadow and Act* (New York: Random House, 1964; reprinted from *NYRB*, Feburary 6, 1964). Unlike those critics who deplore the mixture of sociology and art, Ellison praises this amalgamation as necessary to an appreciation of black culture. But he complains that Jones's militancy interferes with his aesthetic judgment and that the sociological perspective has been carried to a ludicrous extreme. Ellison likewise scoffs at an apparently oversimplified correlation between race, socioeconomic status, and musical preferences, and contradicts several of Jones's separatist contentions, both historical and contemporary. Ellison's arguments implicitly accuse Jones of underrating black contributions to the mainstream of American life by assuming that blacks have always been basically a separate group.

Charles Keil's consideration of *Blues People* in his own *Urban Blues* (Chicago: University of Chicago Press, 1966) praises Jones's book in spite of its shortcomings. The "wild speculations, inconsistencies, misinformation, and absurd arguments that run through his early chapters on blues prehistory" Keil lauds as "a new and interesting 'myth of the Negro past.'" Keil is surprised, however, at Jones's concentration—good as it is—upon recent jazz to the neglect of contemporary blues and at the bourgeois prejudice against religion which prevents Jones from appreciating the foundation of contemporary blues in church music. Yet, Jones is still commended for giving his theme of the correlation between black life and black music incomparable treatment.

A careful reading of *Blues People* informs large portions of Frank Kofsky's *Black Nationalism and the Revolution in Music* (New York: Pathfinder, 1970). His admiration for Baraka's book as one of the "finest and most important books on jazz ever written" is especially apparent in those portions of the book in which Kofsky supports his own contentions that jazz has social content pertaining to the black experience and that jazz is protest music, and in the chapter that evaluates *Blues People* as a sociological analysis of "the role and function of the Negro" in the United States and denounces white liberals. Kofsky's admiration for Baraka the political musicologist, however, does not extend to Baraka the stylist, whom he misunderstands so entirely as to commiserate with him upon

> the publisher's incredibly lax job of editing. Elementary errors of grammar abound, and there are some passages that suggest that they have not even been proofread. With little effort one can find puzzling parenthetical phrases which begin but, due to the absence of a closing parenthesis, never end, appositions lacking commas to set them off, and whole series of other misconstructions that would be absolutely unacceptable in any freshman English class.

Black Music* and *Home Although no other book by Baraka has received as extensive critical attention as *Blues People,* the other nonfiction volumes have not gone unnoticed and have likewise prompted some extreme commendation and condemnation. *Black Music* drew from *The Economist*'s reviewer (September 6, 1969) a description of the text as incoherent and shrill; yet the same book's style won praise from Nat Hentoff in *Jazz and Pop* (January 1968) as almost musical itself in texture, the style suiting the content and the forcefulness "insistently palpable."

Home was the subject of some extraordinarily virulent remarks, such as those in *Newsweek* (May 2, 1966) and *The Observer* (February 25, 1968); some more tolerant views, such as those of Faith Berry (*NR,* May 28, 1966) and Robert Bone (*NYTBR,* May 8, 1966); and some positive praise, such as that of Charles Poore in the *New York Times* (April 28, 1966) and Harold Foster in *Liberator* (June 1966). *Home* has even attracted critical attention in retrospect with Ronald Primeau's "Imagination as Moral Bulwark and Creative Energy in Richard Wright's *Black Boy* and LeRoi Jones' *Home*" (*SBL,* Summer 1972). Unlike the reviews which merely evaluate the book, this article offers a critical interpretation. Each author is presented as a romantic, for both the character Richard and the author Baraka tap their imaginations as a means of coping with life. Primeau does not distinguish between Richard's fantasizing on the one hand and Baraka's stress upon action on the other, but propounds a view of each as similarly concerned with the transformation of reality.

Raise Race Rays Raze Finally, reviews of *Raise Race Rays Raze* range from rejection by Benedict Wengler (*Best Sellers,* August 1, 1971) to enthusiastic acceptance by Jan Carew in "About the Black Accused and the White Accusers" (*NYTBR,* June 27, 1971). The main subject of contention seems to be Baraka's style: Carew praises the sound and rhythm and force of black oral tradition, and E. K. Welsch (*LJ,* June 1, 1971) and George E. Kent (*Phylon,* Winter 1972) likewise admire the prose; but R. Z. Sheppard in "Wait for Ping Pong?" (*Time,* June 28, 1971), Alfred Kazin in "Brothers Crying Out for More Access to Life" (*SatR,* October 2, 1971), and others complain that the style is surprisingly derivative of middle-class white prose. Yet, throughout the reviews there is a deference, an awe of the talent and/or the separatist dedication, which distinguishes these evaluations from the responses to Baraka's earliest nonfiction.

THE POETRY
Preface to a Twenty Volume Suicide Note The first extended consideration of Baraka's poetry was Denise Levertov's "Poets of the Given Ground" (*The Nation,* October 14, 1961), her review of *Preface to a*

a Twenty Volume Suicide Note (New York: Totem Press and Corinth Books, 1961) and of several similar books by Jones's contemporaries. At this early date she appreciates not only LeRoi Jones's promise but also several of the salient qualities contributing to his merit and some of the influences shaping his work. Among the latter, Levertov discerns William Carlos Williams, Ezra Pound, Charles Olson, and Robert Creeley, and she suggests that Jones's natural predilection for the incantatory may have been encouraged by exposure to this magical quality in Garcia Lorca's lyrics. Another formative influence is found in jazz, which plays through the poet's lines. Although Levertov regards some of the poems as "muddled" and contrasts Jones unfavorably with Gilbert Sorrentino on matters of craft and "clarity, logic and restraint," she nevertheless finds much to praise, especially in "The Clearing," "The Turncoat," and "Notes for a Speech." More valuable than her enthusiasm for his work (encouraging as that undoubtedly was to the barely twenty-seven-year-old Jones) is her perception of his special gifts, particularly the "emotive music" which creates a sensual and incantatory beauty, and her request for patience with apparent typographical oddities that might provide us with "precise shades of tempo and inflexion." Yet she cautions us, in a remarkably astute observation for such an early piece of criticism, that Jones's concern with public issues precludes his classification as predominantly a lyric poet.

Levertov's suggestion that jazz can be heard in Jones's rhythms is expanded by M. L. Rosenthal into a metaphor expressive of both the strengths and weaknesses of *Preface.* In "Seven Voices" (*The Reporter,* January 3, 1963), after considering several other volumes, including Levertov's own *The Jacob's Ladder,* Rosenthal turns to a description of Jones's improvisations in the spirit of jazz: "He tries something out, expands on it, repeats effects, drifts dreamily along wispy spirals of suggestion, grows tedious, pulls himself up short and does a beautiful solo for a minute or two." Rosenthal praises Jones's imagery and humor while faulting him for comparative absence of discipline and incisiveness. Perhaps the greatest compliment Rosenthal pays Jones is that of including his book in a review of works by such then more established writers as Levertov, Robert Duncan, Anne Sexton, and Allen Ginsberg.

The Dead Lecturer It was two years subsequent to Rosenthal's brief remarks that commentaries of some substance on Jones's poetry again appeared, following the publication of his second collected edition, *The Dead Lecturer* (New York: Grove, 1964). Another reviewer to remark upon the resemblance of the verse to improvisational jazz was Richard M. Elman. His review, "Moments of Masquerade" (*NYTBR,* January 31, 1965), differs radically from the admiring tone of Levertov and Rosenthal. Elman grudgingly admits to finding some small poetic talent, "however unformed," but criticisms of Jones's technique are his chief concern. These are imaginative criticisms—and, more balanced later articles suggest, perhaps in part deserved. The poetry is judged artificial because of the persona's many masquerades. The poet's possession of any method is questioned. Even his "disconnectedness of language" is deemed "derivative." His "negritude" is termed "posturing," his writing in the manner of Walt Whitman, Allen Ginsberg, Ezra Pound, William Carlos Williams, William Butler Yeats, Dylan Thomas, and T. S. Eliot judged "a rough approximation." His "leaden cadences" and inability "to sustain a thought or mood for longer than a boast" are castigated, and his way with words is judged so inept that he is surely "entirely baffled by the stubborn conceptual basis of the language" and produces sentences a little reminiscent of "McGuffey's *First Reader.*" His poetry is dismissed as "self-advertisements," verse "pretentiously banal, and occasionally trite." Indeed, when the review ends on the accusation that Jones "has apparently never bothered to study his craft" and with the disdainful question— returning to the initial concern expressed by the title—"Will the real LeRoi Jones bother to come forward?"—the concluding jibes seem so tame as to be anticlimactic.

Some of Elman's concerns are reiterated, though with some admixture of praise, in Richard Howard's "Two Against Chaos" (*The Nation*, March 15, 1965). Elman had ridiculed Jones's propensity for "beginning a poem with small letters or interrupting it for a parenthesis"; Howard expands the indictment to include "single parentheses, slash marks, phonetic spellings, Poundian contractions, aberrant punctuation, broken lines, the absence of any 'formality' beyond the decorum of arrangement on the page and, perhaps, a pattern of breathing." Howard seems to have enjoyed *Preface* and to be disappointed by *The Dead Lecturer*, which reveals a poet "much surer of his own voice" but likewise more inclined to exaggerate "the desperation and the fragmentation," perhaps even less in control of form. Howard's appraisal of Jones, though by no means intemperate, is obviously very far from unqualified approval, and his critical perceptions about Jones are much the same as those of his predecessors.

General Considerations of Baraka's Poetry to 1967 The first extended consideration of Jones as poet by a black writer contrasts in some important—though not necessarily racially determined—respects with the preceding responses. Clarence Major, in "The Poetry of LeRoi Jones: A Critique" (*ND*, March 1965), presents the first critical evaluation of Jones's poetry not confined to the limitations of a review of one work. Major insists that Jones's value is as a literary poet, one who handles form and meaning effectively, in contrast to the jazz poet or race poet that others have labeled him. He is spiritual and romantic; he has "a sense of history"; and his descriptions are graphic. Still, formalism can get the better of him and sometimes his rhythms are achieved merely through choppy punctuation. His titles are good, mysterious, and creative. Finally, although his humorous social protest poems are fine, angry protest "is not his forte." This is an interesting judgment from a fellow black poet just at the time when Jones was moving to Harlem and seeking to break off his ties with the white world and to live and write black.

Also published in 1965 was Stephen Stepanchev's similar judgment that Jones is not an "engaged" poet. In *American Poetry Since 1945* (New York: Harper & Row), Stepanchev presents Jones as "too much the cool hipster to trust slogans and programs of any sort"; it is the Jones of "For Hettie" in *Preface* that he knows, the poet who creates fresh images, diction, and rhythms and "enjoys projecting a wild comic sexual fantasy." Douglas Collins's "LeRoi Jones as Poet" (*LanM,* May–June 1966) presents a very different image of the author, a man who in disillusionment has escaped into the world of savage words and become "superbly defiant." Collins admires Jones's ability to turn a cliché "into something powerful and felt." Yet, for all his recognition of occasional talent in the poet, he does not like the poetry; he is, in fact, repelled, rejecting the writing because the writer's soul seems unworthy. Collins insists that Jones's personal drama prevents him from creating works of art and that he is, in any case, derivative.

Roland P. Young's "Black Words/The Death of Yakub" (*JBP,* Summer 1967) quotes several passages from Jones in order to contrast his poetry with that of the less fierce, less revolutionary Langston Hughes. M. L. Rosenthal's *The New Poets: American and British Poetry Since World War II* (New York: Oxford University Press, 1967) expatiates further upon the imagery and humor that he praises in his review of *Preface,* then acknowledges a change in Jones's racial attitudes which seems to permit him greater clarity in expressing hostility to whites in a poem such as "Black Dada Nihilismus." An equally effective contrast to that poem's strength is the "rhapsodic inwardness" of "Crow Jane" and others.

Black Art Of particular importance among reviews of Baraka's poetry is Stanley Crouch's consideration of the 1966 publication by Jihad Productions in Newark of *Black Art* (*JBP,* Fall 1968). Here Baraka is taxed with having thrown together "junk," probably to please "somebody he's worried about: The cats on the block who may throw his past up in his face all the time." Crouch believes that black literature would improve if Baraka set a better example, if he required of all his work the excellence of which he demonstrates himself capable in "The World Is Full of Remarkable Things" and in many of his earlier poems. Not that Crouch wants Baraka to return to the influence of Olson, Creeley, and Duncan. He must develop instead "a style that is swifter and Blacker, more rhythmic and swinging" and also be true to that exoticism and romanticism that are the primary constituents of his natural and very considerable talent. In the same pages in which Young has written of Baraka's ferocity, Crouch assures us that the poet is actually "beautifully gentle." If Baraka must write political poems, he requests, then let them not be polemic and cliché in the style of bad white poets, but the lyrics at which Baraka so excels.

Black Magic The publication of *Black Magic* (Indianapolis, Ind.: Bobbs-Merrill, 1969) prompted responses as divergent as the racial sensibilities from which they emanate. The critics' reactions to Baraka's ideological posture unquestionably color their aesthetic judgments. *Publishers Weekly* (April 14, 1969) dismissed Baraka's merit as being overpowered by his anger. Jascha Kessler devoted an extensive and thoughtful "Poetry Quarterly: Keys to Outselves" (*SatR,* May 2, 1970) in some part to rejection of the book on the two grounds that the content is fascistic demagoguery and that the verse is bad.

In contrast to Kessler's view that Baraka is "tearing himself to shreds as a poet" is Alvin Aubert's opinion that Baraka must be esteemed for "a wealth of wisdom, knowledge and skill" (*BARev,* Winter 1970). Where Kessler pities "an intelligence self-maddened," Aubert extols "the remarkable continuity, a reflection of the poet's unique integrity, his self-togetherness." Where the white critic cringes, the black critic delights: Aubert admires Baraka's thought, his tone, his diction, and his imagery. He especially commends "the movement toward spirituality" evident in "Human to Spirit Humanism for Animals," to which he devotes a paragraph of very perceptive explication. He conceives of Baraka's black humanism as preparing the way for a black aesthetic. And he credits Baraka with elevating black to a position not antithetical to light but eminent in its own right.

Dudley Randall's appraisal of Baraka in his essay "Black Poetry," written for *Black Expression: Essays By and About Black Americans in the Creative Arts,* edited by Addison Gayle, Jr., (New York: Weybright & Talley, 1969), recognizes Baraka's anger and his great talent but details only his assimilation of white culture and techniques, which, although he is "a symbol of black rebellion," he is passing on to the younger black poets for whom he serves as model. The same observation about Baraka's traditional Western verse forms is contained in Arthur P. Davis's "The New Poetry of Black Hate" (*CLAJ,* June 1970). David particularly deplores Baraka's hate-mongering for its contagion to other poets, and he questions the sincerity as well as the artistry of a whole group of contemporary black poets, who have less excuse for despising whites than did their artistic forebears.

Curiously, the first long scholarly analysis of Baraka's poetry is devoted to his use of comics. Lloyd W. Brown's interesting "Comic-Strip

Heroes: LeRoi Jones and the Myth of American Innocence" (*JPC*, Fall 1969) is grounded in concepts previously applied to literature with success by Northrop Frye, Leslie Fiedler, and other critics. Brown considers what Baraka expresses about America's malaise and its dream by means of comic-strip characters, who serve as symbols of both illusory innocence and racial injustices effected by violence. A comic-strip hero such as the Lone Ranger evokes the American hypocrisy whereby the same person epitomizes exemplary goodness *and* the guilty tradition of the nation's repressive, exploitative past.

An altogether different effort at appreciating *Black Magic* is made by Harry James Cargas in "What's Behind Black Rhetoric?" (*National Catholic Reporter*, February 11, 1970). Cargas laments the fact that Baraka's violent lines often are remembered at the expense of those, even in this volume, which more faithfully represent him "as a young man in search of himself." Still another approach, that taken by Edward Margolies (*LJ*, June 1, 1969), acknowledges little difference between "the searing early intensity" and the late Baraka except that in the recent poetry there is "considerably less humor and brooding subjectivity."

Overviews of Baraka's Poetry in the 1970s In 1970, two women published significant materials on Baraka as poet. Carol Bergé's description of him for *Contemporary Poets of the English Language,* edited by Rosalie Murphy and James Vinson (New York: St. Martin's, 1970), is that of a fellow poet and early friend. She says little about his poetry, and that only suggesting an impression, but she evokes the very essence of the man, because "the writing is not separable from the life." She knows him as

> a builder, not a destroyer . . . [a man who] mocks those whose roads even *look* easier. A man who can be wrong, but before you take it in, he's done something else terribly right, some dynamic to set the world's eyes into a new stance. Roi, divided into three parts: memories, nostalgia of when we were young; the present, with the skill taut and extended like madness, writing or speaking truth as if it were the sex act; and the next cycle of time, toward which he is reaching, leaping. An impatient man, of course. A gentle man. Voice breaking onstage as he reads about the death of the lovely black girl he loved: a slim man weeping for all deaths.

The contrast between Bergé's enthusiasm for this "gentle man" and Charlotte Otten's shudders at the same poet's demonic violence could hardly be greater. Otten's "LeRoi Jones: Napalm Poet" (*CP,* Spring 1970) is the first critical article on Baraka published by a poetry journal. Her opening gambit is the unfortunate assertion that Baraka possessed two guns during the Newark riots. In December 1968 (Otten says 1969) Baraka had won a retrial on that charge, and he was acquitted on July 2, 1969, many months before the publication of this article. Otten does refer to the Appellate Court's ruling of judicial prejudice, however, for that decision provides unusual proof of literature's impact: "It was the poetry, not the guns, that got under the judge's skin." Otten quotes the 1967 poem that maddened Judge Kapp, but most of her extensive quotations, designed to prove that Baraka uses poetry "to terrorize and shock," are chosen from his 1964 volume *The Dead Lecturer*. This book is not good evidence of such claims as that Baraka "makes his poetry uniquely black man's poetry, with each poem being an attempt to create a deeper gulf between white experience and black experience. White and black, since they share no common humanity in Jones's world, share no common emotion or vision." Such statements are hyperbolic not because they cannot be supported by the book, but because they can be contradicted by other poems from the diverse same source, by love lyrics and by searching self-examinations in which the poet is more severe with himself than with another. What a pity Otten did not draw upon Baraka's poems for black periodicals and upon the collections *Black Art* and *Black Magic* (the latter published in November 1969—perhaps too late for consideration in her article). And how unfortunate to have regarded as attacks on "white structures" Baraka's unconventional use of "the comma, the double parentheses, accepted capitalization, spellings, rimes, rhythms, even words," all unconventional techniques adopted by Jones under the formative influence of white writers. Otten concludes not with an explanation of her terms "anti-word" and "anti-poetry" or of the characteristics in Baraka's work which qualify it for these descriptors, but with the insistence that his verse is nihilistic because one poem inquires who he is and another seems to fear (Otten says "scream") that he may be "An empty cage of failure." What Otten mistakes for nihilism is the poet's concern during the early 1960s about his racial identity, his worry over whether he is creating the proper essence. Such an existential sense of responsibility for one's acts is optimistic, for it implies that one can control one's character and shape one's destiny.

Two articles that appreciate the affirmation implicit in some of the poetry are "The Dream Motif in Contemporary Negro Poetry" by De-Lois Garrett (*EJ*, September 1970) and A. Russell Brooks's "The Motif of Dynamic Change in Black Revolutionary Poetry" (*CLAJ*, September 1971). The former article considers how to stimulate low achievers from culturally deprived backgrounds in secondary-school English classes with books such as *Blues People* and *The Dead Lecturer* and illustrates the dream of "self-realization" ("Each Morning") and of home (that is, heaven). Here Baraka is used as inspiration for young people whose lives have been so rugged they may otherwise not even try to cope. A. Russell Brooks also sees a positive aspect in Baraka's work—in this case particularly in his post–*Dead Lecturer* verse—inasmuch as Baraka is one of the consciousness-raising writers in whose poetry rings a "note of expectancy, of hope for a better world through the coming into fruition of the black man's national aspirations," as well as a writer whose poems are superior in technique.

Several pieces of criticism from this period concern themselves not with the world view but with Baraka's use of language. The dissertation "Daniel Berrigan and the Ideas Found in Contemporary Anti-Establishment Poetry," submitted by Harry James Cargas to St. Louis University in 1970 (*DAI*, August 1971) and later published as *Daniel Berrigan and Contemporary Protest Poetry* (New Haven, Conn.: College & University Press, 1972), discusses the stylistic affinities among several activist writers, including Richard Eberhart, Allen Ginsberg, Robert Lowell, and Karl Shapiro as well as Berrigan and Baraka; the diction of the black writer is judged to be particularly "shocking," and his use of black rhetorical techniques is explored. Alvin Aubert's "Black American Poetry: Its Language and the Folk Tradition" (*BARev,* Spring–Summer 1971) likewise considers Baraka's use of the black oratorical tradition (in "Sermon for Our Maturity") and pronounces him the preeminent figure in the contemporary Black Arts movement.

It remained for Kathleen Gallagher to provide the first extensive textual exegesis of a single Baraka poem in her "The Art(s) of Poetry: Jones and MacLeish" (*MQ,* July 1971). Gallagher considers "Black Art" a contrast, perhaps even a deliberate response to, Archibald MacLeish's "Ars Poetica." The latter poem, ending with the famous postulate "A poem should not mean/But be," advocates "art-for-art's-sake," whereas the Baraka poem both advocates and exemplifies utilitarian or functional verse. Baraka instructs his readers in his black aesthetic whereby literature must serve the revolution. Gallagher demonstrates in a close, specific contrast of the two poems that the Baraka example employs form, language, and imagery deliberately antithetical to those advocated by MacLeish.

Another article also partly concerned with "Black Art" is Bernard W. Bell's "New Black Poetry: A Double-Edged Sword" (*CLAJ,* September 1971). Bell attributes the renaissance in black literature, particularly in black poetry, to Jones's shift in racial orientation and his subsequent achievements. Maintaining that the new black poetry "is rooted in a love of black people and an affirmation of life," Bell traces the roots of the new writing back to the Harlem Renaissance and then briefly explicates "Black Art" as it embodies what is distinctive about the recent movement: its zeal and its use of art as a "weapon."

As Baraka's fame has increased, so has the polarization of attitudes toward his poetry; reviews of late tend to the extremes of eulogy or insult. Three especially favorable comments have come from black critics, one writing for the large readership of the *New York Times Book Review* and the others for the more homogeneous circulation of *Black*

World. In the first, Ron Welburn ("Reviving Soul in Newark, N.J.," February 14, 1971) acclaims *In Our Terribleness* (Indianapolis, Ind.: Bobbs-Merrill, 1970) as "perhaps Amiri Baraka's greatest book." Its excellence is attributed to his addressing only black readers; white readers may well be puzzled by a book in which both poetry and photographs excel in celebrating black experience, in expressing soul: in uniquely black language and imagery, Baraka endows objects and actions common in black life with vitality. Val Ferdinand's review (*BlackW*, April 1971) is less academic, couching its praises in more direct idiom addressed strictly to other potentially enthusiastic black readers. Ferdinand expresses disgust at the book's publication by a white company and its resulting high price. Kalamu Ya Salaam's rhapsodic praise of *Spirit Reach* (*BlackW*, November 1973), published by Jihad Productions in 1972, is written in a jive diction much like that of the poetry it quotes so extensively. The volume is lauded as Baraka's best, although a complaint is registered that the first three poems are too intelligent, too difficult for easy comprehension. "Peace in Place" is praised for its reliance quite as much or more on sounds as on sense. Baraka's crooning, his affirmation, his titles, even the African graphics receive special commendation, as do two poems in particular, "Somebody's Slow Is Another Body's Fast (Preachment)" and "Snapshots of Everything." If black readers do not like Imamu, they have been influenced by the white enemy or by jealousy, for his work should inspire.

Somewhat more subdued, but sincere, appreciation appears in Stephen Henderson's introduction to *Understanding the New Black Poetry: Black Speech and Black Music as Poetic References* (New York: Morrow, 1973). According Baraka recognition as an eloquent spokesman for the Black Arts movement, Henderson notes his concern with the spiritual. His technical indebtedness to William Carlos Williams and his disciples is explained as less an appropriation of white methods than a return to "the rhythms and phrasings of Black music" which influenced both the Beat writers and Baraka—as well as, a generation earlier, Langston Hughes. Baraka has also tapped the black oral tradition, especially by employing obscenity (for instance, in "Prettyditty") and the game of insults called "the dozens" (in "Word from the Right Wing," for example). Henderson recommends listening to Baraka's poetry in order to grasp fully his use of black speech as poetic reference. The advice is useful, too, for appreciation of every other facet of Baraka's poetic skill.

Another critic to consider contemporary black poetry in the context of music is Bernard W. Bell, in "The Debt to Black Music: Contemporary Afro-American Poetry as Folk Art" (*BlackW*, March 1973). Bell discusses Baraka as the proselytizer of musical inspiration for black poetry, but does not analyze the adaptation of musical conventions to literary needs in Baraka's own verse.

Three extremely fine recent essays on Baraka's poetry consider his development over more than a decade and conclude that his growing immersion in black consciousness has done no damage to his muse. Karl Malkoff, in *Crowell's Handbook of Contemporary American Poetry* (New York: T. Y. Crowell, 1973), acknowledges the decline in Baraka's reputation among white critics, but himself produces an appreciative analysis of poetry spanning the years from Baraka's sharing of his perceptions in concrete images and metaphors to poetry as political action. The writing is now communal rather than personal; the appeal is now more to the ear than to the eye; but the talent, if disturbing, is undeniable.

Lee A. Jacobus's "The Quest for Moral Order," in *Modern Black Poets*, edited by Donald B. Gibson (Englewood Cliffs, N.J.: Prentice-Hall, 1973), traces in specific detail Baraka's transition from the traditional value system (and the poetics of Eliot and even Milton) to faith in action, inverted ethics, blackness, and himself. Jacobus sees in Baraka a sense of mission in the communication of his vision, but Clyde Taylor ("Baraka as Poet," also in *Modern Black Poets*) insists that the poems "carry no argument" and are indeed "anti-didactic." Taylor, although in agreement with Malkoff and Jacobus about the merit of Baraka's recent work, stresses the personal element in even that poetry. He believes that Baraka is probably the finest contemporary American poet, but that he is not suited to the expression of the ethos of all black people.

A Ph.D. dissertation devoted to Baraka's poetry was submitted to Stanford University in October 1973. William Joseph Harris's "Jones/Baraka: The Evolution of a Black Poet" (*DAI*, June 1974) documents the evolution of Baraka the man and is therefore more a biography through poetry than a study of the poetry, and is certainly more concerned with poetic content than poetic form. The poems' views are effectively explicated in the context of tracing their author's changes "from a racially integrated Village intellectual through a Black militant poet to a religious prophet." Although he demonstrates an undeniable progression of this kind, Harris likewise notes, paradoxically but truly, that Baraka has not "exorcised the West" and always was black. A valuable study, this dissertation begins with consideration of Jones's debt to the Beats and to the Black Mountain poets and covers books ranging from *Preface to a Twenty Volume Suicide Note* to *In Our Terribleness*.

THE FICTION

Baraka's fiction has been little analyzed by critics. One attempt to deal with both his volumes is the entry by James A. Emanuel in *Contemporary*

Novelists, edited by James Vinson (New York: St. Martin's, 1973). The factual material is inaccurate, but the description of the two works of fiction provides a usable summary. Emanuel finds Baraka concerned, in *The System of Dante's Hell* (New York: Grove, 1965), with the states of souls in a "death-in-life" unrelieved by the possibility of redemption. He admires several of the narratives, especially "The Heretics," but objects to the prose as sometimes "cryptic or almost perversely obscure." Consideration of *Tales* (New York: Grove, 1967) is arranged according to the categories of the "nine reflective, partly narrative pieces" and the seven "bona fide short stories." In the best stories, Emanuel judges, Baraka "has been both saxophonist and dancer."

Jerome Klinkowitz also treats both volumes in *Literary Disruptions: The Making of a Post-Contemporary American Fiction* (Urbana: University of Illinois Press, 1975). He has a high regard for Baraka, whom he considers together with such novelists as Kurt Vonnegut, Jr., and Donald Barthelme. Although Klinkowitz does not make original contributions to Baraka criticism (he is heavily influenced by his student John O'Brien), his consideration of Baraka in this context may be valuable for informing readers who were previously ignorant about black authors and helping to confirm Baraka's reputation as a novelist the equal of our most talented white writers.

The System of Dante's Hell Other discussion of the fiction occurs primarily in the reviews. Many critics disliked *The System of Dante's Hell;* typical is Richard Gilman's "The Devil May Care" (*NYHTBW,* December 26, 1965), which condemns by quoting Paul Claudel to the effect that the worst form of bad writing "is that which consists in saying obvious things in a pretentious way." Gilman pities Jones as a writer who is at once amateurish and adolescent, fraudulent and arbitrary, and pronounces his book positively "painful to read." Labels such as "fake" and "pretentious" appear in other reviews as well; the cruelty and cleverness of *Newsweek* (November 22, 1965) are unsurpassed. Len Holt (*Liberator,* January 1966) does not even bother to discuss the book, but uses his "review" as an excuse to raise the question of Jones's authenticity as a spokesman for his race.

Another group of reviews expresses distaste and bewilderment mixed with admiration. The style is found here intrusive and there brilliant. Despi Tralis, in "Alone in a Dark Wood" (*Freedomways,* Spring 1966), could be expressing the sentiments of many reviewers when he observes, "In *spite* of himself, passages of unsurpassed exquisite beauty and personal lyrical expression betray these broadsides to be the distress signals of a flashing genius." And few critics were as affirmative and as analytical as Emile Capouya in "States of Mind, of Soul" (*NYTBR,* November 28, 1965).

Several critics consider *The System of Dante's Hell* at somewhat greater length. John R. May's "Images of Apocalypse in the Black Novel" (*Renascence*, Autumn 1970) does not fulfill its intention of contrasting the images of apocalypse in selected novels by Richard Wright, Ralph Ellison, James Baldwin, and Baraka; indeed, May discusses each book separately. Moreover, he seems to have little admiration for *The System of Dante's Hell*, and his connection of it with apocalyptic events is limited to his discerning therein the "realized judgment of hell on this earth." The systems of hell in Dante and Baraka are found to have only the ironic relationship of contrasted "medieval order and contemporary confusion."

Olga W. Vickery's "The Inferno of the Moderns," in *The Shaken Realist: Essays in Modern Literature in Honor of Frederick J. Hoffman*, edited by Melvin J. Friedman and John B. Vickery (Baton Rouge: Louisiana State University Press, 1970), considers several types of novels influenced by Dante's *Inferno* and argues that Baraka's does indeed display such indebtedness. Susanna Campbell Hayashi's "Dark Odyssey: Descent into the Underworld in Black American Fiction," a dissertation written at Indiana University in 1971 (*DAI*, April 1972), examines a tradition stemming from wider mythological, religious, and literary sources. Unlike Vickery, Hayashi confines her investigation solely to black authors. This examination embraces the psychological as well as the literary implications of the time-honored dualistic system which accords "white" and "black" relative positions of superiority and inferiority.

His apparent ignorance of a sizable portion of Baraka criticism, including May's and Vickery's articles and Hayashi's dissertation, fortunately does no great damage to Lloyd W. Brown's fascinating reading of *The System of Dante's Hell*. "LeRoi Jones [Imamu Amiri Baraka] as Novelist: Theme and Structure in *The System of Dante's Hell*" (*NALF*, Winter 1973) is nearly as complex in its insights as the novel it explicates. After attacking David Littlejohn and Edward Margolies for their failure to perceive coherence and artistry in the work and complaining of a widespread critical tendency to divorce form and content, Brown delineates the sort of hell Jones has in mind. It is not the "posthumous reality" described by Dante but the environment which imposes on blacks "social, racial, and perceptual divisions." Hell is the narrator's experience of white stress upon reason rather than feeling and his resultant self-hatred. The traditional systems on which Dante relies to construct his *Inferno* are thus demolished by Baraka in his own, which satirizes Dante's "Western itch to systematize . . . complete with its highly structured complex of paganism and piety, sins and circles." *The System of Dante's Hell* is then specifically analyzed to elucidate the use of irony as narrative structure, the plot of the narrator's denial and later recapture of his ethnic identity, and the associationist images which provide simultaneity of viewpoint or "psychological, as distinct from clock, time." Ironically, Brown's article expounding Baraka's critique of rationalism is itself one of the most intellectually sophisticated essays in Baraka criticism.

Another excellent analysis by Lloyd W. Brown, "Jones (Baraka) and His Literary Heritage in *The System of Dante's Hell*" (*Obsidian,* Spring 1975), examines the novel's use of the Ulysses archetype as it is found in Homer's *Odyssey,* Dante's *Inferno,* Tennyson's "The Lotus-Eaters," and James Joyce's *Ulysses.* Brown identifies elements of Baraka's utilization of each source and shows that this "exemplifies the workings of Eliot's historical sense in that the archetypal mode readily accommodates Jones' simultaneous perception of the past and present, and his awareness of his own relationship with literary tradition." Particularly perceptive is Brown's analysis of the protagonist, Roi, as a figure representing both of Joyce's central characters, Stephen Dedalus and Leopold Bloom. Brown concludes that Baraka's explicit repudiation of the Western literary tradition has not eliminated his extensive use of that heritage.

Noel Schraufnagel's discussion of *The System of Dante's Hell* in *From Apology to Protest: The Black American Novel* (Deland, Fla.: Everett/Edwards, 1973) reduces the book to a story about a young soldier and a prostitute, as though the rest of the narrative did not exist or only an excerpt had formed the basis of his analysis of the "search for identity in an absurd world." The hero is presumed to have been searching for an ordered life; when his quest "fails" and he awakens after his beating, we are told, he is finally in hell. The critic's divergences from Brown's interpretation are predictable, since Schraufnagel describes the novel as "almost impossible to understand."

More enlightening is Paulette Pennington-Jones's "From Brother Le-Roi Jones through *The System of Dante's Hell* to Imamu Ameer Baraka" (*JBlS,* December 1973). Like Brown, Pennington-Jones identifies the book's central problem as the social dichotomies which wrongly force blacks to live white lives. Instead, they must *learn*—it is "an acquired response"—to focus on blackness. Having established the author's social purpose, Pennington-Jones skillfully compares and contrasts Baraka and his model, Dante, and catalogues the circles in the two writers' similar but separate hells. The analysis provides a useful comparison for anyone wishing to read *The System of Dante's Hell* with an awareness of its relationship to Dante's *Inferno* and an appreciation of Baraka's own vision. The interpretation of the eighth ditch section (the play *Dante*) as an inner conflict of a schizoid personality is typical of the article's provocative contributions to the criticism of *The System of Dante's Hell.*

Tales Less critical tribute in the form of analysis has been paid to

Tales, although the reviews are more deferential than those which greeted *The System of Dante's Hell.* The stories are considered by such critics as Donald J. Cameron (*MinnR,* June 1968) and Eugene Paul (*Liberator,* December 1967) to be fine literature clearly written by a black nationalist. Especially enthusiastic is Henry S. Resnik, who in "Brave New Words" (*SatR,* December 9, 1967) hails Jones as "one of the boldest and most vital of contemporary American authors."

The only extended critical examination of Baraka's fiction concerns one of the stories in *Tales.* John O'Brien's "Racial Nightmares and the Search for Self: An Explication of LeRoi Jones' 'A Chase (Alighieri's Dream)' " (*NALF,* Fall 1973) discusses that tale as a montage of sensory images and allusions which foreshadow the action of the other stories in the volume. O'Brien identifies the source of the story's tension in its presentation of the conflict between the romantic boy's yearning and the sordid reality of his surroundings; many of O'Brien's perceptive observations therefore illuminate that source of stress in the running boy.

For further analyses of Baraka's fiction, the reader is referred to those books and articles of wider-ranging critical scope to which we now turn.

GENERAL CRITICISM

Very few attempts have been made to analyze Baraka's work as a whole or even to discuss his writing in more than one genre. Introductions to Baraka's work reprinted in literary anthologies tend to be of little help. All too typical is that in *Black Writers of America: A Comprehensive Anthology,* edited by Richard Barksdale and Keneth Kinnamon (New York: Macmillan, 1972), a mishmash of factual errors and critical oversimplifications or downright falsifications—such as citation of *In Our Terribleness* as a collection of prose essays.

The first real general assessment was David Littlejohn's in *Black on White: A Critical Survey of Writing by American Negroes* (New York: Grossman, 1966). Unfortunately, this book was not an auspicious beginning. Littlejohn is never-endingly judgmental, describing his own reactions rather than the literature. His study is not analysis, not literary criticism, but commiseration with other white readers over how boring, hopeless, sordid, and painful is the literature about which he has, inexplicably, chosen to write. The best that Littlejohn can say about black literature is that by suffering through some of it white readers can correct their "lamentable failure of imagination" about the nature of black life. Given this as his standard of excellence, it is no particular surprise that Littlejohn rates Jones high among black writers, inasmuch as Jones's style is nothing if not vivid. Littlejohn's response to *The Toilet* is mixed, and he dislikes *The Slave,* failing to find in it anything more subtle than "a blatant, unmodulated scream of racial abuse" and judging it "devoid of conflict." But *Dutchman* he praises—as race-war literature—and he esteems Jones as the only black playwright who "has even begun yet to take advantage of the dynamic potential of the living theater in the manner initiated by [Jean] Genêt." As for Jones as poet, Littlejohn describes him as Blakean, antiverbal, antirational, incoherent, difficult, and yet the only black poet who "demands the same degree of poetic respect as Gwendolyn Brooks."

Another critic who considers Jones as poet and playwright is John Tryford, in "Who Is LeRoi Jones? What Is He?" (*Trace,* Summer 1967). A prophetic article, it may have influenced Jones; there is an interesting mixture of predictions that Jones fulfilled and criticisms that he might have set himself to disprove. Tryford suggests, on the one hand, that Jones is dependent on white readers and white publishers, and on the other that in a solely black society "he would be a kind of teacher or prophet"—in other words, one could add later, an Imamu. Tryford says Jones's message in such works as *Dutchman* and *The Slave* is that it is too late for integration. Although he briefly and not entirely convincingly analyzes both these plays, Tryford rejects them as lasting drama on grounds that they are timely but not universal. Jones's poetry, too, he dislikes when it is didactic, preferring his romantic vein and commending "This Is the Clearing I Once Spoke Of" and "As a Possible Lover." Tryford's ambivalence toward Jones is clearest in his concluding remarks, in which he complains of the dwelling on "racial subjects" and yet suggests that by teaching and example Jones could inspire black writers and thereby "entirely change the course of literature."

Another year brought a still less sympathetic consideration in *Native Sons: A Critical Study of Twentieth-Century Negro American Authors,* by Edward Margolies (Philadelphia: Lippincott, 1968). Baraka's more recent writing is compared unfavorably with the poems in *Preface to a Twenty Volume Suicide Note.* His plays and poems of more recent vintage are termed hysterical and, simultaneously, ineffective as propaganda because they are "too erudite and subjective." Again his style is described as incoherent, both in syntax and sense; his rage is termed "a monomaniacal obsession." Margolies's worst epithets, however, are reserved for *The Baptism,* which is "unimaginably bad" and "fails of any movement whatsoever," and *The Slave,* in which "there is little real action and little sense—and the audience gets the uneasy feeling that it has been made privy to an adolescent fantasy." *Dutchman* is Jones's best play—not just best of a bad lot, but really an exciting drama. But if Jones redeems himself with that, he loses Margolies's respect again with *Home* and *The System of Dante's Hell.* What Margolies gives in tribute he snatches back as a tax on that (for him) luxury of praise: "The fair-minded reader must, of course, admit the value of some of Jones's work, despite the hysterical nonsense Jones assumes to be necessary to racial leadership."

Baraka found a somewhat more sympathetic critic in Donald B. Gibson, whose introduction to his *Five Black Writers* (New York: New York University Press, 1970) nevertheless suffers from an apparent lack of familiarity with Baraka's publications since the mid-1960s. After insisting that the work of Richard Wright, Ralph Ellison, James Baldwin, Langston Hughes, and Baraka is not necessarily informed by their racial identity and that, in fact, the "concept of Negro literature" is racist, Gibson describes Baraka's work as similar to that of his fellow academics. He argues that Baraka's roles as writer and "social activist and community leader" have not coalesced, and he supports this contention with examples drawn solely from the early Jones, never mentioning the plays produced since 1964 or any poetry published by Jihad or in black periodicals. Gibson therefore seems to have had insufficient experience with the Baraka canon to form a basis for his generalization that most of the work is "personal and private," unrelated to racial or ideological issues. His observations concerning *The Slave* and *Dutchman* are frequently perceptive, however, in spite of his conclusion that Baraka's social activism does not color his writing, which is aimed at the intellectual elite rather than the black masses.

Taking up where he left off in his consideration of Baraka's response to excessive rationalism in *The System of Dante's Hell*, Lloyd W. Brown, in another perceptive article ("High and Crazy Niggers: Anti Rationalism in LeRoi Jones," [Journal of Ethnic Studies, Spring 1974]), uses the drama, fiction, and particularly poetry to elucidate his theme. Brown considers that antirationalism is one of Baraka's major preoccupations. He identifies this attitude in John Dryden, Jonathan Swift, the Romantics, and in much black writing; he takes his own title from Nikki Giovanni's poem "Short Essay of Affirmation Explaining Why," in which living and feeling are perceived by whites as craziness. What Baraka rejects, Brown demonstrates, is not true rationalism but that pseudo-rationalism manifested in the Jacoub of *Black Mass* which contrasts to "the high and crazy modes of a human wholeness" and the joyous ethnic identity championed by Baraka. From this viewpoint, "Black Dada Nihilismus" describes no more extreme a viewpoint than that which it challenges, and that poem is explained as affirmation in opposition to "a narrowly technological culture." Brown offers other illustrations of his thesis from "I Substitute for the Dead Lecturer," "Green Lantern's Solo," "Rhythm & Blues," "Lowdown," "Race," "K'Ba," "Future Goodness and Social Philosophy," and "Human to Spirit: Humanism for Animals."

Two less successful articles appearing in the September 1973 issue of the *College Language Association Journal* attempt full critical discussions. Each depends heavily on connecting Baraka's writing and his life. This kind of criticism is necessarily difficult with Baraka because of the hiatus between dates of writing and eventual publication or reprinting in book form, with critical use of his periodical publications negligible; both C. Lynn Munro's "LeRoi Jones: A Man in Transition" and Esther M. Jackson's "LeRoi Jones (Imamu Amiri Baraka): Form and the Progression of Consciousness" suffer thereby. Munro observes the shift from "apolitical" to committed writer, but judges that the work is weakened by Baraka's continued succumbing to unduly academic and conventional influences. Munro cites some of the poems as particularly formalistic. Jackson interprets this formalism as indicative of the author's conflicted personality. Baraka's search for form has been expressive of his search for himself, and Jackson concludes that both quests brought him home to his ethnic identity and "to a sense of ethical totality." She traces the journey of Baraka's poetic consciousness in a precarious chronology, yet the overall passage she discerns "from lyrical to moral consciousness" is indisputable. It would have been helpful, however, had Jackson substantiated her numerous judgments of the poetry, drama, and fiction with somewhat more evidence drawn from those works.

The first full-length critical study of Baraka, both the earliest completed dissertation (for Howard University in January 1971) and the first published critical book (for Duke University Press in Durham, North Carolina, in 1973) is Theodore R. Hudson's *From LeRoi Jones to Amiri Baraka: The Literary Works.* This pioneering study is a valuable distillation of much that preceded it and provides some fresh materials, notably those drawn from interviews conducted with Baraka, his parents, and his first wife. Hudson believes that Baraka, a writer of great importance, can be better appreciated by a reader conversant with his life, his usual thought processes, and his habitual literary techniques. Sections which investigate these topics therefore precede his detailed analysis of Baraka's nonfiction, fiction, poetry, and drama. Finally, Hudson argues that Baraka, for several reasons, must be considered a romantic. Of special excellence are the considerations of style and recurring imagery, the shrewd criticisms of *A Black Value System* and *Blues People,* and the perceptive treatment of Baraka's fiction, especially *The System of Dante's Hell.*

Hudson's otherwise excellent explication of Baraka's work is weakened by two deficiencies, both related to the matter of the artist's chronological development. First, Hudson writes as though Baraka's publications were limited to those in his books, whereas there have been scores of periodical publications preceding and sometimes superseding book publication. Ignoring most of those poems in particular which have not appeared in the collected volumes necessarily prevents the complete perspective on Baraka for which Hudson strives. Second, an unacknowledged conflict is precipitated between the view suggested by the title and partially supported by the evidence presented that LeRoi Jones gradually grew into the somewhat altered Amiri Baraka, and the conviction that Baraka has always thought and written in much the same fashion. In his repeated contradiction of his title, Hudson fosters a myth—that Baraka's attitudes and style are consistent—which Baraka himself might like to see perpetuated. The *œuvres,* however, belie such an assumption.

Hudson's dissertation underwent extensive revision before its publication as a book, from rearrangement and adjustments in wording, which sharpen its style, to correction of errors and addition of new matter. A few unfortunate cuts suppress valuable information, so the reader is advised to consult both versions. This study will nevertheless remain, even after the appearance of other book-length appraisals of Baraka, an indispensable aid to appreciation of the artist and his work.

The second book on Baraka, Kimberly W. Benston's *Baraka: The Renegade and the Mask* (New Haven, Conn.: Yale University Press, 1976) combines a singularly impressive grounding in both Euro-American and Afro-American culture with an outdated perspective on Baraka. To Benston's credit are his erudition and intelligence, his precise prose style, his placement of Baraka in appropriate historical, intellectual, and racial contexts, and his sensitive and original readings of a few works of poetry, prose (fiction and nonfiction), and, especially, drama. Benston's book will always be important as a critical tool, especially for its appreciation of Baraka's aesthetic, but its peculiar dating of the plays and its antiquated perspective mark it as one of those brilliant achievements that is at least five years out of date by the time it is published. Unfortunately, Benston treated a 1967 play (*Slave Ship*) as Baraka's most recent achievement and published an entire work predicated upon Baraka's black nationalism more than two years after that political stance had been abandoned. Still, studies such as Benston's began to demonstrate Baraka's considerable artistic stature.

Another full-length study, Mary Diane Dippold's "LeRoi Jones: Tramp with Connections," a dissertation submitted to the University of Maryland in May 1971 (*DAI,* December 1971), attempts a critical biography of Baraka, concentrating on the decade from 1959 to 1969. Although it may prove a useful source of the gist of other critics' views, its unfortunate, often unacknowledged, dependence on previously published materials disqualifies it from consideration on its own merits.

The reader who has time for only one critical article on Baraka should choose William C. Fischer's "The Pre-Revolutionary Writings of Imamu Amiri Baraka" (*MR,* Spring 1973), which considers the ways in which Baraka has changed aesthetically and identifies the foundations in his early work for the later development. Fischer is appreciative but not uncritical, and his article is specific, well conceived, well substantiated, and well written. Fischer discusses the influence of the Beat writers on Jones, including his use of spoken effects (probably prompted by white practice but eventually incorporating black speech), Jones's preference for communality rather than individuality of character, and his distaste for mainstream modes of expression; yet Fischer cautions that in following Beat patterns Jones was imitating writers themselves inspired by black styles, and he distinguishes between Jones's natural adoption of such techniques and the more artificial attempts of white writers. Fischer's consideration in detail of the poetry of *Preface to a Twenty Volume Suicide Note* as exorcism of white cultural myths is the best available interpretation. But no less original and incisive are his extensive sections on *Blues People, The Dead Lecturer,* and several of the plays. Although some of his neat theories of development are based on inaccurate chronology, his conception of individual pieces is not necessarily damaged thereby. His contrast of several poems in *Black Magic* to Jones's earlier work is illuminating; it is to be hoped that he will expand upon this conclusion in another study of Baraka.

Although articles such as Fischer's have much to commend them, unfortunately not a single critic has thus far informed his or her study with a complete knowledge of Baraka's work. Particularly important for appreciation of Baraka's development and versatility as a poet—but essential for any complete evaluation—is familiarity with the many periodical publications which have never appeared in book form. Obviously, mastery of all the work of this prolific writer is time-consuming, but with the aid of the available bibliographical assistance it is not inordinately difficult. Until such a task is undertaken—and completed—the definitive study will not be produced.

I wish to acknowledge those people who assisted in the compilation of my *LeRoi Jones (Imamu Amiri Baraka): A Checklist of Works By and About Him* (London: Nether Press, 1971), and, in addition, Michael Lookretis.

NAME INDEX